TRANS-HIMALAYAN TRADERS TRANSFORMED

Tarang village consists of the cluster of houses near the bottom of the photograph. The route to Pokhara and southern Nepal follows the Jangla Bhanjyang pass which cuts through the snow peaks above.

TRANS-HIMALAYAN TRADERS TRANSFORMED

Return to Tarang

James F. Fisher

Orchid Press

TRANS-HIMALAYAN TRADERS TRANSFORMED
Return to Tarang

James F. Fisher

ORCHID PRESS
P.O. Box 19,
Yuttitham Post Office,
Bangkok 10907, Thailand
www.orchidbooks.com

Cover image: A solar collector has been erected on the roof of a Tarang house. See p. 52.

ISBN 978-974-524-202-9

For the inspirational voices
who helped me find mine

Mike Forrestal
Willi Unsoeld
Dor Bahadur Bista
Ed Hillary
Paul Wellstone
Raman (A. K. Ramanujan)

CONTENTS

ACKNOWLEDGMENTS

I could not undertake a work of this scope without massive assistance from many quarters. First and foremost, of course, are the many Taralis, whether from older generations in the late 1960s or their descendants in the twenty-first century, who helped me understand their lives, even if they never quite understood why I wanted to know about them. As one of them told me once, "We get up in the morning, eat, work all day in the fields, eat again, and sleep. That's all there is to our lives here. What's interesting about that?" But there were exceptions. Several were especially obliging as I attempted to grasp the significance of more recent and current changes. The names Bhim and Sukar, Lank Man and Bisara, and Dhanu are mentioned so often in the text that their appearance here is no surprise. They are hardly typical, but that is partly why they are of such interest. I only wish Chandra Man were still here so that he could see that his extraordinary accomplishments have received the recognition they deserved.

Closer to home, Nancy Wilkie gave the manuscript the benefit of her usual sharp editorial eye, making my words in many places more comprehensible than they would otherwise be. Chaitanya Mishra read the entire manuscript, which benefitted not only from his great knowledge about Nepal, catching my errors about it and explaining cultural and historical features I didn't understand, but also applying his keen sense of theoretical relevance where it was needed—all by email. Finally, the book could never have appeared in its present elegant form without the exhaustive, incomparable, and faultless copy editing performed by Xenia Lisanevich.

In Nepal, Gaurab KC participated in the project from beginning (almost) to end, helping with translation, making sense of what people said when what they said eluded my own understanding, suggesting countless ways in which the points I was trying to make could be made better, and highlighting aspects of life I did not initially detect. As an anthropologist, he helped steer me in productive directions, at points too numerous to mention, rather than letting me follow pointless pursuits. Finally, had he not proposed and then insisted on persevering with his lengthy interview with me, the life history that concludes the book, meant as a counterbalance to those of the Taralis which preceded it, would simply not exist. His contributions to the book are quite incalculable.

NOTE ON GEOGRAPHICAL NAMES

Tarangpur is the pseudonym I gave in the predecessor to this book, *Trans-Himalayan Traders* (1986), to the village known in Nepali as Sahar Tara, Ba in Tibetan, and Tarang in Kaike, the three languages spoken there (Nepali is Indo-European, the other two Tibeto-Burman). Although I use many terms from these languages in the text, I attempt to simplify that process by rendering them without resorting to diacritics. My aim in coining a pseudonym for the village in which I had lived for a year beginning in 1968 was to protect its identity and that of its inhabitants. For example, I wanted readers, but not government officials, to know that villagers poached musk deer (*kasturi*), an activity which might have resulted in their prosecution. In other words, I wanted to express ethnographic truth, but not at the price of harm to villagers. In doing so I was following the American Anthropological Association Code of Ethics, which states that when the interests of research conflict (e.g., those of universities, governments, funding agencies, publications, and people being studied), the people being studied must always be given highest priority.

More realistically, however, even a casual reader of *Trans-Himalayan Traders* could figure out, if not then, certainly by now, by comparing the map in that book with any other map of the same area, that Tarangpur could only refer to Sahar Tara (the only named village on maps), so my attempt at purposeful, but benign, deception was in vain. In this book I have retained the Kaike part of that pseudonym, Tarang, on the grounds that the village deserves to be known by the name that its inhabitants use to refer to it when speaking their own language.

Tichurong refers now, as it always has, to the valley, cut by the Bheri River, in which Tarang and twelve other villages are located. Dolpa refers to the administrative district (one of seventy-five) then and now, in which the inhabitants of Tichurong and other valleys and plateaus in northwest Nepal live. I refer to inhabitants of the thirteen villages of Tichurong, including the village of Tarang, the main focus of my study, by the collective moniker of Taralis.

1

Return of the Non-Native:
You Can Go Home Again

The chapter "Summary and Conclusions" that concluded *Trans-Himalayan Traders* (the book which this one follows, develops, and advances), referred to "the changes that are slowly but inexorably engulfing the people of [Tarang], blurring and maintaining boundary mechanisms between them and the rest of the ever-approaching world beyond their valley." What I stated as a conclusion might have been better framed as a hypothesis. I often wondered during the years since I left the village whether I was right about that or not. After all, it was only an informed guess about the future, and that prediction might have served only to confirm the mocking portrayal of anthropology by some cynics as a discipline whose primary function has been the perpetuation of historical error.

Maybe nothing, or at least nothing other than the mute passing of generations, had changed. Or maybe the village world—how it looks, its economy, its religious practices, its social life—had changed beyond anything I would still be capable of recognizing. Being more empirically-minded than inclined to reason from first principles, I thought the only way to find out was to go back to Tarang and see for myself. I had wanted to make that journey every time I returned to Nepal over the decades, but because it was so logistically difficult to reach, and, more important, because I somehow had always, in the interim, taken on new projects or followed new research interests, I had never quite gotten there. More disturbing to contemplate, perhaps I feared that my original analysis of life in Tarang was all wrong, or even if it was right, that my prediction about what changes would have taken place after I left was wrong. In other words, perhaps I was nervous about what I would find, and just looking for excuses to avoid another difficult, and at my now relatively advanced age, taxing expedition to the wilds of Dolpa.[1]

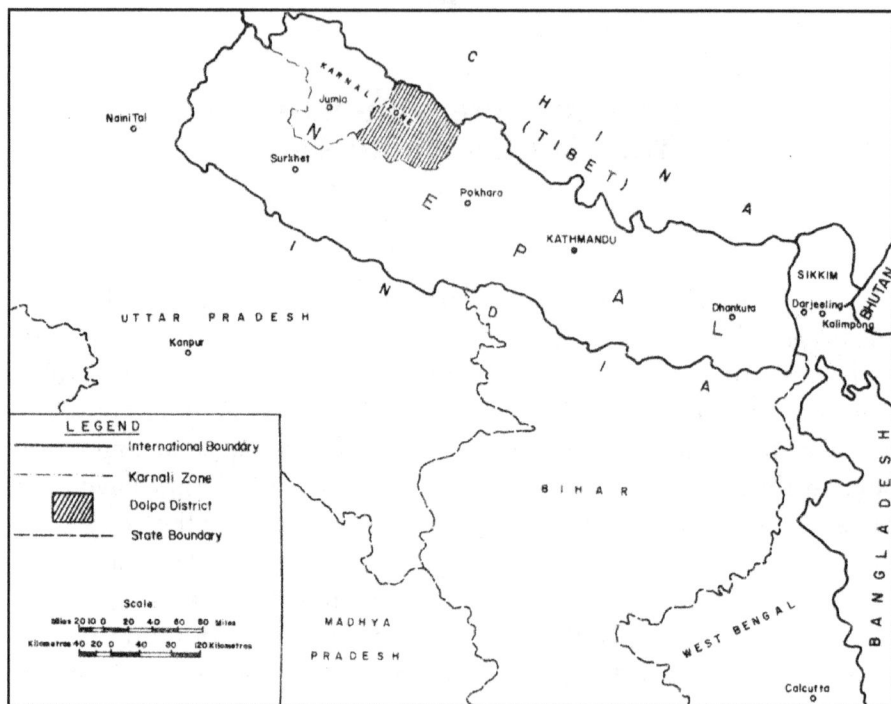

Map 1. Nepal and Neighboring Countries, 1979

At least this was the case until 2011, when some elementary and unavoidable calculations forced me to face the fact that although time moves slowly, it passes quickly, and forty-four years had passed since I had left Tarang. I realized that if I didn't return soon, I would reach a point where I'd be physically unable to get there again. Tramping around the rugged mountains and deep valleys of Dolpa is a young man's game.

---

[1]   When Nepal reorganized itself in the 1960s into seventy-five districts, the biggest one geographically included the area that had previously been referred to by Snellgrove and subsequent British writers as Dolpo, but it now included other parts as well. In Devanagri the district name was spelled Dolpa, and I follow this official Nepalese version of the name.

Map 2. Dhaulagiri Zone, 1969

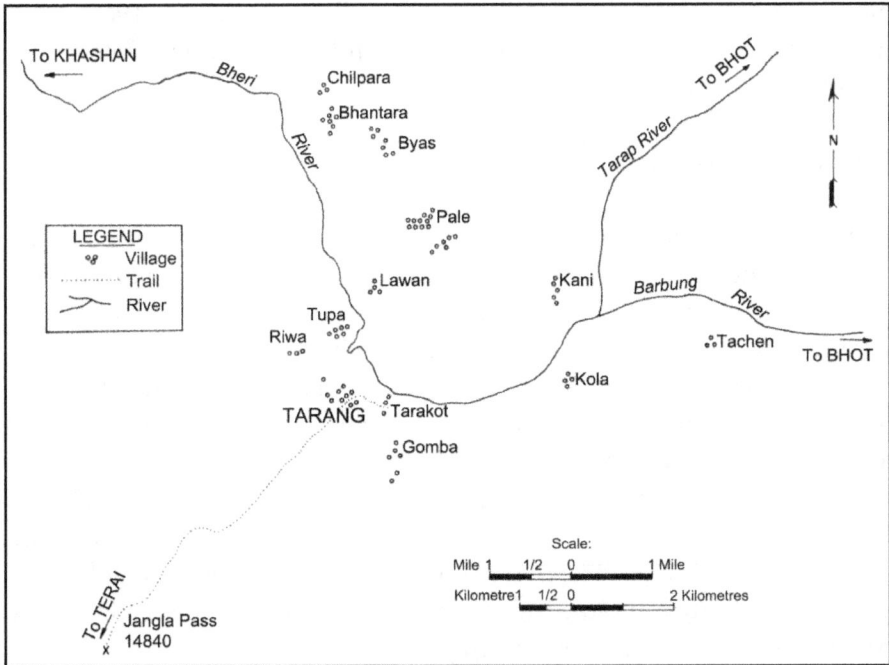

Map 3. Tichurong

Time may be the longest distance between two places, but I finally retired from Carleton College in 2009, after teaching there (when I didn't manage to sneak off to Nepal) for thirty-eight years. I spent the following year in Bhutan helping start Royal Thimphu College, that country's first private college. Although a little apprehensive, by 2011 I was willing, and as ready as I was ever likely to be, to return to Tarang. The truth is that I had run out of excuses not to go back.

In more recent years, as the cyber world began to encroach on Nepal, I had received occasional email messages from children whose parents, or even grandparents, I had known in the village, but whom I knew only through connections I could trace in my tattered and yellowing genealogical charts.[2] We had shared the experience of living in Tarang, albeit in different decades, but they were strangers to me. By 2011, most of the population living in the village had either been born after I lived there, or had been too young to remember me by the time I left. The size of the population of the village was about the same as when I was there, at least that's what I had informally heard, but the people who comprised it were mostly, from my point of view, newcomers. With few exceptions, my friends from the late 1960s were now gone. It was simultaneously a sad milieu to contemplate and a joyful one to anticipate.

Point of No Return

In any case, the die was cast. March 2011 found me back in Kathmandu. Thanks to the extremely helpful assistance of Maya Daurio, a geography graduate student who had spent two months in Tarang at the end of 2008 studying how ecology was related to the Kaike language which encoded and described it, I now knew of some forty-six Tarang contacts living in or near Kathmandu (Daurio 2012: 11). These I could attempt to find and talk to without leaving the valley. Forty-two years previously there had been none. At that time most Taralis had never even traveled to Kathmandu, let alone lived there, although all of them would have liked to visit its pilgrimage sites, and a few of them did so. Many residents of Tarang, including my rather aged landlady (whom I always called Ama, or mother), had scarcely left the Tichurong valley.

---

[2]   See genealogical information in Appendices A and B.

These modern-day Taralis (inhabitants of the Tichurong valley, not just the citizenry of Tarang, as I explained earlier in the Note on Geographical Names) whom I found in Kathmandu mostly reside in the general area of Boudhanath stupa, towards the eastern edge of the city. (This ancient and magnificent stupa has been turned into a lawn ornament by construction of the nearby Hyatt Regency Hotel to its west.) The Taralis generally gather together once a month, for worship or social purposes, in a large hall they rent, so that they can keep in touch with one another and address common concerns. This has made them more connected with each other than most members of imagined communities, even if theirs is not a particularly tightly knit one.

Even more surprising, they all had cell phones, and I was astonished to learn that they talk not only to each other, but also to friends and family in Tarang (and en route to or from it)—all of this in contrast to the two months or so it took to send (or receive) a letter to (or from) the United States in the late 1960s, when for all practical purposes international phone service to the United States did not exist, not even from Kathmandu.

No wonder that forty-four years earlier they would sometimes ask me whether, when it was daytime in Tarang, it was night in my village, and if so, where was the dividing line? They also asked what would happen if the astronauts couldn't find the moon (Apollo 11 was on its way), since the new moon is invisible, and how they would calculate how much fuel and food they would need for the trip. I said it was the same as walking from Pokhara to Tarang: you calculate how much food you will need per day, and how many people need to be fed, and just add it all up. They countered with, yes, but that's easy, because we've already made the journey from Pokhara many times. Obviously, the astronauts enjoyed no such advantage.

My neighbor's son, Darba Ram, also asked if the sun encircled the earth, or vice versa.[3] His father responded that if it were true that the

---

[3] Darba Ram, about twelve or thirteen, was an unusually bright, inquisitive, and charming child. A few years later, sometime in the early 1970s, he left for India and never returned. No one in the village knew where he had gone or what had happened to him. He simply vanished. Such disappearances occur occasionally in remote parts of Nepal. Perhaps the most famous example was that of Dor Bahadur Bista, regarded as the father of Nepalese anthropology, who was last sighted in west Nepal in 1997 and then never seen again, despite strenuous attempts to search for him.

earth went around the sun, we all would feel dizzy. To demonstrate my counter argument, I stuck a piece of straw into a pumpkin, the pumpkin representing the earth and the straw any one person or place on it, then twirled it around so that the straw would be in the shade for part of the time. I also said the earth was so big we don't notice the spinning. But Darba Ram's illustration was better: he picked up a piece of paper, turned it around, and said that an ant in the middle of the paper wouldn't notice if it moved.

Cosmology notwithstanding, gradually a picture emerged of how and when I could return to Tarang. The good news was that there were daily flights to a mountain airstrip at Juphal, only two days' walk down the Bheri River from Tarang, that would spare me the two-week walk from Pokhara—the only way there had been to get there forty-four years earlier. The bad news was that while flights to Juphal were scheduled, no planes were currently taking off because of steep fare increases, caused by large hikes in fuel prices (from Rs. 88 [$0.91] to Rs. 97 [$1.01] per liter) about the time I arrived in Nepal.

Regardless of the availability of flights, in order for me to operate and organize my activities in Kathmandu my first order of business was to acquire a working cell phone. Formerly, one could conduct one's local business by riding a bike or taking a taxi. Now, traffic was so congested that it had become a major expedition to travel from one part of the city to another. After I finally arrived at my destination—the cell phone company office—I was puzzled when they asked for my passport, visa number, several signatures, and even thumbprints. "Why all the red tape for a phone?" I asked. I argued that you don't need thumbprints to buy a hat, to which the riposte was that a hat could not be misused. I still didn't get it, until the cell phone company representative finally explained that cell phones can be used to detonate explosives.

This was a sobering lesson on antiterrorism measures that, after a brutal ten-year Maoist insurgency, had become routine, even after the Maoists had won elections and taken over the reins of government and the multiparty system on which it rested (the monarchy was deposed in 2008). The Panchayat system, ostensibly a government rooted in Nepal's traditional village democracy but actually an absolute monarchy, which had existed during my earlier fieldwork (described in Chapter 7 of *Trans-Himalayan Traders*), had long since disappeared into political oblivion. Obviously, I was facing a steep learning curve.

L E G E N D

Houses
Chorten (Stupa)
Prayer Wall
Walk-in Chorten
Tree (of Religious Significance)
Named Neighborhood Boundary
Political Division
Trail

R   Teachers' Residence
L   Lama
B   Budha
G   Gharti
X   Rokaya
T   Thakuri
J   Jhankri

Village
Development
Committee

Nepal Telecom
Satellite Terminal

Ayurvedic
Clinic

Water Tap

School

Gomba

Water Tap

Damai's House

Shaman Shrine

Map 4. Tarang Village

Now and Then

The original book, *Trans-Himalayan Traders: Economy, Society, and Culture in Northwest Nepal,* relied heavily on a schematic analysis of the transaction circuits which had, over the decades, and probably centuries, drawn Taralis out of the narrow, steep valley (Tichurong) in which they spent most of their lives. As its title indicates, it depended, like most anthropological studies, on the thoughts, words, and deeds of individual human beings, living in real time and real space, in order to find regularities and systems at the larger and more analytically powerful levels of society and culture. With few exceptions, I did not reveal the identity of those specific individuals because I regarded them only as illustrative examples used to explain how the transactional circuits created and exemplified daily life in the village I lived in and knew most about—Tarang. If a critic had argued that I paid more attention to transaction circuits than to the people who enacted them, they would have been right.

But to argue that way is also to come down on the primacy of agency over structure, in the much-discussed debate on that much-contested dichotomy.[4] And for good methodological reasons: history is much more accessible than agency in a largely illiterate place like Dolpa. Transaction circuits seem to have always been a part of life, whereas agents active in them are little known nor long remembered. Those individuals seem to have been more shaped by the economy, itself remotely connected to the expanding world capitalist system through India, rather than the other way around.

This way of thinking envisions cultures, including the most remote ones, passively absorbing the world-system (Wallerstein 2004). The opposite view is of peoples' reactions, inventions, innovations, and transformations of tradition—active attempts to create or recreate a differentiated cultural space within that world-system. This is the view I present here. It assumes that what we need to study ethnographically is not the universalization of modernity, but the indigenization of modernity—how local people integrate the world-system into something even more inclusive: their own system of the world.

---

4   As used by anthropologists, the term 'agency' usually means, roughly, the capacity, condition, or state of acting or of exerting power.

Half of the book is devoted to a new breed of Taralis who have become cosmopolitan and international by responding creatively to new opportunities in the transactional world. The other half presents the extraordinarily detailed story of the exertion of agency by one Tarali—Chandra Man—whose life, although as fully cosmopolitan and international as anyone's, was essentially untouched by transaction circuits.

By contrast to my first trip, which consisted of a year's uninterrupted residence in Tichurong, where I knew no one, this time I returned to Tarang in 2011 via preliminary contacts and conversations with Taralis living in Kathmandu. There were not many—only a little over forty from Tarang itself—and most of them had moved out of those traditional transaction circuits, following a new way of life. They were still culturally, socially, and linguistically Taralis, but they had adopted quite novel modes of urban existence—still transactional, but in an entirely different setting.

It was easy to see that a few individuals had, in a way, broken away from the pack and were now following paths very distinct from those adhered to while growing up in the village. Some of them were very young when I was there in the late 1960s; others had not yet been born. But it became clear that the story of whatever changes had occurred was most evident in the lives of these migrants who lived mostly in Kathmandu but who still maintained close ties in Tichurong and visited there occasionally if they were physically able to. They were migrants whose feet now trod firm new urban ground, but who were not uprooted from their rural village origins.

I began to see that I had two stories to tell. One dealt with those new urban migrants living near Boudhanath; the other revolved around what had happened, or perhaps had not happened, in the ancestral village of Tarang. The more I talked to urban Taralis, the more I came to see that culturally, there was really a single story, but one composed of two quite distinct chapters.

Finding out what was going on with Tarali lives in Kathmandu promised to be relatively straightforward—I could hop in a taxi and go visit and talk to people. Left open still were the big questions of what I would find in Tarang itself. Did I really want to see the changes, whatever they were? How had the advent of those cell phones changed the village, for better or for worse? Had the village joined the larger world in a way that had made it so different that it would be unrecognizable? Would there be anyone still there whom I would remember? For that matter, would anyone be old enough to remember me? Why should they? After all, it had been a very long time, and they had other things to do.

Life Histories

What I slowly, but inevitably, began to realize was that I was going to have to adopt a totally different theoretical stance from the one on which I had relied forty-four years earlier. The questions forming in my mind required a different way of proceeding. To be sure, transactions still existed, but to understand what had happened over forty-four years, it was necessary to look not just at bloodless circuits, but at particular, individual, pulsating lives, especially the most prominent, distinctive, and, at least from an economic point of view, successful ones who had moved out of the traditional circuits.

This is not to deny the ontological clout of the circuits, which continue to operate, whether in the old style (salt for grain, woolen products for rice), new style (carpets and *yarsagumba*, the high altitude fungus sometimes referred to as nature's Viagra, discussed in detail in Chapter 5, for cash), or even the idiosyncratic, intellectually based case

Yarsagumba, the high-altitude fungus that has become Nepal's premier cash crop.

demonstrated by Chandra Man, who acquired advanced education in exchange for his dogged, relentless effort in the academic world. All these exchanges bear on the nature and trajectory of the pulse of life. Whether one starts with circuits and works back to individuals, or from individuals back to the encompassing circuits, both need to be investigated, appraised, and accounted for.

While it is true that in the late 1960s some traders were much more successful than others, I said relatively little about those differences in the earlier book, for no reason other than it hadn't seemed necessary to spell them out when writing about transaction circuits. I wrote as if everyone were more or less the same. I adopted as a working principle the assumption that, since everyone was molded by the same geographic and ecological constraints and the uniform realities of everyday village life, individuals shared more commonalities than differences, which, whatever they were, were trumped by common culture.

Transactions were important, even fundamental, in understanding how Tarali life had evolved, but they did not seem to explain ongoing explosive changes. What follows here, therefore, is less abstract theorizing about transaction circuits than descriptions of change as illustrated, some of them quite dramatically, in the lives of a few of these exceptional 'new' Taralis, whom I place alongside the majority who remain in the village. In doing so, I introduce a new cast of Tarali characters—innovative, entrepreneurial, yet still, in their own way, traditional.

In other words, without consciously thinking about it, I was being drawn back into the world of life histories. Indeed, I had quite forgotten my earlier work in life histories (Fisher 1997). In fact, it was not until I had finished the first draft of this book that my colleague, the anthropologist Gaurab KC, pointed this out to me. In that earlier work, I wanted to produce a person-centered ethnography of an important period in Nepalese political history. Now, I was attracted to life histories not as *dinge an sich*, but because I did not know how to proceed without them. I needed them to illustrate what was happening to Tarali society. Reiterating the details of transaction circuits would fail to do that. What was most surprising, however, was the case of Chandra Man, whose life experience and trajectory were so anomalous as to make his story quite unlike the lives of any of the other Taralis, whether in circuits or out of them, whether in Tarang or in Kathmandu.

Rather than echo Victor Barnouw's characterization of life histories as being fascinating documents with their main difficulty lying in knowing what to do with them (Barnouw 1963), I seemed to want to do too many things with them. In this case, I needed them to confront Paul Ricoeur's position that history is a combination of the system and the singular (Ricoeur 1986). I had the system, but the singular— to illustrate how it actually worked—was missing. Employing life histories provided another way at getting at the perennial anthropological question of human agency. To talk of agency without looking at specific agents and what they do is like talking about poetry without examining specific poets and their poems.

However, human agency needs to attend to the difference between told and lived lives. As Edward M. Bruner put it, "A life as lived is what actually happens. A life as experienced consists of the images, feelings, sentiments, desires, thoughts, and meanings known to the person whose life it is. . . . A life as told, a life history, is a narrative influenced by the cultural conventions of telling, by the audience, and by the social context" (Bruner 1984: 7). What I needed to do was to convert the lived lives that mattered to me into narratives that my audience could comprehend—a task I came to realize was easier said than done.

As in most anthropological studies, sampling of a population is less scientifically constructed than it is the result of happenstance and luck—meeting people who are most interested in talking, or at least willing to talk. This is a procedure that must be utilized judiciously, since those who want to talk the most are often marginal or peripheral to their own society, where the average person is typically less voluble. In any case, the people I was most interested in talking to, initially, were ipso facto available in Kathmandu, rather than still back in Tarang. In both places they were mostly happy to talk, more so than they had been forty-four years earlier, when I, and more specifically, my questions, were regarded as at best mysterious and at worst as alarming threats to their lives.[5] But the selection of these people was not random, since they not only all knew each other but were mostly, in one way or

---

[5]   We were regarded, variously, as 1) government agents looking for information that could increase their taxes; 2) people who would take away the fertility of the soil; and 3) an advance force for Americans who would take over their village the way the Chinese took over Tibet.

another, related to each other. This was the guiding principle behind the methodological reality that one thing led to another, or what might be called snowball sampling.

Most of these people can be traced, genealogically, to a man named Lanku, the most successful Tarang trader in the 1960s, whom I had known well during my first trip.[6] One of his nephews, Bhim, who was born after I left Tarang in 1969 (see Appendix A), exemplifies the transformations apparent in this new urban generation. The similarities and differences between Lanku and his nephew Bhim are illustrative of generational change and instructive in understanding it. Those similarities and differences are also seen in another of Lanku's relatives, Lank Man, who is married to Lanku's sister. Lank Man is the most senior of Tichurong people in Kathmandu and brother-in-law to Lanku. Lank Man is what we would call an uncle to Bhim (Bisara, Lank Man's wife, is Lanku's sister, and two of her brothers are, respectively, Sukar's father and Bhim's father). He served as a mentor to Bhim, so I begin with him.

---

[6]   This Lanku is not the person with a similar name in the next generation, Lank Man Roka, discussed in Chapter 2.

2

Lank Man:
The Carpet Legacy

Bhim's arrival in the business world of Kathmandu followed that of Lank Man, then as now, the most senior of the Taralis living there. The only Tarali to have preceded him there was Chandra Man, who was, before his death in 2000, the first and for a long time the only Tarali resident in Kathmandu. His highly idiosyncratic and unprecedented life history is detailed in Chapter 9, which constitutes the last half of this book.

Lank Man was born in 1954 and lived across and up the river from Tarang, in Kani village, until he was about fourteen—we would have just missed each other in the late 1960s. During this time he spent the six cold

Lank Man at his desk.

months helping manage horses and goats for his father on his trading trips to places like Baglung, Pokhara, Butwal, Tamghas, Galkot, Jumla, and Tansen, which also gave him the opportunity to attend school for six months in those places, wherever his father might be at the time. He and his father followed the same two-week route we had taken forty-four years before, walking from Pokhara to Baglung, then up to Beni and Dhorpatan, before crossing the Jangla Bhanjyang passes directly north of Dhorpatan, and dropping down into the valley of Tichurong.

Lank Man had first gone to school in Dunai, and later attended Classes 7 and 8 in Tansen. For his last two years he enrolled in Banasthali Boarding School in Balaju, on the northwest edge of Kathmandu, where he passed his SLC exams. Perhaps a little atypically, his father had always stressed the importance of education, and Lank Man had ambitions of becoming an engineer or doctor. After graduating from high school he enrolled in Tri-Chandra College in Kathmandu, studying science. His childhood education had been sporadic and weak at best, however, and he didn't score well in the Intermediate Science exams, so he dropped out after three years. However, he retained a commitment to the world of education by returning to his home village of Kani, where he taught for six months, for a total salary of Rs. 150/six months, about $20.

Lank Man has a rather different take on the quality of education I describe in the next chapter. According to him, the quality of schools has deteriorated over the years, rather than improved. He says that teachers drink by day, then go teach. Furthermore, only those who can't afford to leave the village study in the local schools, so the schools are schools in name only. Whether the schools are better or worse now than before, few would argue that beyond acquiring the rudiments of reading and writing in the lower grades, educational quality has never been and is not now competitive with schools in the larger towns and cities to which Taralis travel for further education.

From Education to Business

Following his return to his village, and while he was living there, he began to think about possibilities in business. Lank Man had seen that Manangis made a lot of money, which is of course what he or any trader wanted to do. By this time Lank Man was also becoming familiar with how business worked and the importance of networking, so he used his connections and friendships with Manangis to acquire a passport for himself.

Manangis were successful because at that time only they were given passports to go to Hong Kong. This came about because it snowed during a visit to Manang by King Mahendra during the winter. The king asked them what they ate. The answer was buckwheat (*phapar*, Nepali). So the king decided to help by issuing them passports for Hong Kong. The issuance of passports expanded, and Lank Man acquired one.

He began by buying readymade clothes in Hong Kong (*jhitigunta*—a variety of different items ostensibly meant for personal use). He allowed himself $300 (on paper, for goods, but he needed that much just for living expenses) over two weeks, buying wholesale. Then he returned to Kathmandu and sold them on New Road to big merchants and store owners there. At that time Indira Gandhi prohibited foreign goods from entering India from Nepal, so he had to buy black market dollars in Hong Kong. One pair of pants cost Rs. 40 (about $4.00), for which he would then falsify the invoices, so that the origin of the goods was hidden. He then exported such manufactured goods to India, where they were in high demand, by bribing customs officials, selling them at high profits. Even so, one year he suffered losses—as he said, business sometimes succeeds and sometimes doesn't, and there's no such thing as a sure thing. He also tried dealing in gold, but he was not successful at it, because trading in gold required huge amounts of money—more than he had access to—for bribes.

Having achieved only modest success in the Hong Kong trading networks, he eventually decided to try his hand at the carpet business. Though Nepalese have woven carpets for their own use for generations, Europeans, through the Swiss Association for Technical Assistance (SATA), contributed substantially to the development of the modern carpet industry in Nepal. They gave financial and technical support to Tibetans who had arrived in Nepal after the Chinese took over Tibet, culminating in the Dalai Lama's flight to India in 1959. The Swiss believed in providing skills, rather than just money, so in the beginning the goal of their humanitarian aid was to provide a continuing source of income for Tibetan refugees. The carpets they produced were sold to tourists, who were the only identifiable market at that time, unlike now, when many Nepalis, both individuals and businesses such as hotels, can afford them.

At first Tibetans were not allowed to teach their crafts to others, for fear of competition in the labor market, but slowly these skills emerged among Nepalis too, to meet the high and growing demand for carpets beyond Nepal's borders; refugees alone could not keep up with this increased demand. The first commercial shipment of carpets to Europe took place in 1964, to Switzerland. Carpets proved popular in Europe, especially in Germany, which still imports more carpets from Nepal than any other European country.[7]

From those beginnings, carpets have become a labor-intensive commodity, assuming pride of place as the most important export product of Nepal. In addition to the small, tasteful, artistic, handwoven Tibetan carpets, large, wall-to-wall, machine-made carpets of the kind used in office buildings are also manufactured, but these have only limited, local appeal, and Taralis have not been involved in their design or production. Although nowhere near as large as it was in its heyday towards the end of the twentieth century, the carpet business trails only tourism and remittances (as from workers in the Mideast) in foreign exchange earnings. At its peak the industry employed some 900,000 workers, compared to only 100,000 now. This decline has been due to government policy, which has not been supportive of entrepreneurs, and also to the Maoist conscription of workers in their army ranks and to their support of labor unions. Elvira Graner extensively discusses labor recruitment and conditions in carpet factories in her article on workers in Kathmandu Valley carpet manufactories (Graner 2001).

Meanwhile, Lank Man had learned how to make thread for carpets and supplied other producers with it. At the same time, he began asking others to weave carpets for him. An Indian medical specialist, Sundar Bhawanani, was selling pills through his brother in Germany, but switched to carpets, and gave Nepalis like Lank Man orders to fill. To make carpets, Lank Man first had to buy unwashed wool from Tibet, wash it, and then spin it into yarn, all by hand, before it could be sold to carpet producers. Lank Man hired whatever manual labor he needed to accomplish these tasks. His wife, Bisara (Lanku's sister), provided extensive assistance in promotion of the business.

---

[7] There was a downturn in the European carpet market during several years when carpets made in Nepal were banned because child labor was used in their production. At present, the United States is the primary importer of Nepalese carpets.

The finished wool is packed into bundles, which weigh from as little as 60 kg to as much as 500 kg. Bhim and Sukar need about 1,000 kg per month for their factory at the present, mediocre demand levels (3,000 kg if there is greater demand), or about 12,000 kg over the course of an average year. This enables them to produce 500 square meters of carpet per month, the capacity of their factory, but that assumes there is a demand for that much product, which isn't always the case.

When Lank Man's business was at its height, at the end of the 1990s, he would receive $500,000 as an advance for his carpets. The national labor force then was on the order of 500,000 or 600,000 people spread throughout the industry. Now those numbers have been sharply reduced due to out-migration, principally to the Middle East, where wages are very high, as well as people finding other kinds of work locally.

Lank Man started out by operating three looms in his own house and selling locally through his Indian contacts. As he put it, referring to Indian influence initially before American markets were open to Nepali carpets, "big fish eat small fish" (i.e., large Indian companies began making carpets in Nepal that were stamped "Made in India" and shipped to the United States).

Initially, he hired eight or nine weavers to operate his fifty looms, most of which went unused, but as business increased so did the number of weavers. Two hundred weavers are needed to keep fifty looms busy. He acquired lots of carpet stock, buying in season, August to December. His first international sale was to a Dutch company, Jensen, for $50,000. In Nepal his carpets were sold at such high-end five-star hotels as the Yak and Yeti and the Soaltee. He increased the demand for carpets by distributing business cards to acquire clients. He also successfully made contacts with German clients, and could turn over $500,000 in two or three months dealing with them. Tibetans were even more successful.

Lank Man began exporting to foreign countries in 1985. To further promote his carpets, he travelled to Europe and Asia, for the first time in 1988, and to the United States for the first time in 1993, as part of a twelve-person IMCC (International Management Consulting Corporation) delegation that visited Washington, Philadelphia, Las Vegas, and New York. ABC Carpet Company is one of the big companies centered in New York that they dealt with.

This is the national and international context in which Lank Man's business grew, and to which he importantly contributed. Lank Man is a member of the Federation of Nepal Chamber of Commerce Industries, and at the time of this writing, president of the Central Carpet Industries Association, the main manufacturers' organization in Nepal, which counts 356 separate carpet manufacturing companies as members. There is a publication on the carpets of Nepal, a slick, glossy, magazine-style special issue for the New York International Gift Fair, that contains articles about carpets, advertisements, and full-page letters from such figures as the president of the Chamber of Commerce, the minister of industry, the minister for Commerce and Supplies, and the prime minister (who led the Maoist movement that toppled the government and ended the monarchy). Included as well is a letter from Lank Man as president of the Central Carpet Industries Association (*The Carpets from Nepal, 2009, 2*).

More recently, his business, and that of similar carpet manufacturers, has become much smaller than it had been formerly. He enviously compares doing business in Nepal to doing it in the United States, where people know each other and business contacts are easy to make and sustain. Doing business is harder in Nepal because of *bandhs* (strikes). These are held in opposition to the general political situation, not against carpet manufacturers as such. In these skirmishes, carpet manufacturers appear merely as collateral damage. Union demands also cut into profitability, and even without them, there is competition from the Middle East, where many Nepalis find well-paying work, cutting into the local labor supply. Carpet manufacturing depends on cheap labor, but wages were rising and child labor had also been curtailed. Laws are politically driven, but evaded to the extent possible. Other difficulties arise internationally, including competition in carpet production from India and China, as well as a fluctuating and sometimes depressed international economy that results in reduced demand.

While he has ratcheted down the scope of his own ventures, he leaves behind a legacy which Bhim and Sukar have assumed. Bhim's father was in partnership with Lank Man, whose business was very big and prosperous, and Bhim helped out wherever he could, learning about the business in the process. Lank Man and Bisara nurtured them: they taught them everything about the business, while Bisara provided them with room, board, and advice. With that kind of assistance, which was professional, familial, and even ethnic, success in the carpet business was theirs to lose.

The Next Generation: Lank Man to Bhim

Bhim began learning about carpets from childhood, when he helped his father make yarn. At first, Bhim took over the washing and stretching of carpets, while Sukar owned the building and was in charge of the carpet weaving operation. Sukar had always been industrious, from her early childhood, when she provided a helping hand in her father's shop in Dunai, and Bhim was fortunate to have such an economically capable wife. There were two distinct businesses: Bhim's in Maharajganj (washing), and Sukar's in Bhaktapur (weaving). At this time Bhim partnered with Lank Man for washing, while Sukar partnered with her brother, Heem.

Then Bhim left Lank Man and joined with Sukar, while Heem became independent and returned to Dunai, where he obtained a position with the Red Cross. After five years, in 1996, Bhim and Sukar combined their businesses into one, occupying three buildings on three *ropanis* (a little less than half an acre) of land rented for production (one was used for washing, the other two for making carpets.) Bhim was still partnered with Lank Man to handle the washing of carpets but not the export, which was the lucrative part of the business. He therefore felt the need to be independent. Furthermore, partners always have disputes, and he didn't want to quarrel with Lank Man, who stood in the relationship of *thulo bau* (older father) to him, and whom Bhim always held in the highest respect.

With their consolidated businesses, Bhim and Sukar became joint owners of their carpet business, all aspects of which are located in Bhaktapur. Their company is called RTBM Company. The acronym derives from the first letters (as they are written in English) of the names of their children, in descending chronological order: Ratna, Trishu, Bhupati, and Maya. During the Maoist insurgency, with turmoil raging almost everywhere, exports shrank, and they closed the washing part of the business. It was difficult to continue to operate, much less grow, their business, since Maoists extorted money from them on the order of Rs. 10,000 to 20,000 at a time, although these fees were usually negotiated downward to about Rs. 5,000. These would be paid two or three times a year, for instance on May Day, the universal Communist holiday.

They began exporting carpets in 2007, first to Germany, then to Belgium, where Bhim's cousin, Ram Prasad (another of Lanku's sons), was living, and who has since acquired Belgian citizenship. He had gone with some friends to Belgium, in some kind of government-supported program, and just stayed on there. Bhim followed him to Belgium, where he found a buyer for his carpets near Brussels, so Ram Prasad provides a steady European presence to help manage Bhim and Sukar's carpet distribution, in absentia, in Europe. It has been a profitable business, since $1,000 invested in Nepal yields $1,500 in Belgium. This explains why Bhim now goes to Belgium annually.

Bhim continually attempts to expand his business, and has sent carpet samples to his younger brother Moti (who goes by his nickname of Saman and who is working and studying business management in New York), and to Australia, Hong Kong, and Italy. He has travelled to Italy, Germany, France, and Holland, in Europe, and also to Dubai. Bhim spent $1,500 last year reserving stall space at a carpet manufactures convention in Florida, plus $160 in application fees to the American Embassy, attempting to acquire a US visa. When his visa application was denied, he lost all those nonrefundable fees. Not easily discouraged, he intends to keep trying.

The carpet factory in Bhaktapur currently has twelve to fifteen looms, all being worked by Tamangs, who mostly come from villages near the Kathmandu Valley. When there is demand for more orders, Bhim hires more workers. The workers live at the site rent free, and their pay depends on the quality of the carpets and the kinds of material used to make them. The carpets may be made of hemp and wool, silk and wool, nettles and wool, or just wool or, more recently, just nettles. He acquires nettles from Dailekh, Jajarkot, and Rolpa, downriver to the south and west of Tichurong, and the nettles are transported directly from these areas to Kathmandu. Nettles are in demand in Europe, partly because they are considered to be "eco-friendly." This makes them more expensive than other materials. Nettles, which cost Rs. 150/kg, make a very thin thread, which then costs Rs. 950/kg. The thinner the thread, the more expensive it becomes.

Once the thread and yarn are made, they must be dyed. The dyeing process takes place across the road from the Bhaktapur factory, and only natural dyes are used. The specific design of the carpet (e.g., dragons, flowers, abstract designs) depends on what the buyer wants. It is largely a made-to-order business. Bhim and Sukar have no preferences here and are happy to make whatever their customers want.

The Ingredients of Success

Access to education (including what little was available even in a remote village with not much of a school to speak of), mentoring, supportive kinsmen, and a flourishing national, and then international, carpet business are essential ingredients in this success story, but they do not include one other necessary element: the savvy to prosper in it. That savvy is a critical part of Tarang's cultural legacy—the transaction circuits that pulled them out of the constricted world of Tichurong in the first place.

All those trading trips over the generations, which Lank Man started making as a young boy, nurtured a mentality of commerce that included such skills as the ability to buy and sell products, make deals, negotiate prices, and make economically sensible decisions in a short time, before a profitable opportunity might disappear. Thus the world of traditional transactions, rather than being irrelevant to the modern commercial world, has helped usher it in.

It is difficult to overemphasize the sea change in business prospects between those available before and those available now. In Nepal, someone who has done well financially is sometimes referred to as a lakh *pati sau* (one who is worth at least a lakh or more of rupees), or a *kror pati sau* (one who is worth Rs. ten million or more) or, for someone who has acquired fortunes at Mideastern levels, an 'Arab' *pati sau*. By contrast, in the 1960s someone who engaged in small-scale, long-distance trade might be referred to as a *hajar pati sau* (whose wealth could be measured in the thousands of lakhs, which might amount to hundreds of dollars). By comparison, Bhim now earns about 60 lakhs ($60,000) annually, an astronomical increase in wealth.

Taken together, the combination of these factors (kinship, education, a legacy of commerce, and the birth of a new international business) begins to shed light on how it was possible for a Tarali to begin life in a remote village, at least a two-week walk from anything that could be called an urban, educated environment, then go on to graduate from high school, spend three years in college, and, finally, as a highly successful entrepreneur, start a flourishing and lucrative business.

3

Bhim and Sukar:
Generation X

Finally armed with my new cell phone, I sallied forth to meet one of my far-flung email correspondents, a young man named Bhim Prasad Rokaya (Rokaya being the name of his patrilineal, exogamous clan, or *thar* in Nepali). Bhim was the nephew (one of several) of Lanku, who, although in general lifestyle was indistinguishable from that of his fellow villagers, had been the most financially successful trader in the village during my time there in the late 1960s. For example, his house looked like any other house in appearance, size, and materials. He dressed the same and ate the same as any of his fellow villagers. But he was one of a very few who owned several horses. This was an important difference, since it enabled Lanku to engage in trade on a larger scale than someone whose success as a trader was limited by the amount of trade goods he could carry on his back.

Bhim's mother was Lanku's sister, and Bhim's wife, Sukar, was his father's brother's daughter—an example of the type of cousin marriage match Taralis make if they can find a qualifying partner to pull it off. In this case, it was the marriage of a son to father's brother's daughter (what anthropologists call preferential patrilateral parallel-cousin marriage); more common is the marriage to a mother's brother's daughter (preferential matrilateral cross-cousin marriage). Bhim's marriage only begins to describe his relations with others connected to Lanku (the kinship chart in Appendix A shows some of these connections).

I had hosted Lanku on his first visit to Kathmandu in 1970. Although he was then the wealthiest and probably the best traveled villager, I recall showing him one middling tourist class hotel in Kathmandu during a brief pilgrimage tour he was making of Kathmandu (it struck me as odd that I, a foreigner, was functioning as a guide explaining the capital city to a native of the country). He murmured in amazement as he ran his hands over the brick walls (painted white), so firmly, smoothly, and uniformly built, and so different from the rough, irregular, unpainted and uncemented stone walls of the houses in which he and all Taralis, regardless of economic level, lived.

Bhim and I had agreed, by cell phone, to meet at the Boudhanath stupa. At first he was unrecognizable as a Tarali, dressed in his western sports jacket and open-collar, long-sleeve, button-down dress shirt. I stood out more distinctly as a foreigner, so it was not hard for him to pick me out of the crowd of pilgrims—Nepalis don't hesitate to approach others in poorly defined public situations like this.

Bhim drove me on the back of his motorcycle to his walk-up, seven-story house in the final throes of construction, not far from the stupa. He and his wife, Sukar, and their children (two sons, two daughters), live on the top two floors, along with Sukar's mother, Tshering, who, coincidentally, has the same name as Bhim's mother. The number of different names in use is not great, so many people have the same name—not unlike our system, with its many Johns, Bills, Bobs, Marys, Sues, and Anns. Both Sukar's mother and Bhim's were my age and of course young women when I had last lived in the village.

Bhim stands next to his motorcycle in front of his and Sukar's seven story house, still under construction, near Boudhanath in Kathmandu.

Bhim and Sukar travel occasionally to Europe on business, but most of the time they reside in their top floors and either rent out the other floors as residential apartments to Nepali families (rarely, if ever, from Dolpa), or use them as storage rooms for the carpets they manufacture, while the ground floor is rented by shopkeepers who run small mom-and-pop stores on the street-front. Now, forty-four years after I had left the village, Lanku's nephew had built a "house" well beyond anything his uncle could have imagined. Even I was astonished at its scale. Forty

Bhim and Sukar on a business trip to Europe.

years before, Taralis had asked me about American houses and how many floors they had. I had answered that American houses usually had two or three stories, which were similar, in that respect, to Tarali houses. I also mentioned the Empire State Building and its 103 stories, which were harder to envision, as was the five minutes or so it took to reach the top by elevator.

I had brought along some photos (now digitized on my laptop computer) and my old census notes of the village, so we got to know each other poring over them, looking for pictures on the computer and people's names in my notes. Like Taralis in Tichurong, they were always more interested in pictures than in kinship diagrams. Some of the people we talked about I knew better than Bhim and Sukar, others they knew more about than I did. We both enjoyed telling, and hearing, little stories and anecdotes about people I remembered, which included some of their friends and family, including details such as who was married to whom, who had died, and for those who hadn't, what they were doing now. It reminded me of how, after a year in the village, I had begun to feel a part of the place.

Gradually the details of Bhim's life began to unfold. He was born to Bau Prasad and Tshering a couple of years after I left the village, in

2028 BS (probably 1971 CE, since the Bikram Sambat calendar often used in Nepal (see Appendix D), and which begins in mid-April, is either fifty-six or fifty-seven years ahead of ours). Regardless of which calendar we were using, all the reminiscing made it feel like old home week for all of us.

Bhim began life in the unexceptional way any other Tarang child would. He played with his friends on the rooftops, and sometimes helped out by herding cattle to graze in hillside forests and fields, carrying jugs of water from the tap below the village, or firewood from the forest above the village, to his house. Fetching water was the more difficult of the last two tasks, as it involved going downhill empty and uphill full, whereas collecting firewood, which involves going uphill empty and downhill with a full load, takes advantage of the laws of gravity. As he was his parents' first child, he had no older siblings to help his parents look after him. As is generally the case in Tarang households, his mother took responsibility for most of the child-rearing. She often took him to Tupa, where his father's mother's sister lived, and they sometimes stayed overnight there.

How a villager from an extremely remote village in northwest Nepal ends up living an upscale lifestyle in Kathmandu and building a seven-story building there is a basic question posed by the changes that have occurred in the last forty-plus years. To answer it is to confront the new processes at work in twenty-first-century Tarang, Nepal, and in the world. First, it is impossible to understand the course of Bhim's life without a clear understanding of his position in the kinship system of the village, more specifically his connection to his paternal uncle, Lanku. In addition to kinship, three other independent and interdependent factors are also crucial to this understanding: 1) his education, 2) his ability to capitalize on new, unprecedented economic resources and opportunities that became available to Taralis only after he was born, and 3) the general mentality prevalent in a village and valley whose economy had long included not only a strong agricultural base but active and long-distance trading between contrasting cultural, linguistic, and ecological zones, which was the subject of the original *Trans-Himalayan Traders*.

For his education, Bhim enrolled in Class 1 at the village school, which was just beginning to materialize when I was there. Some sort of rudimentary school had opened in Tarakot as early as 1961, then moved to Tarang the same year, as it was larger and more centrally located than any other village in Tichurong. By the time I arrived in 1968 a school building had still not been constructed, despite fitful, erratic attempts at constructing one, relying on voluntary labor contributed by each house. In theory school classes (through Class 5, which then had an enrollment of three) met in the Panchayat Ghar (Community House), but that building was so dark, dank, and dismal that whatever students appeared just sat outside on the ground, in the sunlight, to go over their lessons. Inclement weather was always a convenient excuse to cancel classes for the day.

At that time the school had an official enrollment of forty-five, of which perhaps a dozen might attend on a good day. Sometimes, depending on weather and competing household work requirements, just three or four would show up. Official school hours were 10:00 A.M. till 1:00 P.M., and 2:00 P.M. till 4:00 P.M. The teacher, from Pokhara, was lackadaisical and indifferent about whether anyone was learning anything; he would disappear for months at a time. He was paid a government salary of Rs. 225/month, and villagers were expected to donate food and firewood to supplement his meager salary. Tuition was charged at the rate of half a rupee per month for Class 1, up to two-and-a-half rupees (about $0.30) for Class 5. Essentially, there was no functional literacy in the village during my time there. (Chandra Man, in his account below, reports that there were four or five literate men in the village in the 1950s or early 1960s—Lanku would have been one of them—which is about what I would expect, but their level of literacy was quite low.)

However, by the late 1960s seven students had completed whatever grades the local school offered and moved on to higher classes in Dunai, Pokhara, Tansen, Baglung, and similar locations (see Appendix C). These students, whom I didn't know because they were off studying elsewhere, formed the initial cohort of literate villagers from Tarang, the first generation of modernity, which has moved into new economic and cultural territory.

Following the same pattern, Bhim moved on to Dunai for Classes 2 and 3. There he stayed in the house of his uncle Lanku (his father's brother), who by that time was entering the burgeoning business world of Dunai. Then Bisara, the sister of both Lanku and his father, brought him to Kathmandu in 2038 BS (1981 CE) to finish Class 3 and then to continue in Class 4, at Sharada Madhemik Vidyalaya, near Pashupati.

For Classes 5 through 10 he attended Pharping boarding school, just south of the Kathmandu Valley, which he liked very much.

It was at Pharping, coincidentally, that I had taught as a Peace Corps Volunteer almost fifty years before and had met Chandra Man, then in Class 8 at Pharping. It was Chandra Man who had told me for the first time about his home village, a place I had never heard of before—Tarang, although he used the Nepali name, Sahar Tara, to refer to it. Chandra Man became the first, and for a long time the only, educated person in the village, eventually acquiring a master's degree in agriculture from an Australian university.

In Chapter 9 he recounts the extraordinary story of his early life in his own words. Except for Chandra Man, almost none of the residents of the village in those days were literate in any language, apart from the few, such as Lank Man, who were in the process of intermittently pursuing higher classes in the hill towns of western Nepal mentioned previously. The itinerant lamas, in addition to the few local ones, who could read but not write Tibetan (a language totally unrelated to Nepali) texts and who would descend from Upper Dolpo to winter over in Tarang were the only exceptions.

After graduating from high school, rather than continuing on to college, Bhim returned to Dunai, the district capital, a day's walk down the river from Tarang, where he was needed to help in the shop belonging to Lanku's brother Siddhi (Sukar's father). Siddhi managed the shop, and Lanku supplied it with goods to sell. He went as far as Calcutta for tea, dye, *boku* (Tibetan coats), and horse tack. He either sold or exchanged his goods for sheep, which he then sold in the south during winter—one of the transaction circuits in which Taralis had been involved for more years than anyone could count.

The Marriage of Bhim and Sukar

The year before his graduation was also when his marriage to Sukar was consummated. His and Sukar's account of it gave me a more nuanced understanding of this life-cyle ritual than the formulaic and binary "capture" versus "arranged" label often used to describe nuptial arrangements in Nepal. Bhim explained that Tarali marriage partners are both arranged and captured, at least most of the time, thus entwining within the practice of ritual or marriage elements that constitute part of Tarali culture, life, and identity.

First comes the *magni* (from Nepali *magnu*, to ask) stage, followed by the capture. The former is to confirm intentions; the latter is to finalize the relationship through stealing. "Stealing" in this context can be construed as a stylized action which is actually staged following the confirmation of intentions. His own marriage was just such a *magnibibaha* (arranged marriage), with the additional complication that he was a *gharjwai* (in which the groom goes to live at his bride's house, in the relatively rare instance when she has no brothers to inherit her parents' land, as was Sukar's case).

What if there are other daughters in the house? In such a case the husband married to the eldest daughter becomes the *gharjwai* and benefits from his wife's inheritance. The other daughters would inherit little, although the parents would extend help if and when needed, and they can continue to reside in their parents' house for a long time. Otherwise, they would benefit from whatever inheritance to which their husbands would be entitled, and live with them. Sukar was the only daughter in her family, so there were no complications, and Bhim was considered quite lucky in this respect.

The capture takes place in an auspicious month. The calendar is a Tibetan one, but similar to Hindu marriage months. Marriages never take place in the month of Kartik, because that's considered to be the month that dogs mate. Baisakh, Jestha, Asar, Mangsir, Magh, and Falgun are auspicious months, but only during the fifteen days before Purnima (full moon).

Divorce is rare, but when it occurs, *porchya* (compensation) must be paid by whoever leaves the marriage. If a husband brings another wife, or even if an unmarried man brings a married woman into his house, *jari* (a fine for adultery) must be paid to the former husband. Amounts depend on the economic status of the parties. Unwanted pregnancies occur rarely, and then only if a boy reneges on a promise to marry. Birth control and family planning have entered through the provision of pills and injections by NGOs operating out of Dunai.

Bhim and Sukar explained that the advantage of capture is that it makes everything easier: few expenses, although a *bhoj* (feast) must be given afterwards, no problems with long distances between partners, and no misunderstandings. The parents make the agreement secretly, but they try to select partners who are not likely to object to their proposal. If grown children fall in love, there can be a simple elopement, without either *magni* or capture, and they cannot complain to their parents if there are problems later. Once made, m*agni* can not be violated or rejected, otherwise a huge fine (*porchya*, Kaike) will have to be paid, which includes payment for legal proceedings.

The matrilocal arrangement entailed in a *gharjwai* marriage gives women a package of rights they do not normally have in the more typical marriage, in which the wife shares in her husband's inheritance by going to live in his house. It gives rise to the question, sometimes discussed by villagers, of whether Tarali social structure is based on matriarchy. In terms of access to education and commercial wealth, men unquestionably do better than women—it is they who study at higher levels and go trading. Appendix C lists only men's names. However, as is often the case in Nepal, decision-making power within the household (concerning finances, for instance) is dominated by women. They largely control the agricultural sector, doing all the work except for plowing, although decisions concerning what day to plant, and in which field, for example, are made jointly. Women have also made notable contributions in the business world, although not always publicly recognized, as will be seen below. However, probably at least the initial push towards "modernity" (e.g., schooling, trading, migrating) has very often empowered men more than women.

In Bhim and Sukar's case, the *magni* was performed when they were in about Class 4, and they found this out when they were around twelve or thirteen. This results in some teasing, since it is also generally known in the village at that time. While Sukar knew about the arrangement, she didn't know, nor did Bhim, when the capture would take place, and she didn't find out until just a few days before the actual event. Bhim didn't know when the capture would take place until he was actually captured. This secrecy ends with a grand feast for the entire village.[8]

When Bhim was seventeen years old he was enrolled in Class 9 at Pharping Boarding School near Kathmandu. At this time he received a message from his parents asking him to return home quickly as they were both unwell. He was worried about them and therefore headed for his village at once, where he discovered his parents both in very good health. He was surprised, but it would have been considered to be bad form to ask about their health.

---

[8]   The entire village is invited to the *bhoj* feast, regardless of personal relationships. Enemies, if any, must decide whether they will attend or not.

One evening he went to stay the night at a friend's house. The bride's side (Sukar's family) knew where he was and sent some young men to capture him. Both sets of parents would have known about this, but not the principals. Although he knew about the arrangement, which had been made when he was in Class 4, once he realized what was happening to him, he escaped briefly to his own house, but they followed in hot pursuit and finally took him to his wife's house (Sukar was sixteen at the time).

The main event which consecrates the marriage is the feast. For the feast, a Kami (Carpenter caste) comes to apply *dubo* (grass) behind the ears of the participants. The *dubo* symbolizes auspiciousness and just generally positive feelings, or as Bhim put it, *"suva sait ra khusiyali"* (good luck and happiness, Nepali). This is an expression of well-wishing by a member of the community, and in return they expect, and are paid, something for their contribution to the occasion.

Also at the feast a lama chants from a text, called *dhomo*, to give blessings for the couple. This same text is used at *bartaman* (the coming-of-age ceremony for boys at around puberty), death, and other rituals.

Marriage among Taralis in Kathmandu is similar, with some urban modifications—for example, the bride (or groom, in the case of *gharjwai*) might arrive by car or taxi to the relevant house. As in Tarang, parents would generally execute the *magni* arrangements. It's hard to say whether urban modifications are temporary adjustments or harbingers of a future, more permanent urban version of Tarali culture.

Thus, most marriages are made both by arrangement and subsequent capture, whether in the normal case in which the boy's side captures the girl, or the rather rare *gharjwai* case in which the girl's side captures the boy. However, it is also possible for a genuine capture to take place in which a girl is taken without *magni*, or prior agreement, of any kind (a girl capturing a boy in this way would never happen); such cases will likely be followed by legal challenges, and I observed one in the late sixties when the aggrieved girl's parents filed a complaint with the local police checkpost.

After his marriage, Bhim continued his education but continued to stay at his parents' house when he was in the village, after which he lived in his wife's home, which by this time was in Dunai, where she was running her shop. Similarly, a married girl will continue residing in her parental home for a year or so after marriage, before moving to her husband's house. Bhim spent two years in Dunai, helping Sukar in her shop. This obligation as *gharjwai* also demonstrates mobility in rites of passage.

Two years after their marriage Bhim and Sukar both came to Kathmandu. By this time Bisara (sister of both their fathers as well as of Lanku) was already established there with her husband, Lank Man. She helped Bhim and Sukar get started in the carpet business, in which Lank Man was already well established. They first rented a three-story house in Bhaktapur as center for their operations. They were in partnership with Heem (one of several of Lanku's sons), and the business grew bigger. Eventually Bhim and Sukar separated their business from Heem's, so then Bhim and Sukar each had their own businesses. All along they had helped Lank Man where they could, but they were never full business partners with him, the way Bhim's father had been.

These carpet-weaving enterprises were among the most important and lucrative business ventures to have taken root in still relatively provincial Kathmandu, because the manufacture of Tibetan carpets, which were exported worldwide, had become a prime source of foreign exchange in Nepal. These Tibetan carpets are woven by Nepalese, but according to mostly Tibetan designs.

Thus it was that Bhim returned to Kathmandu to enter the carpet business, with Bisara's husband, Lank Man Rokaya, as his mentor. Sukar was still mostly in Dunai (with occasional visits to Tarang during holidays to visit family, etc.), and Bhim later passed on what he had learned from Lank Man to her. This was not an entirely new venture, since Bhim's father, Bau Prasad, had also spent time in Kathmandu beginning in 2029 BS (1972 CE) making yarn for carpets. Lank Man and Bau Prasad were partners, and Bhim, only in Class 3 at the time, assisted them in chores such as energetically taking care of the Tibetan wool and spreading it in the sun to dry and later spinning it by hand into a circular shape, and storing it properly. Had he stayed in Tarang, he would have learned the ins and outs of agriculture and small-scale trading. Based more in Kathmandu, in addition to attending school, he learned a lot of the carpet business by doing it as he was growing up.

Bhim remarked that dealing with carpets was his family business, as he saw himself as heir to his father's business. In Nepali, Bhim proudly and confidently claimed that his family had been well-to-do from the beginning: "Hami hune khane paribarka ham" ("We belong to a well-to-do

Bhim Prasad in Kathmandu, standing
in front of one of his vertically
stretched carpets.

Bhim's father, Bau Prasad, and his
mother, Tshering, on their front porch.

family"). By that he meant that his family had been traders in Dolpa for a
very long time, well before the rise of the carpet industry in Kathmandu.
In other words, business was not just an opportunity, but a legacy.

Lanku's prior commercial success was essential to that of Bisara and
Lank Man. But his was also part of the traditional transaction system,
leaving it to them to become the first true entrepreneurs from the village.
They divided their labor so that Lank Man exported (managing orders,
handling financial transactions) what Bisara produced (supervising
workers, helping Bhim spin and spread out the wool). Bau Prasad and
Lank Man (both married to Lanku's sisters) had formed a business
partnership. Lank Man described Bhim's father as a profit partner;
that is, the investment was Lank Man's, but shares were distributed to
Bhim's father and others, who contributed various skills in producing
the carpets. Bhim and Sukar joined in the operation by supplying carpets
to Bisara, who transferred them to Lank Man to handle the exporting
part of the operation. This was a familial operation in which each person
played a well-defined role and cooperated with everyone else. This
simultaneous learning and earning enhanced the prospects for success
and growth of the business.

Subsequently, Bhim and Sukar established a factory in Chabel (Handigaon), and later moved their operations to Bhaktapur. What had been more of a family operation now became separate and somewhat competitive, although in an overall cooperative fashion. Bisara contributed much and thinks that those she and Lank Man have helped over the years have not always been very grateful. She doesn't always feel fully appreciated. But she admits she likes the business now because it's so prosperous and, compared to formerly, an easy way to make a lot of money.

Bhim and Sukar's business site, Bhaktapur, was, coincidentally, the site of my first Peace Corps assignment in 1962. At that time I hadn't a clue that the entrepreneurial way of life of someone from a very remote village, in a very remote district in northwest Nepal, neither of which I had ever heard of, would eventually take shape behind and beneath the medieval, magisterial, and imposing Newari temples of its then decrepit and unrenovated Darbar Square. It's probably fair to say that at that time no one else in Nepal, including the Taralis themselves, imagined such a chain of events either. Only at the present can I look back and see how what was then the distant future inexorably emerged, over time, from a world which now seems unimaginably archaic.

Bhim's story is one of several that, collectively, show how a new generation of traders has expanded the traditional notion of transaction, one which is both true to its previous forms and simultaneously novel, going far beyond the earlier ones. It also shows how Bhim, as an able, skilled, and successful Tarali businessman has transcended his *gharjwai* role. He sees what he's accomplished as part of a familial tradition. His education was certainly an essential part of it, but in addition his success is due in no small part to the various kinship connections in place that assisted him in moving into this new commercial world. In this, his link with Lanku's sister Bisara (sister of both his father and Sukar's father) and her husband, Lank Man, was critical. Bhim and Sukar could not have achieved what they have without that long mentoring relationship in what would otherwise be the alien world of Kathmandu.

4

Modern Migrants:
Life in Kathmandu

Like Bhim, his wife, Sukar, was born in Tarang. Since her father (Siddhi, Lanku's brother) had opened a shop in Dunai, she grew up mostly there. Her schooling, from Class 1 through Class 10, took place at Saraswati Higher Education School in Dunai. Her school and street language were Nepali, but she spoke Kaike at home. All of her four children understand most of the Kaike spoken to them, but they speak it rarely. They lead asymmetrical linguistic lives: Sukar and Bhim speak Kaike to each other and to their children, but the children answer, and speak to each other, in Nepali. This is the classic, near-universal adaptation children make to such bilingual or multilingual situations. They also understand Tibetan, since they hear it often spoken by non-Kaike-speaking Taralis for whom it is their mother-tongue, thus giving them multiple home as well as school-and-street languages. When asked if a Kaike district should be established as part of a government decentralized along ethnic lines, the parents said that would not be possible, and that even if it were, they don't want it; the main point of government, they say, should be to prosper humanity and provide opportunity for all.

All of Sukar's children were born in a Kathmandu hospital. The oldest son, Ratna, was, at the time of my visiting, just finishing his bachelor degree at the Nepal College of Travel and Tourism Management, and waiting for results of the exam. He has also picked up considerable knowledge about the carpet business over the years while growing up with both parents in the business. Maya was studying biology in Trinity International College (and in 2016 left for the United States to study nursing). The younger daughter (Trishu) and son (Bhupati) were in secondary boarding school in Classes 9 and 5 ("boarding" in the Nepali context simply means private). In appearance, demeanor, and language they are indistinguishable from most other middle-class Kathmandu kids—that is, they speak several languages, as almost all Nepalis do. I have never met a Nepali who spoke only one language. Class, a term more associated with things modern and global, trumps ethnicity in these urban circumstances.

The daughters struck me as uncommunicative teenagers, surfing through channels on the TV to which they were glued much of the time, while their parents and other adults carried on a conversation with me. They follow their parents' example in some respects, such as eating with a spoon instead of with their hands, although eating by hand is practiced, and often preferred, by even the most highly educated and widely traveled Nepalis. They have all been globalized, in somewhat random and inconsistent fashion, into a new slice of the nation of which they're now an integral part. They self-identify, to the extent that they engage in that process, more as Nepali nationals than as Tichurong regionals, although they do not see those identities as being at all incommensurate.

Recreating Tarali Culture in Kathmandu

Choputa is the Kul Deuta not only for Tarang but for the entire Tarang and Lawan VDCs (Village Development Committees, administrative units consisting of neighboring villages; Dolpa district consists of several VDCs; Tichurong consists of two, as noted above, one on each side of the Bheri River). Choputa is the major deity present in various rituals and festivals, referred to collectively as Rung.[9] In the middle of the month in which a puja is held, before the full moon, all participants observe a cluster of six or seven stars, side by side with three vertical stars, on the other side of which is the moon, all adjacent to each other. If the sky is clear so that they can be easily seen, it is perceived as a rinpoche in the form of a deity, Rungpacha (Midu, Tibetan). The major Choputa *puja*, Lapsol (lit: *La*, god; *sol*, day of worship), lasts two months, starting in Pus and ending in Magh (mid-December till mid-February).

The day before the *puja* begins, they create a *pakhi*, symbolically an ancestral figure, made with *ghiu* (clarified butter), wheat, and honey (or sugar). A flame is lit in the *pakhi* for the entire month. The last day of the

---

[9]   *Rung* includes whatever is done ritually (including the New Year and Kul Deuta Puja) in the Nepali months Pus to Baisakh.

month they drink fresh *chang* (regarded as a sacred libation) and finally eat the *pakhi*.

According to the seasonal calendrical festival, after the winter rituals, Choputa will go to the southern plains. The belief is that Choputa comes during the winter season festival to give them blessings; after that, during the month of Falgun (mid-February till mid-March), Choputa goes to the Tarai to play Holi. This case demonstrates exchange and syncretism between the Tarali Magars and Hindus, as opposed to mere ethnic difference.

The next major ritual occasion is Chaite Bokne. It occurs in the month of Chait (mid-March to mid-April), as part of the coming of spring. As before, it involves the *puja* of Choputa, for which two families out of the entire village who take part in the ritual in Tarang take their turns as hosts on a rotating annual basis. The rotation turns over again about every thirty years. If a host family happens to live in Kathmandu (as Bhim and Sukar do), they have to return to Tarang to fulfill their ritual obligations. Whoever is the organizer in a particular year is carried (*bokne*, Nepali to carry) during the month of Chait from house to house. Chaite Bokne is celebrated by consuming *jad* (Nepali, beer), *rakshi* (distilled *jad*), and meat, the expenses for which add up to roughly 25,000 to 30,000 rupees each turn.

The singing and dancing take place after the host is carried by the villagers. Chaite Bokne is now performed in Tichurong mainly in Kola village because the ritual requires so much time that it is felt the younger generation is involved in so many activities that they don't have the leisure the older generation had. Also, after the *patum* (title of the traditional ritual leader) died, there have been only two people available to organize the music, as opposed to a dozen in Kola, where there is still a *patum*. It is performed twelve days after the Kul Deuta Puja for Choputa, and lasts for three days. The Kul Deuta Puja reveals the faith and devotion every member of the community feels. Chaite Bokne, by contrast, is more in the nature of a festival in which the main objective is to have a good time.

Tarali Community Organizations in Kathmandu

Bhim and Lank Man are active in Dolpa affairs, particularly in two Kathmandu organizations promoting Dolpa culture: one is called Dolpa Rung Samaj, started originally by Chandra Man Rokaya, whose life history is presented in detail in Chapter 9. Its members gather once a month in a rented hall near Boudhanath.

They also help organize the observance of the major festival (*chad*, Nepali) Chaite Bokne, in the month of Chait.

Those who are not hosts but who live in Kathmandu take part in the festival by placing a Tibetan flag (*lumta*, Kaike) at a sacred place on top of Swayambhu hill. They cook bread (*roti*, Nepali, including an oily bread, *puri*) and worship their Kul Deuta, Choputa. As mentioned above, they mold dough made from wheat flour, honey, and sugar in the shape of a mountain—a generalized mountain, not a particular peak—in which the Kul Deuta, Choputa, resides. This overall process takes place in Kathmandu, but Chaite Bokne hosts resident in Kathmandu have to return to the village to carry out their ritual and social obligations.

Other Taralis go to a second, similar organization, Chaigo (referring to the New Year) Samaj, founded by Bhim's uncle (*kaka*, Nepali), Lal Prasad Rokaya, from Kani VDC, up the river. The latter organization is more politically driven, but there is no substantive political divide between the two organizations. The difference seems to be primarily generational, with younger people tending to affiliate with the Chaigo Samaj, the more recently founded of the two. Bhim said Chaigo, being newer and established by younger people, is more active, compared to Rung, which is older and less active. This relative passivity is what gave rise to the creation of a new organization.

Now, it is Chaigo, with Lal Prasad as its chair, which organizes the monthly *puja* in Dashami on the tenth of the month, the birthday of Guru Padmasambhava (Guru Rinpoche). They also organize their New Year's picnic (in Pus) every year (for Tarang and Lawan VDCs), enabling Bhim to say proudly, "We are preserving our culture." Just as in Hindu culture when sisters are respected and honored during Bhai Tika, a part of the Tihar celebration, similarly Taralis celebrate their sisters during the winter season (Pus and Magh). Chaigo Samaj is raising a fund to support this.

Bhim and others seem to share a broad agreement that it would be better if the two organizations were combined into a single one: "I think it would be good" (*malai ramro hunthyo*, Nepali); "Two societies should be one" (*duita samaj ek hunu parcha*, Nepali), since the aim of both organizations is identical: to preserve the traditions and culture of the Taralis who have migrated to or are living in Kathmandu. Membership in either organization does not preclude membership in the other. Bhim emphatically stated, "We belong to both organizations" ("hami duwai ma cham," Nepali). Sometimes the actors are more important than the institutions, as different individuals will disproportionately support one or the other. Either way, the intent is the same: promotion and preservation of Tarali culture.

Despite the agreement that the two organizations should merge, neither Bhim nor anyone else has a concrete plan to do so. What everyone seems to agree on is that the two organizations should be combined into a unitary organization that would be given a new name. Asked whether such a united organization should be called Rung or Chaigo, Bhim laughed and said they would have to search for a common or alternative name, and stressed that social unity was much more important than nomenclature.

Bhim also serves as the Kaike vice president of Nepal Magar Sangh (Magar Society of Nepal), one of the organizations that promotes the interests of indigenous peoples, in this case Magars. The Sangh has divided Magars into three linguistic groups: *barha* Magarant, *barha* meaning 12, refers to historical areas or districts where the Magar dialect of Dut is spoken by villagers in such locations as Syanja, Gulmi, and Palpa (Hitchcock 1966); 18 Magarant Kham, referring to the Kham Magars in the west, whose language is called Kham (Oppitz 1981); and the Kaike speakers of Tichurong, which comprise the third group. The Tibetan-speaking Magars of Tichurong are not included in the Magar Sangh's tripartite linguistic categories, although their status as Magars is not contested. Similarly, many Magars in 12 Magarant and 18 Magarant no longer speak any language other than Nepali.

Budhamagar (2014) has discussed in some detail the history and geographic spread of 12 Magarant. Before the unification of Nepal in the late eighteenth century, these were part of the twenty-four Chaubisi Raja kingdoms. Similarly, the 18 Magarant included the areas of Beni, Baglung, and Dhorpatan today. What seems to unite the three areas is the commonality of clans (*thar*, Nepali) found in them (e.g., Budha, Gharti, and Rokaya in Tichurong, plus many more not found in Tichurong). It is commonly said that there are a thousand clans and subclans found in the various Magar areas. This is no doubt an exaggeration, and it is also true that *thar*s are not fixed, eternal entities. Some *thar*s are subdivided into still other *thar*s. Members of the Jhankri *thar* elsewhere in Tichurong (but not in Tarang) have recently started calling themselves Rana Magar instead of Jhankri Magar.

Tarali Culture and Other Cultures

Partly because of these two organizations that have collectively raised consciousness of Tarali culture, some Taralis in Kathmandu have self-consciously stopped observing some parts of Hindu culture, such as performing certain Hindu rituals, over the last dozen or so years. The aim is not the negative one of pursuing an anti-Hindu agenda, but rather the positive one of preserving Tichurong culture. But such matters remain personal options. For example, some no longer observe Dasai, although others, such as Chandra Man's widow, Paljum, who has lived for decades in Kathmandu, still celebrate it. One afternoon Bhim and Sukar's youngest son returned home covered with vermillion powder, after playing Holi with other neighborhood kids. Attempts to cease practicing Hindu rituals, festivals, and holidays do not apply to children having fun.

Thus many ethnic groups, like the Taralis, celebrate some Hindu rituals, or parts of them. In the same way, many Nepalis, Hindus, and others nowadays celebrate occasions such as Losar and Sakela (a Kirat festival celebrated twice annually), as well as Christmas, English New Year, Valentine's Day, and Halloween. Some more nationalistically inclined people argue against this on the ground that Christmas and Western New Year are not part of the Nepalese heritage. They want to maintain a cultural dividing line between what they regard as traditional Nepalese customs and imports from elsewhere, an ideological demarcation very difficult to sustain in everyday life.

Taralis engage in other cooperative activities in which various members help one another. As mentioned above, most of the Tarali families meet once a month and worship together, regardless of Rung or Chaigo membership. On the day I visited the hall rented by Dolpa Rung Samaj, they were celebrating Guru Rinpoche's birthday, which they do on a regular monthly basis. Their main secular motivation is to work for the welfare of people in Dolpa. Attempts along these lines were initiated originally by Chandra Man and, after him, Lank Man. Like others, Lank Man has a strong interest in preserving Tichurong culture, and he's particularly interested in making a documentary, noncommercial film about celebration of the Chaite Bokne festival in the three Kaike-speaking villages, but sees no way to raise the $20,000 to $30,000 it would take to finance it. Bhim has started a Dolpa Development Foundation, motivated by a similar interest in attempting to improve the quality of Tichurong life.

Part of the interest in promoting Tarali culture centers on Kaike—not only on continuing to speak it, at least among the older generations (in the younger generation it seems to already be a lost cause), but on the transformation of their opinions and evaluations of it. Forty-three years ago my queries about Kaike generally elicited negative responses: Kaike is not a good language because you can't compose songs in it, there are no proverbs in it (although I found a few), you can only count to twenty in it, you can't write in it. They regarded Kaike as some sort of primitive, or at least unsophisticated, language spoken by uneducated people. Now, in marked contrast, there is strong interest and pride in it and in its divine origins (Fisher 1986; Daurio 2012).

The question of counting to twenty is complicated. It was a commonly held belief in the 1960s, often repeated by Taralis, that one can count only up to twenty in Kaike. A closer examination shows, first, that there is a regular counting system up to and beyond one hundred, similar to that in English and Nepali, such that one can stipulate the exact quantity of countable things (houses, head of cattle, people, number of potatoes). Second, there is a kind of "shortcut" system also in use by which, for example, ninety is represented as "four twenties plus a ten," or fifty-one is represented by "two twenties plus an eleven." When Kaike-speakers say they cannot count beyond twenty, I believe they are referring to the "shortcut" system, which they frequently utilize in daily life.

Another instance of interest in Kaike is that of a boy from Samtiling, Nima Tsering, who is studying to be a monk and also writing a Kaike dictionary. Interest in Kaike has also reached professional linguists such as Ambika Regmi, who has two works on the subject: *A Grammar of Magar Kaike* and *Analyzed Texts in Magar Kaike* (Regmi 2013 and 2014). People notice and remark upon small dialectical differences in Kaike even within Tarang. For example, there are differences between Samtiling (the upper part of the village), where they say *tai jing pao?* (for 'What is this?') and the main part of Tarang, where they say, *tai jing pa?* As mentioned above, though, the attempt to keep Kaike alive in Kathmandu among the younger generation has been almost entirely unsuccessful, at least as an actively used language, as opposed to being only passively understood.

While the interest in preserving Tarali culture has been gradually and generally expanding among Taralis in Kathmandu, this interest does not extend to some of the material aspects of daily life. Somewhat along the lines of Bhim and Sukar's lifestyle, Bisara and Lank Man also live near Boudhanath, in an eight-story house. Neither of these houses displays any of the architectural features whatsoever of Tarali houses, and both of them survived the 2015 earthquakes without damage. Bisara also built a ten-story house which she and Lank Man now occupy, in addition to renting out lower floors to a private bank. She is presently installing an elevator to take them up to their living quarters on the top floor.

Living in colossal houses does not mean that Bisara has forgotten her origins or abandoned her emotional attachment to them. As I talked to her about what it was like growing up in Tarang, and

Lank Man and Bisara's eight-story house near Boudhanath in Kathmandu.

Lank Man and Bisara in Kathmandu several years ago in their 10-story house. Bisara would not wear these earrings now, except at special Tarali occasions.

showed her my pictures from that time, she began to cry, as she remembered her relatives and friends who have died. She hasn't visited Tarang for ten years; her sister, Pyari, lives in Tupa and never comes to Kathmandu, so the two sisters haven't seen each other for all this time.[10] She misses people who are (at least from her point of view) left behind in Tichurong. Despite her palatial and comfortable surroundings, she feels lonely and complains that even friends and family in Kathmandu don't come to see her very often.

She also recounted how she and her brother Lanku, and Lanku's mother (among others), came to our house for Christmas dinner in 1968, an event I had totally forgotten. Although I didn't notice it at the time, they were extremely careful about what they ate and did not eat. They ate our potatoes but not our vegetables, because, in typical American fashion, we had tasted the vegetables in the process of cooking them, to see if they were done. In doing so traces of our saliva, however minute, would have polluted the cooking pot and all the vegetables

---

[10] Bisara's ability to travel is limited by her diabetes; the insulin she needs costs around Rs. 4,000/month. Lank Man is also worried about diabetes and watches his own diet accordingly.

in it, transforming them into *jutho* (polluted food), so that eating from the pot would have contaminated anyone who did so in a serious and compromising way.[11]

All this concern about food was so subtle and unspoken that it took me quite some time to realize the strength and ubiquity of these beliefs about pollution. Thinking that contamination beliefs and practices were far more pronounced among Hindus than among non-Hindus, including Tibeto-Burman-speaking peoples such as the Taralis, among whom I imagined they didn't exist at all, I simply wasn't looking for them.[12] This observational blindness, to coin a methodological oxymoron that characterizes much anthropological fieldwork, caused me to miss them even when they were staring me in the face.

---

[11] See Chandra Man's reference (in Chapter 9) to his own worries about a rumor circulating in the village that he had eaten Hitchcock's "*jutho*" (food contaminated in the same sense as our Christmas dinner was).

[12] Nor is contamination belief (and behavior) conspicuous only among Nepalis, whether Hindu or non-Hindu. Although highly variable, it is a ubiquitous notion, however the contamination is believed to be transmitted: by air, saliva, or even by shaking hands.

5

Dhanu:
Yarsagumba and Politics

The more Bhim, Sukar, and I immersed ourselves in Tarang history, poring over photographs and genealogical charts from more than forty years previously, the more we wanted to keep at it. But, agreeing to resume our retrospective discussions where we had left off soon, Bhim and I eventually left their house and wandered over to the nearby hall, hired by the Dolpa Rung Samaj, where three lamas were chanting in celebration of the birthday of Guru Rinpoche.[13] About twenty people had gathered, and I was introduced around. One of those attending was Kwinkep, another of Lanku's sons, wearing a black motorcycle jacket; I remembered him the way he was at the age of five.

We sat around chatting and exchanging pleasantries and drinking tea, more or less oblivious to the chanting lamas, but in doing so we were just following the usual protocol. What is important is that the lamas chant, since the power lies in the sounds of the words themselves, not in understanding or even necessarily in hearing them. In addition to the efficacy of the chanting itself should be added the attraction of the comfort and valorization of a living tradition that has been part of life as long as anyone can remember. That is what continues on a monthly basis.

This is the same phenomenon I had observed during my first trip, in which I found that the power of sacred, written Tibetan texts, which are not considered public documents, is contained not in the meanings the words convey, but in the palpable, audible form taken of the visible words on paper. Even the physical books containing the words are powerful, which explains why the Taralis refused to allow me to take one or two with me, or even to write down the name of a text so that I could show it to a textual scholar who could properly identify it. By a

---

13   Guru Rinpoche's birthday is celebrated monthly, not annually.

similar logic, the power of agriculture is contained in the actual soil, so much so that they were very upset that I wanted to take a soil sample to Kathmandu to have it analyzed. In both cases, these actions would deplete the power that they very much relied on.

This time I discovered yet another example of this belief: cutting a small tuft of hair from cattle and sticking it in some arbitrary corner of the cowshed. Doing so brings good luck, but it also preserves the power of the cattle. To sell cattle denotes loss of wealth, rather than accumulation of it, which is praxis for everyone. Selling cattle means the loss of something, but the hair clipping demonstrates that the cattle are still symbolically there. This not only effectively cancels out the loss, but it also reminds one of what specifically has been lost, functioning as a kind of low-level mourning, somewhat akin to the ashes one keeps of one's ancestors.

Good luck might enable the number of cattle to increase exponentially in the future, which is desirable, since cattle are a form of capital. Previously, to rear and increase a herd of cattle was a sign of wealth and respectability—a matter of pride and self-esteem. Now, people rear cattle primarily for unadorned economic reasons, since hard cash is also a sign of wealth and pride. It has trumped the unfinanced dignity of animals. However, holding on to a tuft of hair from cattle that have been sold allows the owner to both profit economically and preserve their wealth symbolically, thus retaining the best of both worlds.

Therefore, since the language of the chant we were listening to was classical Tibetan, which Taralis don't understand, it does not matter if anyone listens—somewhat like Catholics listening (or not) to a Latin Mass. While the chanting continued in the rented hall in which we had gathered, during the casual chitchat among the Taralis, a stylishly dressed, modern-looking, confident young man arrived: this was Dhanu, whose reputation as a big man (*thulo manche*, Nepali) had long since preceded him. No matter whom I had been talking to about modern developments in Dolpa, Dhanu's name invariably came up, approvingly and admiringly. In terms of respect accorded to community leaders, he clearly occupied a higher than normal level.

Dhanu (another of Lanku's sons) had been, like Bhim, one of my email correspondents. Like Bhim, he has achieved considerable financial success, not so much in carpets—but more about that below. However, unlike Bhim and other Taralis, he has also blazed a political trail no other

Tarali has achieved, and very few
have attempted. He is not only
the most successful businessman
in Tichurong (in this regard he is
a chip off the old block), but he is
also the major political leader not
only in Tichurong, but in all of
Dolpa District.

He has translated his economic
good fortune into political capital
by throwing his hat into the ring
and making a prominent name
for himself politically. Before his
victory in the November 2013
election for the Dolpa seat in
Parliament, he told me there are
33,000 people in Dolpa, of which
20,000 are voters, 70% of whom
support him. In that election,
running on the UML ticket (a

Dhanu celebrating his victory in the
2013 election to be Dolpa's representative in the national parliament.

relatively moderate party, despite its leftist-sounding name: United
Marxist-Leninist), he won 62% of the votes (99% in Tarang, where he ran
as a favorite son). His tally was 7,000 votes, a very substantial margin
over the runner-up Maoist candidate with 2,700 votes (a scattering of
eleven other parties shared the approximate total of 13,000 votes cast).[14]

This result did not come without costs—not necessarily money
for buying votes, a common previous political practice, but for the
expenses of running a campaign, including the day-to-day support of
700 cadres who roamed Dolpa attempting to stir up support for their
candidate. Dhanu tends to think big: one of his projects is to build a
road from Tibet to India, which is already being accomplished with the
help of Tarang labor.

What is unusual is not the political interest, but the degree to which
it has been successfully pursued. Lank Man, for example, like most
Taralis, indeed like most Nepalis, has political interests and keeps

---

[14]   The Maoist candidate had married out of Dolpa District (into nearby Jajarkot), so
that she was considered to be somewhat of an outsider, which cut into her vote
total.

Like most Taralis, Lank Man has an interest in politics, but he does not take himself too seriously.

abreast of them (to be successful any businessman would have to), but he does not take himself too seriously.

Since it was dark and noisy in the rented hall, Dhanu took me in his spanking-new Japanese SUV (driven by his personal driver) to the nearby Hyatt Regency Hotel, probably the most elegant of the 5-Star hotels now sprinkled around Kathmandu. As the son of my old friend Lanku, he was no doubt trying to send me a signal, to show that he runs with the best and fastest horses. An important part of the impression he wanted to make was the appearance that he does this sort of thing routinely. Indeed, he seemed to know many of the waiters and was familiar with and entirely at home in these opulent and regal, polished, Greco-Roman marble surroundings. As I had done with Bhim earlier in the day, we pored over my census records, names, houses, and photos. He ordered coffee for himself, but insisted that I have a beer. I ordered a local brew, which, like several other domains in Nepal these days (publishing, textiles, carpet manufacturing, wood carving, metal statuary, haute cuisine) is of international standard.

The Kathmandu Valley–based carpet business represented a new economic direction Tichurong residents could follow, and some were doing so, but it wasn't the only one. It was, in a way, predictable in the context of growing European and American interest in Asian culture generally and Asian aesthetics specifically. Tibetan carpets were an important, and profitable, piece of this interest; apart from tourism itself, carpet manufacturing was the largest piece of the new economic pie in Nepal, and one which attracted thousands to try their hand at it.

Carpet commerce was nothing new in Nepal; other carpet commerce had preceded that of the modern era. Woolen blankets and carpets were exported to Tibet, China, and Myanmar from the fourteenth to

Dhanu with his new Japanese automobile.

the sixteenth centuries. Before that, woolen blankets were exported even during the fifth century BCE, according to Kautilya's *Arthashastra* (Kautilya, 1915).[15]

And today the carpets were there for the taking, provided only that the taker was clever enough to compete with others possessed of similar ambitions. Lank Man, Bisara, Bhim, and Sukar were not part of a long-established ethnic group that had for entrenched generations controlled and profited from proprietary trade routes (Thakalis, Sherpas, and Newars are well-known examples of such groups). Nevertheless, they were strategically positioned to capitalize on this economic opportunity from the small-scale, long-distance trading culture in which they had grown up, from their education, and from their familial and kin-supported networks. Their commercial skills, acquired from the transactional backgrounds from which they came, compensated for their modest economic and educational backgrounds.

---

[15] The etymology of *Nepal* derives from two Newari words, *Ne* (woolen) and *par* (house).

Dhanu had finished Class 10 in Dunai and passed his SLC exams from the high school there. He enrolled in a Kathmandu college (ASCOL campus, or Amrit Science College) and, like Lank Man, earned an intermediate degree before dropping out to pursue possibilities he believed were present in the business world. Like his predecessors, he was interested in continuing and supporting what had been a relatively small-scale family business that was the sole professional aim of life. There was never an interest in becoming part of the government bureaucracy, and business was the traditional and obvious alternative to it. That is all now in the process of dramatic change, as the example of Bhim's and Sukar's children—each of whom is pursuing higher education (one daughter in the United States) beyond what their parents had achieved—makes abundantly clear. Bhim's sentiments are echoed by others who hold that formal education has now become essential to advance in life, whether that is in business, agriculture, government, international work, or anything else.

The *Yarsagumba* Revolution

Unlike Bhim and Lank Man, Dhanu made the bulk of his fortune from the pioneering and even revolutionary new crop—*yarsagumba*—growing above the village. Because it is so lucrative, it has not only transformed his life, but has also transformed, and continues to transform, life for run-of-the-mill villagers in Tichurong and elsewhere high in the mountains of Nepal. Unlike carpet manufacture, which is part of the bubbling commerce of Kathmandu, *yarsagumba* is available right at home in Tichurong, in the backyards of Tarang. It is not really new, since it was there all along. It was scarcely noticed, though, since it was used only as fodder for grazing horses during the summer months. It was so insignificant and unremarked that when I lived in Tichurong in the 1960s, no one ever thought to mention it to me, and I therefore had no reason to enquire about it.

Yarsagumba (*Ophiocordyceps sinensis*) is a fungus that parasitizes larvae of ghost moths and produces a caterpillar corpse, valued as an herbal remedy for various ailments, including, most famously, male impotence. Signaling its international appeal as an aphrodisiac, it is sometimes referred to locally as nature's Viagra. The fungus germinates in the living larva,

Dolpa villagers harvesting *yarsagumba*.

Yarsagumba fungus emerging from the caterpillar's corpse.

kills and mummifies it, and then the stalk-like caterpillar emerges from the corpse.

It is known in English colloquially as caterpillar fungus, or by its original, and more prominent Tibetan name: *yartsa gunbu* or *yatsa gunbu*. In Tibetan, *yar* means summer and *tsa* means grass, hence *yartsa*, or summer grass; *gun* means winter and *ba* means worm, or winter worm. *Yarsagumba* (to use the Nepali spelling in Roman letters) stays underground in winter, in the soil, where it is relatively warm. It develops slowly, and sprouts in the summer, neither grass nor worm, when it is harvested.

The profit margins even of lucrative occupations such as carpet manufacturing are less attractive when compared to the harvesting of *yarsagumba*. By climbing up to the top of the ridge above and behind the village, toward the snow-covered Jangla Bhanjyang passes leading to the
rest of Nepal, and digging around in the ground for a good part of May,
June, and early July, a Tarali family can fairly easily gather one kilogram
of *yarsagumba*. In 2011, that would be worth about Rs. 400,000 (depending on the size of the caterpillars, the larger ones being preferred), or
roughly $4,000, depending on exchange rates.

It is not easy work, but compared to the preparation of their fields,
and the plowing, weeding, and harvesting of crops from them that is
required in their former largely cashless agricultural economy, this is
a sum of money the average Tarali could not have expected to earn
over many years, but can now acquire in a couple of months. Even the
poorest households now have savings of five or so lakhs (about $5,000)
to fall back on, and few daily expenses, if they live within the village,
that they need to worry about. Although their lifestyles have not
changed much—not of those who have stayed in the village, anyway—
it is this income which enables them to have cell phones, DVD players,
and solar collectors on their roofs to power them (see cover image) and
thus make use of the phone transmission complex that has been built
just above the village.

Among other local repercussions, Tarali labor is now partially derailed
from traditional occupations such as farming during the beginning of
the planting season and trading in the traditional transaction circuits
during the winter. *Yarsagumba* has dramatically raised incomes, but
because of the time needed to harvest it, which falls during the spring
planting season, villagers now typically spend about a month's less time
tilling fields, leaving some of them, formerly planted and productive,
now fallow. The result is a decline in agricultural production. This new
"crop" has given the traditional agricultural economy, which put food on
the floor (tables not being part of Tarali household furnishings), a minor,
but weakening, jolt. Villagers still grow enough to feed themselves, but
not always enough to power the transaction circuits at previous levels.

Dhanu's father (Lanku) is Bhim's father's brother, so they both occupy
prominent places in the socially and financially advanced kinship
network of the village. In Nepali kinship terms, this makes Dhanu and
Bhim brothers. Dhanu acquired only an intermediate college degree, but

Part of the telephone communication system which has been located just above Tarang village.

again like Bhim, he has achieved enough education to carve out a place for himself in the business world, whether in Nepal, Asia, Europe, or America. He has done so by moving aggressively in this new *yarsagumba* part of the economy.

After relaxing at the Hyatt-Regency for a while, Dhanu and I drove to his current residence—not the one he's in the process of building, which, like Bhim's and Bisara's, will be something like nine stories when completed. We walked up several flights of stairs to his comfortable flat, where handsomely varnished wooden bookshelves were lined with bottles of high-end wine and whiskey, including Johnny Walker Red Label and Black Label, as if it didn't matter which was which as long as it was imported. Perhaps he offers different-quality Scotch according to the rank of the visitor; since he didn't offer me any, I was unable to test this hypothesis (this was in the middle of the afternoon, which is traditionally more of a tea-drinking time).

Dhanu is never far from the political world, with which he is in constant cell-phone contact, and our conversations were frequently

Dhanu's new house in Kathmandu. Such modern architecture was unheard of until relatively recently.

interrupted by calls—incoming and outgoing. A few days later I met him again at Boudhanath, along with two political leaders from Tarap (in Upper, or Inner, Dolpa). His agenda was to straighten out an argument over who could legally collect the *yarsagumba* crop there. I was surprised that they spoke entirely in Nepali, and surprisingly good Nepali, whereas I had expected that Dhanu would have spoken to them in their native language, which is Tibetan. When I asked Dhanu about this, he said, only half seriously, that his Tibetan was broken, his Nepali was broken, and his English was broken. That would leave Kaike as his only intact language, but of course of no value outside his own and the two other villages where it is routinely spoken.

Whether in the quiet, gilded seclusion of the Hyatt or out on the crowded, hustle-and-bustle streets of Kathmandu, Dhanu seemed at ease in the world he now occupies most of the time, perhaps more so than Bhim because of the wider network of social, economic, and political contacts in which he comfortably moves. On the way out of Boudhanath he casually donated Rs. 20 to a beggar sitting by the side of the road, and he bows in obeisance, as most Nepalis do, when we drive by Hindu temples such as Pashupatinath. He clearly feels at home in Kathmandu, whether with the largely Hindu population, with whom he has social and political dealings, or with his Kaike- and Tibetan-speaking Dolpa countrymen, for example at the monthly get-togethers of the Dolpa Rung Samaj, or even with the Tarap politicians quarreling over *yarsagumba* collection rights.

How does Dhanu manage to cash in on the new *yarsagumba* business so successfully? Not, one can be sure, by living and shivering in a makeshift tent a few thousand feet above Tarang for a couple of months and rooting around in the cold, hard ground for *yarsagumba*. The development of Chinese demand, whether in China itself, Hong Kong, or Singapore, fueled by its reputation as an aphrodisiac, transformed it from horse fodder into something more like a miracle drug. It is believed to be a strong herb that activates 106 types of cells of the human body, in addition to increasing sexual potency. It is also thought to erase the wrinkles in one's face and to filter out toxicity from the body. There are some direct sales to China over the border from Dolpa, and some from Kathmandu (this is where Dhanu concentrates his commerce), whence it is exported around the world.

Late May, June, and early July constitute the gathering season, and beginning in May most schools and stores shut down while village populations ascend to higher ground to collect *yarsagumba*. It is harvested by villagers who carry their cooking gear, food, and tents to live below the Jangla Bhanjyang passes for the month and a half any family might spend during the three-month total harvesting season. The amounts harvested are small: perhaps 300 grams per person. Per-capita production has declined now that everyone in the village is engaged in it, and a single family can not now expect to collect more than one kilogram. Villagers then sell whatever they have to a middleman, or, alternatively, they take it to the border to sell themselves. Additionally, Tibetans (from Tibet) sometimes come secretly as far as Tichurong to buy it, and Taralis also go into Tibet. Recognizing the beneficial economic reality of *yarsagumba*, in 2015 the border was officially opened for fifteen days to permit these transactions.

Price depends on quality and venues of sales. One kilogram of *yarsagumba* could yield 15 lakhs for low quality ($15,500), 22 to 25 lakhs for average quality ($23,340) and for best quality, 31 lakhs ($32,158). In general, quality depends on size (the larger the better) and color (golden color is preferred). These sample prices, which fluctuate widely and wildly over time, are those commanded for *yarsagumba* sold in Kathmandu, where businessmen transport it after collecting it in Dolpa and similar locations. This is where Dhanu comes in. He buys it in Dolpa from individual collectors (Bhim is one of his minor suppliers), consolidates it in larger amounts, and brings it to

Kathmandu, from where he takes it to Hong Kong and Singapore. He might buy and sell 200 or 300 kilograms per year, yielding a profit of one and a half crores (150 lakhs, or 15 million rupees), equivalent to $155,000. Sold internationally, the price per kilogram increases by two lakhs ($2,075). Dhanu is the only person in Tichurong whose operations are big enough to be involved directly in this international trade. He's an international dealer and has to be dealt with on that basis, including the respect accorded a figure who moves in those worlds.

Against these large sums must be assessed the difficulties such as competition (since so many people want in on it), unpredictable risks (such as high market volatility), expenses (such as travel), security risks (e.g., theft), and corruption. Bhim opined that profit margins are greater in other businesses, such as carpet manufacturing, than in *yarsagumba* trade which, though apparently spectacular, cannot escape all its attendant uncertainties. One way of putting this is to say that margins in *yarsagumba* are spectacular if all goes well, but it is a high-yield/high-risk crop. Another attraction of dealing in carpets is that it can be carried out over an entire year, whereas *yarsagumba* is strictly seasonal.

Markets in Nepal can be difficult to negotiate, because consumers have little idea of actual prices and costs of such exotic products, and therefore feel compelled to pay whatever is asked. Competition is also intense, even in harvesting the crop. Nepalis from other districts are free to enter Dolpa to collect the crop, but they must pay a Rs. 1,000 fee per season to do so. While they compete for the crop, the fees they pay of course result in increased income for local needs.

At ground level—the actual collecting of the crop—various relationships among the participants have evolved. Businessmen try to cultivate collectors by offering advances, which can be used to purchase logistical supplies for food, cold weather clothing, tools, etc. An advance would be an amount worth at least two kilograms. Some collectors receive only this much, some get enough to cover the acquisition of five or more kilograms, and an advance of as much as 20 lakhs (about $20,000) is sometimes offered.

Various taxes are levied on the collection and sale of *yarsagumba*. Rs. 10,000/kg must be paid to the District Forest Office, and a *yarsagumba* collector from a village must pay an additional Rs. 1,000/kg to the local DDC (District Development Committee). Previously, there was a penalty of Rs 1,000 per piece when trade in it was illegal. Similarly, a fee of Rs. 1,000/kg is now due the Nepal Chamber of Commerce. During the Maoist insurgency the rebels bought *yarsagumba* pieces for Rs. 150 each, but now tax is based on market rates per weight. Bhim has sold in the local market whatever *yarsagumba* he's acquired, but plans to export in the future, as Dhanu does, to clients in Singapore, China, Korea, and Hong Kong. Chinese traders also come to Nepal to buy *yarsagumba* locally. One way or the other, China (or, more accurately, Chinese buyers) is where the money is.

Before he began dealing in *yarsagumba*, Dhanu, as some other Taralis, conducted traditional, small-scale business in Dunai, where his wife even now continues to live and operate their little shop. He also now has financial interests in construction projects like the road coming up the Bheri River from Jajarkot, which will eventually result in a motorable road from the Indian border in the Tarai all the way to Tarang, or at least to the side of the river flowing directly below Tarang, on its way to the Tibetan border. This will make possible the export of items such as apples, which are now plentiful in Tarang (there had been none until Chandra Man brought seeds to the village). Another of Danu's construction projects is the continuing expansion of the little airstrip at Juphal. Dhanu has an eye for large capital projects and seems to jump into them before others are aware that they are there, or at least he has the capital that allows him to do so.

Since he buys *yarsagumba* from whoever has it to sell, Dhanu's success in that market does not depend on the vagaries of who has the good luck to find it in large amounts or high quality, or both. That depends partly on weather—ample rain and snow produce higher yields. *Yarsagumba* and horoscopes are connected, too, as villagers decide when and where to look for it according to their zodiac signs, which are calculated in Tibetan horoscopes according to the year (Year of the Tiger, Year of the Dog, etc.). Lamas consult the horoscopes for those in business, whether the business is *yarsagumba*, carpets, or anything else. This does not affect those who do the actual collecting of *yarsagumba*. If the horoscope is not favorable, it is up to the individual whether to submit to the risk of ignoring it or not.

Bhim, Dhanu, and Lank Man and their scattered relatives represent the upper edge of Tarali society in Kathmandu, the segment that has moved farthest from the traditions I had been trying to learn about

and understand in the late 1960s. Chandra Man had been my student
in Pharping, and Lanku my friend in Tarang, but the next generation
(Bhim, Sukar, Dhanu, Lank Man, and Bisara) I met only forty-four years
later. They constituted a new class, socially and culturally, that did not
exist before. What strikes me is that, as I believe is the case in other
trading groups (Thakalis, Sherpas, Newars), those who have settled in
urban areas continue to feel as much at home in their ancestral villages
as they do in the urban environments where they spend most of their
time. Rather than flee their past or deny it, they seem to want to nourish
and strengthen it, and probably the more successful they are, the more
they are inclined to do so.

These are not the only financially successful Taralis, just the ones
whose origins are in Tarang whom I met and know more about. Other
Tarali families in Kathmandu are managing well financially also, but
my aim here is to describe a few people in some depth from a village
I know well because I lived in it for a year in the late 1960s, rather
than many people in a more encyclopedic fashion. Not all of them
have built multistory high-rises, but Paljum (Chandra Man's widow),
for example, lives in a substantial house with her son (her daughter
is in England) and earns some money by renting out parts of it she
doesn't need.

Lank Man feels that the former golden days of great opportunity
are now gone. There are more hurdles, more competition, which have
put what he has accomplished largely out of reach for most Taralis,
who nevertheless do work as employees. As he pointed out, they own
carpet facilities and build houses, so they have all achieved a measure
of success. None of these Kathmandu-based Taralis is living in poverty,
although some, such as Kwinkep (another of Lanku's sons) are
politically active as members of the conservative RPP party, without
any particularly visible means of support. They are perhaps indulging
in watchful waiting, in order to catch "the next big thing" in which a
fortune can be made.

How the individuals mentioned so far ended up in the situations in
which they now find themselves, including the broader repercussions
for the way of life they come from, are a result of taking paths that
are partly idiosyncratic and partly a pattern consistent with the
nature of Tarang life as I first encountered it in the late 1960s. Their
accomplishments were not in any sense predictable, yet in retrospect

one can see how they track cultural precedents. It's no accident that some Taralis have been adept at moving successfully into an economic way of life that, I have argued, despite lacking large amounts of capital and degrees in higher education, they were culturally prepared for. The way they act and conduct themselves in everyday life—their personas, temperaments, ambitions—are all of a piece. They have all achieved some kind of success, though of different degrees. Given their similar cultural backgrounds, the success was theirs to lose.

6

Return to Tarang

Meeting the Taralis in Kathmandu opened my eyes to dramatic changes in the lives of a few, which reverberated at least to some degree to the many who continued to carry on with their lives in Tichurong. They constitute but one small example of the ways all of Nepal had changed by 2011, since I first encountered it in 1962. Urban Taralis are still a community, however geographically scattered around town, and small enough that its members mostly know or at least recognize each other. Although I have no hard statistical data to prove it, the number of degrees of separation was certainly very small, and probably almost always close to zero.

To determine how life in the Tichurong part of that new distribution of Taralis had changed, or even if it hadn't, was my next challenge. After all, that was what I had really come for, since I wasn't fully aware of the migration to Kathmandu that had taken place until shortly before I arrived there. Thus, the part of my project that was the hardest was yet to come—far from the electricity, plumbing, taxis, and haute cuisine of Kathmandu, but also, serendipitously, far from the material rubbish, political corruption, and demographic and automotive congestion and chaos that had engulfed, overtaken, and overwhelmed that city. In the perhaps overly optimistic hope that aviation fuel supplies would become more readily available and that planes would eventually fly again to Juphal, I proceeded to apply for a trekking permit, which was the governmental sine qua non for going anywhere even near Dolpa.

Since permits for foreigners to visit Dolpa are not issued unless the party consists of at least two people (there was no maximum that I was aware of), a "ghost" Japanese woman was listed on my application as my companion. I refer to her as a "ghost" because although such a person did actually exist, and was physically present in Nepal, I never met, saw, or talked to her (not even on cell phone). My only worry was that police at check posts I would pass by in Dolpa who would see her name on my permit might ask me where she was, in which case I would have to quickly make up some sort of story to explain her absence. I wasn't sure I could concoct a false but convincing story on the spot, quickly and credibly, that would account for my missing companion. I thought perhaps I could say that she fell ill and was recuperating behind me on the trail, but I didn't know how persuasive that would sound. What would I do if they deputed a constable to go find her and render whatever assistance she needed? Meanwhile, Dhanu, who, as far as I could tell in these murky circumstances, had arranged for my ghost companion, had also arranged for my flight. So I had my ticket to Nepalganj, an urban center in the western Tarai, which served as something of a hub for flights throughout western Nepal. I would spend the night there before flying on to Juphal the next morning.

March 25: My flight on Yeti Airlines touched down at Nepalganj late in the afternoon. Two minutes after I stepped onto the tarmac, I had cell phone calls from Bhim and others in Kathmandu who hadn't realized I was gone, bringing home the compelling realization that I would never be out of communication with contacts in Kathmandu. The gleaming image of the anthropologist going to the ends of the earth to expand our knowledge of humanity had vanished. Reliance on such antiquated means of communication as the Nepal postal service, as I had done in the 1960s, or indeed any postal service, had become a memory out of the distant past.

Near the airport I ran into an elderly man who lived not far from Dunai, who had been a friend and political ally of my old friend in Tarang, Tagla. It was Tagla who finally decided that I was not a threat to the village and therefore convinced the villagers that they could talk to me without fear of reprisal or retribution. This gentleman whom I met near the airport kept insisting, over my protestations, that I had lived in Tarang for six years (instead of the one, to the very day, that I was actually there), that my son had been born there (instead of at Shanta Bhawan Hospital in Kathmandu), and that I spoke fluent Kaike (I compiled lists of several thousand words, but with very little ability to actually use them in conversation). These and other myths that had been fabricated seemed to have become more fanciful and extravagant the longer I had been away. It was enough to make me question the reliability and legitimacy of ethnohistory as a legitimate field of inquiry, instead of what might otherwise be cynically described as the garbled memories of toothless informants.

I spent the night on a hard bed in a hotel a short walk from the airport. The bed consisted of bare wooden slats supported off the floor by four posts, but for amenities I at least was issued a pillow and a blanket. An overhead fan kept the warm, musty air circulating. Whereas in Kathmandu, "load shedding" resulted in the shutdown of electricity during most of any twenty-four-hour period, here, at least, I could rely on my fan running all night. I was told to report to the airport at 6:00 the next morning for my flight.

March 26: When I arrived at the time stipulated, I was the only person there, because the airport had not yet opened. But after I had hung around for a while, someone showed up and let me into the small, unadorned cement building. While waiting I had a cup of tea for Rs. 20 (20 cents), compared to about a dollar at the Kathmandu Guest House. I couldn't help wondering what a cup of tea would have cost at the Hyatt Regency—several dollars, no doubt. Income inequality had grown substantially since Chandra Man's time as a child in Kathmandu in the 1950s, when there were virtually no tourists. Then, only a few families such as the royal family and others connected to it by marriage or employment possessed sums of money sufficient to buy tea in such an establishment. This was only a hypothetical consideration, however, since at that time there were only two hotels in Kathmandu in which to spend such amounts of money.[16]

Household income inequality has grown within towns and cities in Nepal as well as between rural and urban households. At the national level, however, household consumption inequality substantially decreased between 2005 and 2011, and probably even more since then. Reasons for this decline include the expansion of migratory employment for rural labor (including large-scale migration to the Middle East), substantial increase in agricultural and other wage rates (including wage rates in the carpet industry), and economic diversification.

---

[16] The Snow View Hotel, in Lazimpat, and the Royal Hotel, kitty-corner from the Royal Palace, were the only hotels, in the Western sense of that term, in Kathmandu in the mid 1950s.

Destination: Dolpa

I was ticketed for the second flight of the day to Juphal, which meant that I had to wait for the first flight to take off, land at Juphal, and return. When the little Cessna Caravan, a nine-seater, finally arrived, I boarded it with two pilots at the controls: one American and one Nepalese, who I guessed was still in training. Soaring over those harsh and unforgiving mountains down below in a small single-engine plane was a chilling and unnerving experience, no matter how many times I had done it elsewhere in Nepal or Alaska. The pilots somehow found the Bheri River and flew a course following it upstream until I realized we were gradually descending towards the airstrip, or so I fervently hoped. As we landed, the propeller created a fierce squall out of the loose dirt, gravel, and stones we were rolling and bumping our way over as we slowed to a stop at the end of the uphill slope. As I stepped out of the plane, the fresh mountain air felt cool and bracing after the heat blanket of the Tarai in Nepalganj. Forty-four years later, I was finally back in Dolpa.

I was amazed at my first sight: tall steel towers supporting power lines strung between them led up to the airport from a hydroelectric plant below that captured the energy not of the Bheri River itself, but of a stream that empties into the Bheri a little above and beyond Dunai. The trail from the airstrip led unrelentingly down to the river and then upstream to Dunai, now as then, the capital of Dolpa District. Dunai has become a large bazaar town of some two thousand or more people, as opposed to perhaps a few hundred, at most, forty-four years ago. In the bazaar I ran into Mangali, one of Lanku's daughters, who was twelve the last time I saw her. I would not have recognized her, but she knew me immediately. She is the girl in the photograph facing page 114 (first edition) or page 108 (2017 edition) of *Trans-Himalayan Traders*, carrying her younger brother on her back while preparing to throw a snowball at an adversary on a nearby roof, a common winter amusement for children.

There is also a street crossing (*chok*, Nepali) in the middle of Dunai marked by a larger-than-life statue of former King Birendra. If I hadn't known otherwise, I would never have guessed from the presence of abundant statuary and posters that anything had happened politically since I was here—for example, that virtually the entire royal family had been assassinated in June 2001, and that the 231-year-old monarchy was formally and legally abolished after a ten-year Maoist insurrection in 2008. After continuing on through the busy bazaar, I finally arrived at the "Blue Sheep Inn," a combination campground (for those with tents) and austere, bare-bones sleeping rooms (for those without them), about like the one I had slept in in Nepalganj. I booked one of the latter for the night.

Arriving in Tarang

March 27: As yesterday, the fresh mountain air is invigorating as I head up the Bheri River on the familiar and well-trodden trail to Tarang. It's familiar but not the same, since I shared the trail with short columns of mules along the way, many carrying stones for construction of the new road being built along the river upstream from Dunai—virtually complete in some places, still very much under construction, or not even started yet in others. New so-called hotels have sprung up, and others are in the beginning stages: I counted over half a dozen diminutive lodges that have been built along the river, usually offshoots from villages perched on the steep hillside above them. It's amazing to see (particularly pronounced in Dunai, but also along the trail) people walking around with a cell phone, or "mobile," as they call it, pressed to their ear.

I moved along at a steady-enough pace, but I felt tired compared to the energy levels I remembered, or thought I remembered, from forty-four years before. Exhaustion was more than balanced simultaneously with relief and thankfulness that I needed to walk only two days this time, instead of the two-week-long haul from Pokhara, as before.

Late in the afternoon I finally rounded a bend in the river and could see in the distance, above the opposite left bank, the down-river edge of the spur on which Gombatara village sits. Then, nearer still, Tarakot was perched on an adjacent ridge below Gombatara. Finally, even closer, more or less directly across the river, was a house in the tiny hamlet (about five houses) of Beluwa, above which I knew had to be, although I couldn't yet see it, Tarang. I saw the hotel and police check post that were built down by the river about twenty years after I left, the check post replacing the one that had been established in the village just a few months before my arrival in 1968. The hotel and check post are still the only signs of habitation anywhere close to the river, neither apparently generating much business—hotel guests and miscreants were apparently in short supply.

I noticed a few local people eating and drinking by the side of the trail, apparently taking a break from whatever they had been doing. One woman (in a group of about a dozen) called out and asked if I was Jim Fisher. Astonished, I said yes, and she replied that the group of men I had just passed a few yards before (the two resting groups were slightly separated by gender) included Budhi Bahadur, my landlady's older son, about my age. Somehow they had gotten word of my arrival before I arrived. Since I had come almost straight from the Juphal airport, I couldn't imagine how they knew, unless, I wondered, could the news have been transmitted by cell phone?

I couldn't believe it. I threw down my pack and went over to greet Budhi Bahadur, and, for that matter, the rest of the men gathered there. To say that everyone's response (including my own) was overwhelming would be to put it mildly, even though few of them would have been alive when I was last there; for example, one of the young women was the granddaughter of the *dhami* (shaman), who had long since passed away.[17] There was lots of laughing and joking, as I dug the copy of my book I had brought along out of my pack and showed them pictures of people and places from forty-four years earlier, just as I had done with the Taralis in Kathmandu. I had sent a couple of copies of the book to the village when it was published, but what their fate had been was not clear; even if a copy was still there, no one seemed to be aware of it. A village in Dolpa is not an ideal location to protect a book from the ravages of time and nature, at least not unless it is protected by cloth wrapping and sturdy wooden covers, as Tibetan religious texts sensibly are.

My curiosity about them and theirs about me was mutual—nothing new about that. Many people remembered my son Kim's visit about twenty years before, as well as Maya's (I am referring to Maya the geography student, not my daughter) only three years before, in 2008; they were curious about both and wondered when they would return. They wanted to know how many children I had (two), what they were doing, what, and up to what level, they had studied, their marital states, whether I had grandchildren, and so on.

---

[17] It was expected that his son would then become a shaman, but so far he has failed to become possessed, while an unrelated villager has become possessed. There is no limit on the number of shamans, but at any given time there is unlikely to be more than one. In the late 1960s the wife of my friend Tagla started becoming possessed. Tagla put a stop to that on the grounds that it causes much difficulty and expense.

Someone asked about the Mrs. I forget if they used the English term or the Nepali, *budi* (old lady), since that would have matched their term for me, *budo* (old man), although contrary to my case, they would have never known her as anything other than a young woman. I told them we had divorced. They asked why, whether we were speaking, if she went with someone else, if I did, where she lives now, where I live now, where our children live now. That the four of us all live thousands of miles from each other (the two coasts, the Midwest and the Southwest) was simply incomprehensible, although the two days it would take them to walk to Juphal and then a day of flights to reach their friends and family in Kathmandu was considerably more time than it would take any of the four of us to reach any of the others in our far-flung family. The Taralis regarded their own equivalent trips to see their families as quite routine, unremarkable, and quotidian. They had come to their own terms with the air age.

Their main curiosity about the Mrs. was about why she seemed so quick to anger, a query that I'd heard before, from Chandra Man and Paljum. They seemed puzzled by this, but I was even more puzzled by their puzzlement. In my experience, my wife was no match for the Tarali women, whose flaring tempers were on almost daily display, as, operating at full volume, they hurled insults at each other from their respective rooftops, sometimes from opposite sides of the village. When it comes to venting anger publicly, Tarali women (but not men) were without parallel. They were in a league by themselves.

They also wanted to know how long it takes to get to the United States, how much such a journey costs, whether it's hot or cold where I live, what crops I grow in my fields (a fertilized but inedible grass lawn drew uncomprehending, and perhaps unbelieving, stares), what I eat, how much I make, and whether I get a pension—all topics (except the last) they were just as curious about forty-four years ago. What little I had said about world geography before did not seem to have had much lasting impact: Budhi Bahadur still thought China and the United States are neighbors, and he didn't know about the existence of the ocean that separates us. He likely had forgotten about such details, as well he might, since they had no impact on or relevance to his daily life in Tarang, where a plethora of questions about local conditions demanding his attention was far more pressing.

Just as they repeated questions they had asked me before, during the next two weeks I put the same sort of queries to them that I had posed forty-four years earlier. In a way I had not thought of very explicitly or consciously previously, we were each subjecting the other to an anthropological interrogation, even though I was the only one displaying the label. We reciprocated each other's curiosity, with the important difference that my life depended on asking them questions, to which the lives they lived provided me answers. Apart from being a brief, sometimes amusing appearance in their lives, my presence had no lasting significance for them whatsoever.

The reason they were all gathered down by the river is that they were working on the new government-funded roadbed, so I walked over to the hotel where we agreed that I would wait until they had finished their work at five o'clock, prior to returning to their houses up the hill. The hotel proprietor and manager, Tshering, charges Rs. 50 (about $.50/night) for locals, and Rs. 300 (about $3.00/night) for the occasional foreigner. He said that during the insurrection the Maoists would come at night wanting food, and during the day the Nepal Army would do the same. What could he do? he asked in the typical plaintive Nepali way. The Nepali question, which almost all Nepalis often pose when describing difficult situations in which they find themselves, is simply: *ke garne?* (what to do?)

But the hotel owner said the Kamis (so-called untouchable carpenters, now also referred to as Dalits, or oppressed, who live in Riwa village, an hour or so walk from Tarang) liked the Maoists because they championed the Kamis and opposed the discrimination against them. I could readily understand why this alliance was a natural one that had materialized all over Nepal. Maoists did not oppose Buddhism as such, but they would occasionally paint a hammer and sickle on large rocks and cliffs along a trail. Some monks retaliated by painting "Om Mane Padme Hum," as they have traditionally done on rocks for millennia, over the hammer and sickle.

When the villagers had finished their day's work on the roadbed, we all walked up the hill together, passing a handsome new *kani* along the way, commissioned, I later learned, by Lanku before he died.[18]

---

[18] A *kani* can be thought of as a walk-through chorten, adorned with paintings on its interior walls and ceiling. It does not contain the items, such as the purported or actual physical remains such as bones, pieces of clothing, or objects associated with saints or other religious figures that a solid chorten, a reliquary, possesses.

Someone insisted on carrying my pack, for which I was grateful. It was a happy ending to a long, hard day, and I appreciated the gesture. I also appreciated Budhi Bahadur's invitation to sleep on the floor of a small storage room on the edge of his roof. This was a different part of the same house I had lived in earlier. The part we had lived in forty-four years previously had been inherited by Budhi's younger brother, who had died, and his children were living elsewhere, so that section of the house, which had just been refurbished forty-four years before (which was an important reason we wanted to live in it then), had been abandoned and now lay in almost total ruins. It was a rude reminder that continuous attention to maintenance and upkeep is required to protect houses, and the local building materials used in their construction, from the destruction that accompanies the harsh weather conditions that are simply an unavoidable part of life in Tichurong.

During the Maoist insurgency, monks painted the mantra "Om Mani Padme Hum" over the hammer and sickle Maoist cadres had applied to a rock slab.

7

The Next Day

March 28: Arriving at the village yesterday afternoon, I had the overwhelming impression that everything looked just the way it had forty-four years before, as if I had walked away and everyone had agreed that nothing should be done that would ever change its appearance, transforming it into a modern-day Brigadoon.

Ambling around the village early the next morning reinforced this first impression: the houses and their construction, the trails and paths connecting them, people working and socializing on their flat roofs— talking, quarreling, and laughing—children horsing around under their parents' eyes, and everyone doing (whether enjoying or disliking) whatever they had to do to make a social, political, and economic life in the village.

As before, a significant part of life in Tarang took place out in the open, on the rooftops in full view, as if the inhabitants were playing parts in a public drama whose lines they knew well, after lifetimes of practice. Except for indoors, there was no privacy and therefore few secrets. Also unchanged, no matter where I looked, were the fields spread out from the village edges in every direction—up, down, sideways, all around— on the steep hillsides. The crops planted in them were still the same (mostly varieties of millet and buckwheat—details are in Chapter 3 of *Trans-Himalayan Traders*), and the chortens along the trail entering the upper edge of the village were not only still there, but also still in the rather dilapidated state I remembered from so long ago.

On each rooftop stands a long pole with a pine branch lashed to its top and two white flags, one from the prior year, one for the present year. The flags are a symbol for the Choputa (Kaike) deity, which is part of the object of the celebration of the Rung festival (*chad*, Nepali and Kaike).[19]

---

[19] Choputa is the Kul Deuta for everyone in the Tarang and Lawan VDCs (Village Development Committees).

It is Choputa who is responsible for everyone's health and avoidance of harm. It is not worshipped in a corporeal form, but is thought to reside invisibly in the mountains. Despite its importance, it bears no relation to Buddhist practice, which, with the assistance of lamas, is followed during birth and death. Each house puts up a new flag during the winter months (Mangsir, Pus or Magh), but replaces the poles only every other year in order to limit destruction of forest resources.

This sounds like a progressive ecological view, but the reasoning is more along the lines that a cloth flag wears out sooner than a wooden pole. Tibetans do something like this too, but according to a different calendar. When the flags are raised, the villagers also *lipnu* (Nepali, resurface floors and walls by smearing them with mud made from soil and dung, which dries to a hard surface) and generally spruce up at the same time. Other flags (blue, red, white, yellow, all Buddhist colors) are found on just a few houses, and are put up by lamas.[20]

One of anthropology's central tenets, though it's not always explicitly stated, is not only that things deep down are never the way they seem on the surface, but also that even after peeling back layer after layer, you never find the core of the anthropological onion. In my case, I found that the longer I was there and the more I walked around, the more I could see a number of changes that had taken place after all, even if they weren't immediately obvious. Many peach trees and apple trees were growing where none had existed before; maybe a dozen solar collectors were attached to tops of poles installed on the flat roofs; black plastic pipes drained rainwater from roofs; fresh water was available from new taps within the village; poison (available in Dunai and in Bau Prasad's shop) makes possible the killing of rats by means other than traps and cats.

More obvious to an outsider, there is much more nonbiodegradable refuse lying in and on the trails that meander through the village connecting the houses: discarded old clothes, torn cloth, rubber shoes falling apart, food packaging, garbage, tin cans, flashlight batteries, cigarette packages, and so on. The Brahman schoolteacher from Nepalganj, Yamuna, agreed about the debris, but she pointed out the important distinction between the commons (the trails and paths in and around the village which belong to no one in particular and are

---

[20]   Not raising the Buddhist flag is not a sign of disrespect towards Buddhism; once the Kul Deuta flag is up, some just don't want to be bothered by having to raise yet another flag if its presence is optional.

therefore not tended by anyone) and the insides of houses that are swept scrupulously clean. Similarly, five-gallon plastic jugs (called "gallon," a new word in village lexicon whether the language being spoken is Kaike, Tibetan, or Nepali), as opposed to the heavy metal ones (*gagro*, Nepali) which were used formerly, are carefully washed out before filling at the tap and then carried inside the houses, providing water for washing and cooking.

The filth in public spaces is no one's responsibility and therefore ignored, whereas keeping indoor areas clean is a priority, but one neither very visible nor so easily accomplished. One evening Budhi Bahadur was sitting by his household hearth holding a grandchild, who then unleashed a torrent of green diarrhea on Budhi's clean clothes, which

he had just put on that morning. This annoyed him, although his wife, Pasang, found it amusing. The solution, which worked quite well, was to call the dog over to lap up the diarrhea. Similar situations develop with small children who haven't been toilet trained and who generally crawl or toddle around naked, at least from the waist down, whether inside or on the roofs.

Forty-four years ago changes in women's fashions over the previous forty years (say, the late 1940s) were very obvious. This can be seen particularly in the length of the *patuka*, or waist sash. Its folds function as "pockets" in which women carry small items they need during the day and it conserves body heat in cold weather.[21] The size of earrings also changed noticeably.

Chandra Man's wife, Paljum, and her mother pose to display changes in dress fashions from the 1940s to 1969. Note cloth patterns, size of waistband (*patuka*) and size of earrings.

---

[21] The *patuka* has also been found to reduce back pain (Shah, 1994). For many of the same practical reasons, men also wear *patuka*s some of the time.

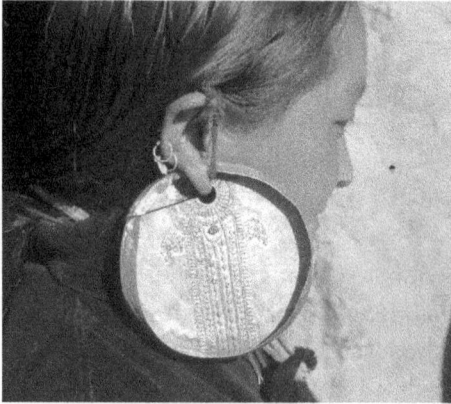

Paljum's earrings of solid gold have reached their anatomical limit – the top of her shoulder.

Forty two years ago women's earrings had been growing to the size of saucers over the previous 40 years; now they have shrunk to a modern, more international size.

Now again, the *patukas* are even shorter than they were in the late 1960s, continuing the miniaturization process already underway previously: barely visible underneath the blouse now, compared to prominent and obvious in the 1960s.[22] The earrings also are now miniscule and modern looking, whereas forty-four years ago they were still in the process, ongoing for decades, of becoming as large as could be physically worn—that is, the anatomical limit was reached when the solid gold circular earrings hung to shoulder level. They could hang no lower without resting on the shoulder. Attitudes towards clothing seem casual: it looks similar to what it had been before, but many women now sometimes wear tee shirts instead of the blouses prevalent earlier, and men alternatively wear traditional *suruwal* or modern slacks.

Innovations

Much more visible is the change evident in the large elementary and middle school complex (what would almost qualify as a campus in the United States these days) under continuing construction at the

---

[22] Women's *patukas* are thought to have originally been ninety *hat* (Nepali, length of hand); fifty years ago twenty *hat*; forty years ago, ten or twelve *hat*; presently, eight *hat*.

upper edge of the village. It consists of about three buildings where no building had existed previously. Upgraded now from an elementary to a middle school, the complex offers all eight grade levels, but with the number of students steadily declining as the class level rises. The school is now staffed by eight teachers instead of one (often absent) in the 1960s. All the teachers come from west Nepal: three are from Syanja, one from Parbat, two from Nepalganj, one from Dunai, and one from Tarang. Most of them live in the new Village Development Committee (also an administrative novelty) building at the top of the village. The two who do not are the very capable young Brahman woman, Yamuna, from Nepalganj, who teaches Class 7 and lives separately (in the spare room of a friend) in the village, and the teacher who is a Tarang native and lives at his ancestral home. Except for Yamuna, all the teachers are male. Pay is Rs. 10,000/month, plus Rs. 5,000 in allowances, or a total of about $150/month, the same for all. As a Peace Corps Volunteer in 1962, I earned Rs. 350, or $46/month, which was approximately what our counterparts received; the monthly Peace Corps stipend is now Rs. 15,100, or $150.

Surprisingly, the total number of students spread over the eight grades, 103, is equally distributed between boys and girls (52 and 51, respectively), but the number of girls falls off precipitously in Classes 6, 7, and 8. In Class 1 girls outnumber the boys 15 to 12. Even in Class 5 girls outnumber boys, 3 to 1. But boys outnumber girls in Class 6, 5 to 1, in Class 7, 9 to 1, while 5 boys and no girls are enrolled in Class 8. The division of labor underlies the gender differences of students attending school, although, to a lesser extent, early marriage does too. Women do almost all the household and agricultural work (except for plowing, which is men's work, and harvesting, which men and women do equally), including taking care of younger siblings. Girls start learning to work in the fields (*khetipati*, Nepali) about the age when they would enter the upper grades, which is also when they begin to drop out.

Therefore, girls typically don't attend school for as many years as boys who, as Lank Man did, can manage to attend classes even during the winter, while they're helping with trading expeditions. Those who pass Class 8 will usually go on to higher grades if they haven't done so already at lower grades in Dunai, Baglung, Beni, or Kathmandu, depending on where they have someone who can take them in or where they can afford to board. Thus village education described earlier, when people like Bhim and Lank Man, not to mention Chandra Man, were of school-going age, has been much enhanced by opportunities outside the village, as well as inside it.

There is also now an Ayurvedic doctor with his own building not far from the school, at the top of the village. There are lots of medicines on his shelves, but it's not clear how effective he and his medicines are. Villagers still blame illness on ghosts (*bhut*, Nepali) and witches (*boxi*, Nepali), as they used to. When I met with the doctor and teachers and a couple of villagers (all male), just hanging out together late one afternoon at the top of the village, they struck me as coarse and boorish, as they made juvenile (or, rather, in the United States they would be classified as juvenile) jokes about penis size. The doctor seemed absorbed in the pornographic videos he had stored on his cell phone.

An Ayurvedic doctor notwithstanding, health conditions have remained fairly constant. Because of dirt, dust, and pollen constantly being blown into the air, and probably also because of chronic colds, children and adults have trouble controlling nasal mucus. When a child was blowing into his glass of tea to cool it, at the same time mucus from his nose would drip into the glass. Tea is not always available, as when the fire in the fireplace goes out during the day. On one such day Budhi's wife, Pasang (age sixty-six), offered her breast to one of her grandchildren to quiet him, as a pacifier.

Except during festive occasions, faces are often almost black with soot until they can be washed. Staying clean is more difficult for women than for men. With a husband and grandchildren to look after and cook for, and almost the entire agricultural cycle to take responsibility for, women don't always have enough time and water to keep themselves as scrubbed as they would like to be. As before, women bear the lion's share of whatever work (domestic and agricultural, but not trading, which takes place outside the village) gets done throughout the annual cycle.

Surprisingly, but not immediately observably, Tarang has now seen the emergence of what might be called a laboring class. Five households now employ young boys from places as far away as Pokhara as servants; they perform menial jobs such as carrying wood and water to the households who have hired them. Or they look after mules, which are a recent addition to the list of domesticated animals kept in the village; mule owners are the most regular employers of these boys. As salary they receive three or four thousand rupees (about

$35/month in addition to room and board), which they are given when they leave. It is the relatively few wealthier households who employ these boys. Such employment of outsiders as domestic labor was unheard of before, although it's long been common in urban centers such as Kathmandu.

March 29: I went down to the old water tap below the village, which is rarely used now because of the two new ones that have been installed in the gully next to where the Ghartis live. For this to come about, the government built a covered concrete tank at a spring about

Women line up at the new water tap, in the middle of the village instead of at the old one far below it.

Black plastic pipe drains rain water off the roof, helping preserve the roof and providing a source of drinking and washing water for the house.

two hours' walk up the hill, which allowed the flow of the water, using black plastic pipe in a gravity feed, down to the new tap in the gully. This is a far more convenient arrangement than the long hike to the old tap at the bottom of the village (with empty jugs going down the hill, full jugs coming back up). Also, Budhi Bahadur and some others have attached short pieces of black plastic pipe at the corners of roofs to drain the rain that falls during the monsoon—an excellent technique for helping preserve the roofs and preventing leaks as well as collecting water right from one's own house.

One of the houses next to the one I used to live in, which belonged to Mata and Kancha, is now occupied by a woman from Lawan (a village directly across the river) and a man who is from a village below Juphal. The heir of the house, Sher Bahadur (Mata and Kancha's son) lives in Dunai where he manages his business; he has these people living in the house so it won't become dilapidated or broken into during his absence. Such absentee ownership and rental is another new phenomenon, the result of small demographic shifts not apparent to the casual visitor.

Formerly, a member of the family, or a neighbor, would help take care of such houses. These are some of the barely noticeable ways the slow trickle of villagers out to other places (residence in Kathmandu, Dunai, work on trading trips, marriage) affects current patterns of house holding.

While the houses are structurally and architecturally unchanged, they don't display as much decoration made from whitewash on the walls as before. Some now display writing in Nepali, usually people's names, and, even in English, words such as *welcome*; such writing on walls in either language is a novelty. The ubiquitous, randomly spaced white dots are smaller now than they used to be, and there is a greater variety of designs. The dots are applied using the branch of a *dhupi* (Himalayan cypress) tree, with honey applied to it to which the whitewash adheres. The significance is that the white dots safeguard the house against evil spirits and other malevolent forces. But some kind of whitewash painting, regardless of artistic flair or lack of it, seems to be a requirement for any Tichurong house, inside and outside.

This painting on the exterior wall of a Tarang house in 1969 is considerably more imaginative than the white dots typical then and in 2011.

So much of life takes place on rooftops that it's not surprising to find change occurring there. I saw a bright orange tent on a roof, and was told that it keeps the harvested grass dry (every square inch of roof is used to dry grain or grass after it's harvested), and that anyone who wants such a tarpaulin can get one. Another change in rooftops is the appearance of solar collectors. These can be used for powering a dim lightbulb, barely bright enough to read by, but at least powerful enough so that it is not as dark indoors as a coal cellar, even at high noon, as it was previously.

More important than providing illumination, the collectors can

Houses are still painted with whitewash decorations, nowadays including writing in Nepali and English. This house says "welcome".

also power cell phones and DVD players. One result of this is that young boys and girls don't have evening parties anymore, which popularly took the form of nocturnal singing contests, involving spontaneously created songs used as weapons (boys and girls, each grouped on opposite sides of the room, have to sing a clever putdown in answer to the last sortie from the other side). Instead of these remarkably creative responses, they now prefer the easier and more modish activity of watching DVD movies, mostly of Indian provenance, but such songs are still sung on festive occasions such as marriage, *bartaman*, Chaite Bokne, and Lapsol.

Another aspect of rooftop life is the quarrels that take place there; one could hardly spend a day or two in Tarang without witnessing a shouting match from a rooftop. The one I saw on this trip involved a woman who had given a man new clothes to plow for her, but he did his own plowing instead, hence the quarrel, which sounded just like the quarrels of old. Similarly, Yamuna gave a woman her watch to carry a big load of firewood for her; the woman took the watch but didn't bring the firewood, claiming she couldn't because she had a small child to take care of. The arguments continue, in the same mode (yelling from rooftops), and about the same sorts of issues. But as before, amidst the difficulties that daily life brings and the flaring of tempers, people make up quickly most of the time (but not always—sometimes disputants will not speak for years after an argument), and continue the more normal process of appreciating life, laughing and joking at the vicissitudes it throws their way. In that sense, too, the core processes of confronting life and getting on with it haven't changed.

Unlike Bhim's spanking-new, six-story mansion in Kathmandu, the house of his father, Bau Prasad, is unchanged from its earlier design and construction. Taralis renovate their houses whenever they need to—once every twenty years or so, whenever they begin to collapse. Bau also has a little stone chicken house that he can close at night so cats won't attack the chickens. Another defense for chickens is dogs, which bark during the night when foxes come down from the jungle in search of chickens. Along with one or two others, Bau was innovative in placing a hollow log on his roof that serves as a beehive; he harvests honey at night, when it's cold, covering himself with long sleeves and facial plastic to prevent being stung. Villagers had not collected much domestic honey in this way before, not because of a lack of bees but because of a lack of courage or skill to extract honey from the occasional hive that might appear.

In a house next door to Bau's, two men were cutting up round logs, which I guessed were for a new house, but it turned out they were actually logs from an old house they were renovating. They were cutting up the old logs to use as firewood, and they'll bring fresh wood from the forest for the new house. This illustrates an implicitly understood but unstated fact of life: since wood is heavy and has to be carried a long way, villagers use all of it in any way they can. Local forests have a seemingly inexhaustible supply of trees, but wood is never a throwaway item. With its small population and relatively huge land area, Dolpa has not experienced the overcutting of forests that has resulted in deforestation in much of Nepal.

That innovations in Tarang exist, limited though they may be, does not mean they are evenly distributed, as can be seen in the example of solar collectors, which are owned by only a small minority of householders—so far. A solar collector setup costs Rs. 20,000 to 30,000 (about $200 to $300). With the increased income from *yarsagumba*, which has resulted in wealth of five or six lakhs for even the poorest houses, this would be affordable. But the electric world does not stop with solar collectors. The national grid is slowly making its way up the river, which, when it arrives, will supplant the need for solar. Therefore excess cash is now being invested in land purchases in Dunai, or even farther away in places like Pokhara.

8

The More Things Change...

Economic Changes

While mega financial ventures such as carpet manufacturing and commerce in *yarsagumba* have been under way in Kathmandu, and *yarsagumba* harvesting has been taking place in Tichurong, many smaller-scale economic changes have also developed in Tarang that generate new sources of income. My landlady's son, Budhi Bahadur, received Rs. 700 (about $7.30) per day to work on the government-funded road project below the village. Each house was entitled to contribute one person to work for up to ten days at Rs. 700/day. About sixty-five villagers took advantage of this, leaving fifteen houses with no one working, either because their inhabitants were too old or because they had young children to care for—in other words, because of lack of manpower to take advantage of this new source of income. While government pay scales are equal between men and women, privately contracted work (e.g., in fields) provides a somewhat higher wage to men than to women on the theory that men, possessing superior muscular strength, can perform more difficult and strenuous manual labor.

In addition, Budhi Bahadur was among those who also used to engage in small-scale trade (for about seven years, in Budhi Bahadur's case), taking sheep, goats, and woolen products (sweaters, *patukas*) to Pokhara, Baglung, Beni, Butwal, and Nepalganj—the traditional places for such trade. The relatively lightweight woolen items are carried by those who sell them. They also use mules and horses on the trail between Dunai and Tarang, carrying market goods (tea, oil, sugar, chewing gum, rice, and clothes). I was an unexpected and highly irregular source of income; upon leaving, I gave Budhi Bahadur Rs. 10,000 (a little over $100) for his hospitality and friendship during the few days I stayed in his house, and he seemed pleased at this unexpected remuneration.

I was surprised to learn that in addition to the proliferation of small shops and stores in Dunai there are now four shops even in Tarang, where there had been none before. One of these *kirana pasals* (grocery shops) is run by Bhim's father, Bau Prasad. As in the shop Sukar used to help run in Dunai, one can buy basic staples there such as cloth, salt, rice, cigarettes, matches, or whatever small items are in demand. Bau Prasad said that among these more-or-less standard items available in Dunai, he sells razor blades to men for shaving, which is surprising, since what little beard the men have they seem to bother with shaving only rarely. Bau Prasad's "shop" consists of a room in his house which is usually locked, but which he will unlock if someone needs to buy something he has in stock. He acquires whatever goods he has in Dunai. Prices for goods are twice what they are in Dunai, and in Dunai twice what they are in Nepalganj, from where they are flown when flights are available.[23]

Many people now take mules to Butwal and buy up provisions which they bring back to sell or use for themselves. Bhim has four mules which he owns in absentia. Using mules to transport goods is beneficial also because any mules kept locally during winter would have to be fed grass, when what little grass might be growing is mostly covered with snow, as opposed to more readily available grass in the warmer, snowless lower hills. Grass for mules kept in the village in warm weather, after their return from Butwal, is not a problem. In winter, Bhotias still come south from Upper Dolpa to the relative warmth not only of Tichurong villages like Tarang, but also to Dunai and even to Kathmandu, so there are not as many who winter over in Tarang as there had been before. A few still stay home in Upper Dolpa to take care of cattle and snow removal.

No one in the village keeps yak anymore,[24] but Bhotias still bring theirs down to graze above the village. Mules (for those who have them) are now used to carry manure to the fields, in addition to the former method of transport on women's backs. Of eighty-eight houses currently in Tarang (by Budhi Bahadur's count), twenty houses are involved in trade with horses and mules. Generally, mules carry loads and horses carry people. Mules on average are more expensive, but a good galloping horse is the most expensive of all.

---

23   Goods are also occasionally flown in from Kathmandu.
24   Yak are still kept in the village of Tachen, across the river.

All engage in barter to satisfy their own salt requirements, using the old salt trade route to barter (*satta patta*, Nepali) millet and buckwheat for Tibetan salt. Nowadays many people use iodized salt supplied from Kathmandu rather than the hard rock salt from Tibet, although Tarang people occasionally go to the Tibetan border to bring back sheep and salt for themselves, and Bhotias bring Tibetan salt to Tarang, which they trade for *phapar* (buckwheat), *kodo* (millet), and *chinu chamal* (another variety of millet). One kg of salt buys three kg of phapar. The price of one kg of *phapar* is Rs. 30, so the equivalent of 1 kg of Tibetan salt is Rs. 90 (therefore 3 kg of phapar = Rs. 90). Tibetan salt is never sold for cash, but only traded for edible grains like buckwheat and millet, buckwheat being preferred because it can be used in bread and also fed to animals. It is also therefore not always available in unlimited quantities.

Indian salt (fortified with iodine, which prevents goiter and cretinism) is also available, subsidized by the Nepal government. One kg of Indian salt (subsidized for up to two packets) goes for Rs. 10 ($0.50/lb.); beyond that, it is Rs. 100/kg on the market. Tibetan salt lacks iodine but tastes better, so villagers prefer it and consume more of it if they can, but it's not always readily available, as is salt in a shop. All in all, the consumption of Tibetan and Indian salt is about equal.

Another source of income is government-issued coupons which provide each person with three kilograms of rice per month. Such coupons are responsible, serendipitously, for the almost-universal registration of births, because a registered birth is required to be eligible for the coupons. Babies are registered at a district office in Dunai; an official comes from Dunai to do the paperwork at frequent but irregular intervals. The rice and registrations are entirely new—neither had ever been suggested or even thought of formerly.

Rice can also be bought at the subsidized rate of Rs. 30/kg ($0.14/lb). These arrangements were all facilitated through the good offices of Dhanu; nothing remotely like them existed before, when there was almost no government presence in the village, except for the police check post and, minimally, in the case of the erstwhile village school. The rice ration results in its increased consumption at the expense of the traditional millet and buckwheat diet, partly because it is higher status, but also because cooking it eliminates the tiring manual labor required to prepare the latter grains, pounding the grain in a mortar and pestle system to separate chaff from it. Budhi and Pasang still drink salt tea with *ghiu* every morning, which is what people in Tarang (and the rest of Dolpa) mostly drink, rather than sweet tea.

Improvement in basic infrastructure is reflected in the new road being constructed along the way up the river from Dunai, as well as lesser projects such as trail maintenance. I made an excursion to Tato Pani (Nepali, hot water), the spring an hour's walk or so above the village, with Yamuna, the Brahman schoolteacher (sometimes referred to as Madam), Budhi Bahadur and his wife, Pasang, and one of their grandsons. Formerly, this excursion involved hiking over a rough trail to a spring and mud hole. The trail is now vastly improved, and the mud hole has been replaced by two large cement tanks to hold the hot water, so that one can ease one's aching joints and bones by soaking in it. The government paid villagers with rice and dal to improve the trail to the spring above the village. Not far above the spring are the wilds of the *yarsagumba* grounds.

A cement tank has been built, with government help, at the hot spring two hours walk above the village.

On the way back to Tarang from a visit to Riwa, the Kami village, Yamuna and I passed many Tarang men getting started on their spring plowing, including Budhi Bahadur, who was rebuilding a retaining wall made of rocks of all sizes that were lying haphazardly in the middle of the fields. When I stopped to lend a hand, it reminded me, in a close and visceral way, what hard work it still is to plow these fields and struggle with the rocks that border them and even largely comprise them. Cell phones, DVDs, solar collectors, fruit trees, and literacy, while all radical in their own ways, have not altered the technology of agriculture, the most basic and time-consuming component of their economy, nor have they reduced the fundamental physical difficulty of practicing it, nor, I should add, the danger of doing so. In early 2016 Budhi Bahadur died when a stone wall he was trying to repair collapsed on him. It is in this central and dominant sense that life in Tarang continues, and sometimes ends, much as it always has.

Budhi Bahadur and I pause to rest while preparing his fields for spring plowing and planting.

Ritual Changes

Hindu and Buddhist rituals and festivals often overlap, in Tichurong as well as in other parts of Nepal. In Tichurong, Buddhists celebrate Saun Sankranti (the first of the month of Saun, which occurs in mid-July), as Hindus (e.g., in Dunai) do. But the latter celebrate the occasion with *puja*s, whereas Buddhists in Tarang just light their rooftop fires on the specified day to get rid of skin diseases such as scabies (*luto falne*, Nepali), and more generally to rid their houses of whatever is bad and evil in life (bad luck, ill omens, disease). The day to get rid of scabies takes place just after the rainy season when people have been working in the fields and are somewhat predisposed to fever and diseases. It is thought of as a kind of medically prophylactic ritual. This is accomplished by casting the ash and embers from fires off the rooftops, and with them bad luck, ill omens, and diseases, into the filth of the open cowshed below. The fires are visible in villages across the river from each other (*waripari*, Nepali) and form a visual component of the mutual scolding that takes place across the river at this time.

Nowadays people don't celebrate this festival to the extent they did formerly, in that they have stopped the chicken sacrifice, because a highly respected reincarnate (*tulku*, Tibetan) lama from Shey Gomba (in Inner Dolpa) preached against it on the grounds that animal sacrifice goes against the grain of Buddhist theory and practice. But the lighting of rooftop fires is still a universal practice. After strenuous work during the spring and summer—plowing, getting the crops in the ground, weeding them and nurturing them—everyone is in a mood to celebrate during the month of Saun by observing these rituals, relaxing by drinking substantial amounts of *jad* or *rakshi* even if they no longer sacrifice a chicken.

Taralis don't celebrate major Hindu holidays such as Dasai, Tihar, or Holi, but *bartaman*, nominally the first haircut for boys, is a major ritual event. It is conducted at the age of seven in Tarang, the most typical celebration age among Hindus, who may also celebrate it later, at thirteen or fifteen. *Bartaman* is a major ritual (*thulo chad*, Nepali), and it is celebrated lavishly, especially for an eldest son. The topknot (*tupi*, Nepali) is left after *bartaman*, but is routinely cut afterwards except in the case of the *dhami*, who keeps it for the rest of his life. The *tupi* has no apparent connection to the similar practice among Hindus.

Expenses for the big feast that accompanies the ritual are paid by the community, but later these expenses have to be repaid, with interest,[25]

---

[25] The interest is not calculated as for a bank loan. Rather, individuals are expected to contribute a little more than they have borrowed. The amount also depends on economic status; the impetus to repay is felt to be a community obligation that one would regret reneging on.

so all the villagers are invited and contribute money for it. If repayment is delayed, the interest due increases (like filing tax returns late), but the communal sponsorship applies only to the *bartaman* for the first son. On the female side, like Hindu women elsewhere, Tarali women celebrate full moon days (Purnima, Nepali) by circumambulating the chortens scattered around the village, but even here the observance is quite irregular.

In the midst of gently and uncertainly wondering about how I might promote and protect the Tarali way of life, I thought that asking how I could contribute to village welfare might also reveal some cultural preferences. Education is a high priority—by all accounts the highest among civic needs and "development" (*bikas*, Nepali), but that was a nonstarter because of the government's already substantial support for the school.

I therefore asked about the need to improve the condition of the chortens. They are commissioned by wealthy people (for example, the new *kani*, which I saw on the way up to the village from the river, which had been commissioned by Lanku), but once built, there is no provision for maintaining them, and, though sturdy, they are left to deteriorate over the years. Maintenance of chortens is problematic because if they are not maintained well, responsibility would fall on whoever took on the task. As long as nothing is done, no one can be blamed for anything. To explore a similar but alternative form of merit-earning philanthropy, I asked about interest in constructing a resting place (*chautara*, Nepali), especially for those carrying loads, at the new water tap, which would provide a platform where "gallons" can be placed before and after filling. I was told that such a *chautara* had been built, but that people then stole the stones used to construct it to use in their own houses.

Similarly, villagers cut the black plastic pipe installed to supply the school with water, but for an understandable reason. The pipe developed a leak, which reduced its usefulness, and it therefore made sense to cut it into smaller pieces that could at least be utilized to drain water from individual roofs.

Villagers that I talked to are discouraged by the stealing of stones (but not, presumably, the ones doing the stealing). There is agreement that this is a deplorable practice. However, as a community they seemed unable to come up with any way to effectively deal with these predicaments. Administratively, each of the two wards of the village is represented by a single person, as before. Tarang has a villagewide budget to provide for the school, water supply, improvement of trails, and whatever other projects come up that need financial support. But one reason why the stealing is allowed to take place is that in the present period of political instability, all local political bodies are temporarily disbanded, so no official is in office to deal with it. Dharma accrues to those who construct such useful structures as a *chautara* or a *kani*, but because of the size of the stones, those from a *chautara* are useful in household construction, while those in a *kani* are not. Moreover, there is more dharma involved in building a religious monument such as a *kani* than in constructing a practical structure such as a *chautara*.

The existence, and sometimes coexistence, of various Hindu practices and rituals notwithstanding, the primacy and strength of Buddhism has never been a matter of debate. Indeed, Buddhism, along with other aspects of Tarali culture, including language, has become more than ever a center of attention. This could be seen in the excitement generated by the arrival of a highly respected lama from Upper Dolpa for his once-in-twelve-years visit, when he dances for three days. Late one afternoon, ten monks accompanied him to the upper edge of Tarang, where they set up camp and performed a brief introduction to ecclesiastical music and dance. Many villagers came to see the lamas, all men at first, followed later by women, who, unlike the men, brought offerings of millet (*chinu*, Kaike) and prayer scarves (*kata*, Tibetan). The tops of the poles holding up the tents the lamas were using were Shiva tridents, as cross-incorporation of iconography between Buddhism and Hinduism is as common as is the variety of belief systems, such as the primacy of beliefs about karma and dharma.

In addition to this visiting lama, a local lama from Samtiling chants annually for sixteen days (Niunnya, Kaike) for the benefit of all people, and specifically to bring about peace for the entire world. On alternate days the lama and a few lay villagers either speak and eat, or remain silent and fast. They take turns rotating the ceremony in Tarang, Tarakot, and Gombatara.

There is thought to be a marital relationship of very long standing between Gombatara and Tarang, which explains why the two villages unite in this ritual (for this ritual purpose, Tarakot is considered to be part of Tarang). The relationship is traced to the assistance citizens of Tarang gave long ago in the construction of the landmark eponymous gomba still standing in Gombatara. The exchange of course ensures that some Gomba villagers who marry into Tarang will learn Kaike (even if imperfectly) and some Tarang villagers will improve their Tibetan if they marry into Gombatara.

Alongside Hindu and Buddhist rituals and influences, the indigenous religious traditions continue. In place of the Chaite Bokne celebration that used to be conducted by *patum* (the title of the traditional ritual leader, now deceased), villagers take turns (two houses at a time) hosting it. The old Chaite Bokne required one month during the months of Pus and Magh (the middle of winter, when snow and frozen ground bring a halt to all agricultural activity), when *patum* would dance, holding and beating his shaman drum, with young boys dancing around him, beating their drums. Chaite Bokne involved much dancing, drumming, playing, and acquiring new clothes, as well as feeding *jad* and *rakshi* to all comers.

The new version of Chaite Bokne also takes place, by turn, for five days during which time, with the hosts wearing *patuka*s and *khukri*s, all houses acquire and wear new clothes. Without the *patum*, the special, archaic, ritual form of Kaike he chanted is now gone forever. Both the old and new rituals are dedicated to Rungpuki, the Himalayan cypress (*dhupi*, Nepali) and Rungpacha, two of the four sacred trees above the village; the ritual takes place in Chait or Baisakh (spring). The other trees are Tamuna (*diyar*, Nepali), and Sisuru, which like Rungpacha, uniquely represent those species in the area. No one knows how they got there. The trees are not considered deities, but are regarded as natural symbols that serve to eliminate evil spirits, diseases, draught, and any other kind of disaster, protecting the entire village.

The Outside World

In addition to the economic and ritual changes mentioned above, other transformations have penetrated Tarang from the outside world in ways I would never have expected or even imagined, including some that affect children's lives, without being transmitted directly through the parental or grandparental generation. Budhi Bahadur's grandson likes to pretend he's doing Japanese-style karate, which he has seen on DVDs. One morning he was crying because his grandparents wouldn't give him chewing gum, which couldn't even be obtained previously. He didn't like going to school, and got into fights when he did go. A couple of years later he was sent to Kathmandu in the hopes that he would acquire more discipline and schooling there—and not from his parents. That option would have been unavailable before.

Hindu/Buddhist differences have become more complicated by politicization of ethnic and religious differences following the downfall of the monarchy and abolition of Nepal's definition as "the world's only Hindu state." For example, the dichotomy between Hindu and Tibetan personal names is less clear-cut than it was before, or at least than I had originally thought it was before. People continue to use Hindu names at times, but they averred that this was for pragmatic reasons—because they are easier to write and more familiar to people Taralis meet in the Nepali-speaking *purba* (east). Thus, use of Hindu names instead of Tibetan ones does not seem to reflect an ideological preference of one over the other, as villagers certainly do not try to hide or disguise their Buddhist identity the way they might have before,[26] and as Chandra Man did as he cycled through his various name changes (detailed in Chapter 9). The influence of the self-conscious Tarali cultural resurgence, ironically initiated from Kathmandu, has begun spreading to Tichurong.

I could see how the Kathmandu, Tarang, and other far-flung branches of a family are maintained in Bhim Prasad's case. In addition to Bhim in Kathmandu, his sister Rubi is in Australia, and his brother Moti (who goes by his nickname of Saman), is in New York. His sister Kabita is studying nursing in Kathmandu, and his brother Om is a contractor constructing roads and buildings in Kathmandu. Saman's family helped him financially during his first days in New York, but now he is earning his own way, working in an upscale lower-Manhattan hotel.

Bhim looks strikingly like his father (Bau Prasad). Both of Bhim's parents had come to my house in Kathmandu in 1970, when I feasted all the villagers who had come there on pilgrimage that year. Before the feast I showed them the USIS film of the Apollo 12 moon landing. One of the villagers had expressed serious doubts about whether the moon landing had taken place at all: "Even the Dalai Lama has not gone to the moon, so why should anyone believe the Americans had?" He changed his mind after seeing the film, asserting that it would be impossible

---

[26]   Furthermore, the either/or distinction might be too facilely drawn. Sukar's name, for instance, is of uncertain origin; Bhim thought it might derive from her birth on a Friday (Sukrabar), but he admitted that he was just guessing.

for a film not to be true since films show real people (or even deities) doing things. This is the same reaction Chandra Man had had as a child watching movies in Kathmandu in the 1950s. Perhaps it is a reaction anyone who has never seen a movie would have at first, unless television had intervened (television first became available in Nepal in 1985).

Bhim hadn't traveled to Tarang for three years, nor had his parents gone to Kathmandu, but they talk on the phone once a month. In 2013 he returned to take part in Dhanu's campaign for the parliamentary seat allotted to Dolpa in the November election for that year (which Dhanu won handily). I had lunch at Bhim's parents' house, and while I was there, we called Bhim in Kathmandu. It was amazing (at least to me— they seemed to think it was nothing out of the ordinary) to see how easy it is to talk by mobile phone over such logistically difficult terrain. After the call we had a long discussion of how Bhim's father recharges his phone by having Bhim transfer money over his phone to pay for a recharge card in Dunai, which Bau Prasad then picks up. For example, if Bhim transfers Rs. 100, the intermediary charges a fee of Rs. 2, leaving Rs. 98 to pay for his father's calls. They were thrilled with the photos (still present in my camera) that I had taken of Bhim and his family at what could only be called their highrise house in Kathmandu. When a picture of Bhim popped up on the camera screen, his mother was so happy she kissed the screen.

There are about as many uses for mobile phones as there are people who own them. For example, a mobile phone is very useful for Yamuna to keep in close touch with her husband and son; they live in Kathmandu, where her husband is stationed in the army. Anyone who has a cell phone manages to find a use for it. Or perhaps the reverse is more the case: anyone who needs a phone will find one to use.

My old friend Tagla had three sons and two daughters, of whom two sons and one daughter were living. The daughter lived nine years in Bhaktapur, working in the yarn business, but now has returned to Tarang. Her house is unique in that it has screens on the windows to keep out insects such as flies, and a metal stove (unlike the usual open fireplace made of rock) with chimney (instead of an open hole in the roof). The stove had been manufactured in Korea, and had cost about Rs. 7,000 ($73), plus transportation to fly it in from Nepalganj. I asked Shanti, a young woman, why she doesn't have a stove like that, and she said the gods would be angry if she acquired and installed one, but that if a new house were built it would be all right to install such a new stove in it. Tagla's daughter's diet has also changed as a result of time away from the village. She keeps no local food (millet, buckwheat) in her house, only rice and lentils. Yamuna says she had gotten used to eating in Kathmandu and in hotels, thus acquiring the taste. Her house is only three years old (hence the lack of problem with having a stove), and she will probably start cultivating her own fields soon.

Hierarchical Changes

As described in the original *Trans-Himalayan Traders*, social hierarchy exists on a variety of different levels. Taralis have hierarchical relations with Bhotias from Upper Dolpa, with high Hindu castes in Dunai and points west (Khasan, or land of the Khas), the low-caste Kamis in nearby Riwa, and Magars belonging to different marriage classes in Tichurong. Chandra Man speaks of his relations with all these groups, sometimes positively, sometimes negatively.

A further complicating element is that villagers refer to the lamas in Samtiling (the upper part of Tarang) casually as Gurungs, rather than by the clan names of Budhas or Rokayas or Ghartis, a status they claim for themselves. In other words, they do not grant Magar status to the lamas, or rather, they do not do so privately. Although they refer to the lamas as Gurungs, that is only a placeholder tag. They think of them as Bhotias, like the Bhotias from near the Tibetan border, although they don't say so to their faces. Yet lama girls don't marry socially up (geographically down) into the village, while village girls, if there is no better match available locally, marry socially down (geographically up) to Samtiling. All inhabitants, other than the Kamis, are incontestably classified, at least publically, ethnically as Magars. In the more important domain of marriage, the distinctions of separate marriage classes come into play.

Any villager would agree that people of Upper Dolpa and Tichurong are both Buddhist and both follow the teachings, instructions, and proclamations of lamas; on those liturgical and dogmatic grounds they should be of equal rank. When I asked a young woman why Magars don't wear Tibetan clothes in Tichurong, despite the importance of the lamas from Upper Dolpa and the use of Tibetan language as a first language in all the Tichurong villages except for the Kaike-speaking ones, she said that "they are Bhotias and we are Chetris—and then immediately corrected herself and said "we are Magars" (i.e., not Chetris). I think it was a careless slip, but I also think people here don't think much about such matters, at least not as much as I do in my attempts to find an ethnic or hierarchical slot into which I can comfortably and unequivocally place everyone.

One of the activities lamas undertake in Tarang is to give babies their names, but this is not as significant as it sounds. First, they do not give names to everyone, since they are not always available to do so. Even when they do give a baby a name, they sometimes give it a Nepali name. Furthermore, these lama-given names do not always last. When Budhi Bahadur went to Phoksumdo at about age ten, the Bonpo lama there gave him a new name, but it didn't stick. By now, no one even knows about the existence of Budhi's alternate, lama-given name, let alone what it might be.

Government and Maoist Presence

Government presence is a mixed blessing. In addition to providing employment in road and trail building, improving resources such as availability of potable water, in the form of two new taps, one within the village and one at the new expanded school site (see Map 4), and facilities at the hot spring, and making rice and salt available at subsidized prices, the government pays most of the teacher salaries. But these government contributions are not accomplished without a hitch. At the time of my visit, a teacher's strike had just gotten underway, which was launched because the teachers hadn't been paid recently. The Tarang teachers went, en masse, to Dunai to take part in the strike and to show their support for it. No one seemed to know what the outcome would be, except that the teachers said they wouldn't continue to teach unless they were paid according to the schedules in their agreements.

Grasping the impact of Maoists on Tichurong is not easy; answers to my questions about it were guarded. On the one hand, during the insurgency, the Maoists demanded Rs. 500 from each teacher per month. Each teacher handed this over to the principal, who then passed it on to the Maoists. The government was unaware of this arrangement, as no one could safely tell them about it for fear of harsh reprisals for what would be considered cooperating with the enemy. Maoists also took food without paying for it, as did the army, but not as much as they did in other parts of west Nepal such as Nepalganj. In demanding these payments, Maoists apparently took into account the economic circumstances of those being assessed.

On the other hand, Kamis would have been a natural constituency for the egalitarian-minded Maoists, but the consensus opinion was that the Kamis had voted for the UML candidate (i.e., Dhanu). At the time of my visit the general opinion seemed to be that there were probably no more than one hundred Maoist supporters in all of Tichurong. Everyone in Tarang voted for Dhanu except for one man, who gave his vote to the Maoist candidate. This was odd, since Dhanu had let him stay in his house while studying for exams. If there were some idiosyncratic reason for withholding his vote from Dhanu, no one was able to figure it out.

One incident has left a stain on the immediate Maoist reputation and legacy, whatever that may turn out to be in the long term. Maobadi (Maoists) are thought to be behind the theft of a statue from the temple in Gombatara village. No one knows for sure, but one widely believed rumor is that some members of the YCL (Young Communist League) stole it. The motive is imagined to be the same as that behind many of the thefts that have taken place in the Kathmandu valley over the years: the financial value these artifacts have for collectors and museums outside the country. The Gomba statue is believed to be eight or nine hundred years old, which gives it very high value in international art markets. The YCL members were all local Magars, not outside organizers. The case is not closed and may yet erupt on the political scene. In any case, the YCL is no longer actively functioning in Tichurong.

As evidence for the increased prosperity due to *yarsagumba* and government help, I found little response to my interest to hire someone to help me on my trip to Phoksumdo. Kamal Dai wanted Rs. 1000 ($10)/ day for himself and a horse, so instead I took a Kami from Riwa, who was willing to make the trip for Rs. 500 ($5)/day. This arrangement had the added advantage for the Kami that he could moonlight by bringing back a load of goods to Tarang from Dunai for Yamuna, after I flew from Juphal.

Kamis

Despite the dramatic differences in caste rank and religious practice, the challenges facing life in Riwa, the Kami village, are much like those in

Tarang. Like the school in Tarang, the school in Riwa is being expanded to include a new building which uses translucent plastic sections in part of the roof (one per room), which is a great improvement over 100% zinc or tin. In 1964 plastic roofing was used on Sherpa schools in Khumbu, because they provide diffuse lighting even on a cloudy day, but now, fifty years later, they're only beginning to catch on in Dolpa.

Thus, without priests, Riwa seems like any other Tichurong village in its housing, fields, crops, and general architectural appearance and layout. Despite the villagers' Hindu origins, Buddhist flags fly from the roofs. Unlike Buddhist Taralis they do celebrate Dasai (but not Tihar or Holi), in addition to Saun Sankranti and Mai Sankranti. Otherwise they accept the authority of the lamas when they encounter them, and no Bahuns (Brahmans) ever visit Riwa—there would be nothing for them to do there. The Kamis worship several deities (Deorali, Indu, Sukuti, Kailash, Otari, Bwani, Mamadeu, Lati Deorali, Patanni, and Lachin, among others), but not the "Great Tradition" Hindu deities such as Shiva (Mahadev), Krishna, Vishnu, or Ganesh.[27] The deities that are worshipped are located in various houses, rather than in a temple. Taralis in the other Tichurong villages take no interest in any of these Hindu deities. Lamas don't come to Riwa for ritual reasons, except to help erect the auspicious rooftop flags, and for the same reason: they don't worship these deities. Thus, without priests of either Buddhist or Hindu persuasion, Riwa is substantially without ritual specialists, except for a Kami *dhami* who performs occasional rituals. Indeed, to a limited extent Kamis act as ritual specialists at events such as a Magar marriage feast, *bartaman*, and death. Each Tarang household has a "family Kami" who is called when needed for these events. They also act as non-ritual specialists, performing services such as keeping knives sharp and other household implements in good repair. These Magar/Kami relationships are of course analogous to *jajmani* relationships, which have been much described in India.

Yamuna, the Brahman teacher, seemed to fit right in and feel at home when we visited Riwa, but later, as we were walking back to Tarang, she said she was relieved that I had declined the Kamis' offer of tea, because she is very aware of her high caste and attempts to preserve and protect it at every opportunity. She says that when teachers from the area are

---

[27] Some of the names may be local versions of more standard nomenclature: for example, Mamadeu for Mahadev, and Lachin for Laxmi.

brought together for meetings and training sessions, she and other high caste Hindu teachers will consume tea or rice with the Kami teacher, because it would be openly insulting not to do so. But she is unable to feel comfortable in such situations, and declines offers of commensality when she can get away with it.

This sentiment was reflected when I was chatting casually with a few villagers, and Kamal Dai opined that Riwa was a nice village but not the people in it, who speak falsely and are of a low caste (*sano jat,* Nepali). I asked Budhi Bahadur and others in the group if they would eat rice cooked by Kamis, and they emphatically, if laughingly, said no, because they were Kamis, whereas Magars are a high caste like Bahun, Chetri, and Thakuri, showing the extent to which the Magars of Tichurong buy into the conventional but dominant Hindu hierarchy (when they can do so to their advantage) found outside its borders. All this echoed Chandra Man's experience on the other end of the hierarchy, when these same high Hindu castes in Jumla and elsewhere cast aspersions on him because of his low caste, variously identified as Magar or Bhotia.

Economically, Kamis have fared well recently. They have earned considerable income, whether from installing solar collectors, or from building the village schools and a hospital, doing house construction in the area, and the like. No wonder I found it difficult to find a porter; they can usually do better practicing their traditional crafts and skills, which are in rising and considerable demand.

When I asked the Riwa people about politics, they seemed hesitant to commit themselves. They said they were for "*swatantra,*" which I took to mean they were "independent" and unaligned with any political party, rather than that they were for the conservative political party known by that name, which is not active in Dolpa.

International organizations have not made their presence felt locally either. Neither Yamuna nor others had ever heard of the Peace Corps, which was not surprising since the Peace Corps had never assigned a Volunteer to work in Dolpa. But even in Kathmandu, I never encountered a taxi driver or restaurant waiter who had ever heard of the Peace Corps. The identities of specific organizations like the Peace Corps are swamped now in the thousands of NGOs operating throughout the country, including those working in road construction, poverty reduction, and education in Dolpa.

Local Interest in Local Culture

I encountered one exciting development I had not even remotely
expected. I found more intellectual curiosity about local life: how it
originated, how it worked, and what its prospects are, than before when,
if it existed, I couldn't detect it. The manager at the Blue Sheep Inn in
Dunai asked what I'd written in my book. I tried to make my answer
simple, explaining that I had written about the language (Kaike), the
crops (millet and buckwheat), trading (the transaction cycles), food,
religion, *pujas*, houses, kinship, family, etc., and he responded, in a way
I had not anticipated, "Oh, you mean the *culture*?" This exchange was
conducted entirely in the Nepali language except for the English word
culture—anthropology had truly arrived in Dolpa.

Then Angad (son of Laxmi Saran, the venerable and highly respected
Brahman who lived in Dunai in the 1960s) told me that all of Dolpa is
Nyingmapa (as the Sherpas are), which coexists easily with Bonpo (the
pre-Buddhist religion of Tibet), whereas Gelugpa (the Dalai Lama's
sect) might have local disagreements with Bonpo.[28] Recent years have
seen the establishment of a big Bonpo presence in Dunai, as well as of
traditional Buddhists, but they all get along well whatever doctrinal
differences they may have. Santaram Thakali, a Dunai resident and
author of a book on historical Dolpa that he gave me titled *Wigatako
Dolpa*, or Old Dolpa (Thakali, 2007), is married to a Tarang woman and
came to the feast I had hosted in Kathmandu in 1970. He said there
has been a kind of Buddhaizing of Dunai, citing the big new Bonpo
buildings as evidence of fresh energy. Since Dunai is the capital of
Dolpa District, many of its residents are government employees and
mostly Hindu. They therefore outnumber Buddhists, but the Buddhists
are exerting their influence in the town more than the Hindus are, who
have only one small temple at which to worship.

Angad also entertained a theory I'd not heard before on the etymology
of Sahar Tara, the Nepali name for Tarang: it had originally been Sadar
(major or capital) Tara, which morphed over time into Sahar (city,
which, stretching things a bit, it is, compared to other Dolpa villages).
Either word would fit, structurally, grammatically and semantically.
Also, he maintained that Tarakot might have gotten top billing on maps

---

[28]   H.H. the Fourteenth Dalai Lama has formally approved Bön as one of the five major
spiritual traditions of Tibet.

because as a *kot* (fort) there might have been some sort of king there, although I could find no local story or legend to this effect. Wherever the king lived would automatically have been accorded some kind of special status and recognition, including the cartographic one of being recorded on a map.[29] These local intellectuals in remote areas are an as yet untapped resource for the development of further knowledge about Nepal. Kathmandu-based intellectuals, and those working in campuses affiliated with universities, can profitably pay attention to intellectuals who have, for a variety of idiosyncratic reasons, ended up in remote places like Dolpa.

Finally, my long-awaited return to Tarang had reached its culmination. I came, I saw, and to a limited extent I understood. Maybe I could have conquered too, intellectually, by staying another year, continuing to learn more and more, cutting ever further into the omnipresent onion of culture, and peeling back its multiple layers, but without ever reaching its center. As in my first trip to Tichurong, however, circumstances dictated that another phase in my life had reached its inexorable conclusion. It was time to move on.

Leaving Dolpa

After a one-week side trip to Phoksumdo, I was back on the windblown airstrip at Juphal. Two flights were scheduled in and out of Juphal that day, both of them returning to Nepalganj, but the weather on the flight path to Nepalganj was so unstable they were both rescheduled instead to the western hill town of Surkhet. The first flight landed at Juphal, took off promptly early in the morning, and returned. I then boarded the second flight. The plane was loaded and the engine was revved up and ready to go when the pilot (Captain Bhattarai) turned off the engine, saying the weather was too stormy to attempt a take-off. We sat at the top of the runway, waiting for half an hour before we tried again. It was still raining, and although the winds seemed extremely high to my amateur eye, Captain Bhattarai apparently saw things differently. Or maybe he had just lost patience—I'll never know for sure.

---

[29] An alternative theory, which I heard about only in 2016, is that Tarakot had been selected as the first district capital; if so, nothing came of it, and Dunai soon became designated the Dolpa District capital.

There's nothing like that final moment, bouncing and swerving uncertainly down the runway and hoping against hope that the plane is going to leave the ground soon, since otherwise there's no place for it to go other than into the narrow ribbon of a river gorge thousands of feet below. This time we took off right into that horrendous rainstorm, winds tossing the plane around as if it were a butterfly in a stiff breeze. I was sitting next to a Tibetan man with long, braided hair whom I had happened to meet earlier in Kathmandu. I was relieved that he was energetically fingering his rosary beads, praying fervently, and chanting vigorously at what seemed like a faster tempo and louder decibel level than usual. I intensely, if silently, urged him to keep doing all the things he was doing.

Captain Bhattarai somehow managed to steer us through all that and we proceeded on our way to Surkhet, where I caught a public bus for the four-hour ride to Nepalganj. There I would pick up the connecting flight to Kathmandu I had intended to take directly from Juphal. In Surkhet they handled all the bureaucracy of issuing a new ticket very efficiently, charging me nothing for the service. I got to the Nepalganj bus station and from there, on the back of a motorcycle, rode on to the Nepalganj airport. The airline provided the motorcycle free of charge. After the mid-trip change in flight destination, they went all out to get me from Surkhet to Nepalganj in time to catch that last flight of the day to Kathmandu. It could have been both a disaster and a ripoff, and it was neither. In the days before deregulation, Royal Nepal Airlines, then the country's only carrier, would not have extended itself one iota on behalf of a beleaguered passenger.

Airplane crashes in Nepal are not common, at least not as a proportion of all the flights flown. When they do occur, they probably follow the pattern of airplane crashes in the rest of the world generally: about half due to pilot error, 22% to mechanical failure, and 12% to weather. Rather than repeat the arduous and exhausting two-week trek from Pokhara to Tichurong, I was more than willing to take a chance on these small aircraft and their brave and experienced pilots operating on airfields of minimal dimensions, with uncertain surfaces, and at maximal altitudes. These upcountry airlines deserve great credit for performing a difficult, dangerous, and important job well—maybe not entirely unfailingly, but at least reassuringly a large portion of the time.

Nevertheless, in the interests of full disclosure, I should mention the sobering aeronautical fact that in 2013 the European Union banned all Nepal-based carriers, citing their inadequate safety precautions and procedures, from flying in the twenty-eight-nation EU bloc.

9

Chandra Man Rokaya:
Rags to Riches

I would not want to give the impression that the remarkable accomplishments of Lank Man, Bisara, Bhim, Sukar, and Dhanu (and others like them, unnamed here) are culturally and structurally overdetermined by the fortuitous circumstances of their particular lives—that education and kinship and prior trading experience are what is required to break into the new class forming in Kathmandu. This would be the conventional, one might say even traditional, anthropological way to look at it. To show how social, cultural, economic, political, and symbolic arrangements mesh together (or not) to form systems is what anthropologists, in one way or another, generally do.

That is certainly a valid way to proceed, as far as it goes, but it is not the only way. Indeed, the final example is of a Tarali who has succeeded outside the village in a way that seems to be not only in a different world from, but even at odds with, that of virtually all other Taralis. His case to a great extent belies my social, cultural, and economic analysis in the preceding chapters. It is even, to the extent that it flies in the face of the anthropological grounding and reasoning of the book so far, anti-anthropological, in a perverse sort of way.

Chandra Man Rokaya left Tarang for Kathmandu and followed coping strategies so different from those of Bhim Prasad, Sukar, Lank Man, Bisara, and Dhanu as to be unrecognizable among these scions of wealth, education, and powerful, supportive kinship ties. His circumstances were anything but fortuitous. His case shows that the auspicious conditions in which those I've described so far found themselves were not necessary to explain their success, and not even sufficient, because my portrait of them is not complete. In a substantial and significant way Chandra Man contradicts the very picture I've been trying to paint of an almost inexorable march toward prosperity by some, and the relative stasis that characterizes the majority whose lives have continued much as they always were, the miracle of *yarsagumba* notwithstanding. In that sense I present him as a counterexample, even a refutation, of the analysis I've been promoting thus far.

I first met Chandra Man in 1963, when he was one of my students in Class 8 English at Pharping Boarding School. I saw him again in 1969 when he returned to Tarang during a vacation from his university in India. In the meantime, he began telling his story in 1966 to John Hitchcock (in English), who passed it on to me decades later. I have updated the narrative beyond the point where Hitchcock had taken it and edited a few parts of it very lightly, but the words and the organization of them are almost entirely Chandra Man's. Because Chandra Man has told his own story in his own words, it is full of details unavailable in my accounts of the others, and certainly not in my earlier book about transaction circuits.

His story shows how the idiosyncrasies of an individual case—a sociologist might think of him as a statistical deviant—can completely override what would normally be culturally expected or required to accomplish what he accomplished. His background and the life he eventually lived not only do not easily match up; they seem self-contradictory. The latter does not follow from the former, in the way that I have argued they do in the examples of others who have begun settling in Kathmandu much more recently. Additionally, his case brings to the surface many aspects of Tarali culture so subtle that I have heretofore missed them, or at least failed to mention them. These aspects do not necessarily differentiate Chandra Man from the others, who may share them, but I simply lack the relevant, comparable details in the other instances. In any event, it is now time for Chandra Man's case to assume its place in the portrait of Tarang—and Taralis—that I have developed thus far. However uncharacteristic, or even deviant, his case is, it cannot be denied. It demands to be heard.

His narrative is undeniably unique, but it also illustrates how some of what I've written about Tarali life at a more systemic and abstract level looks from the vantage point of an individual living through it and surviving in spite of it all—what it's like to herd cattle, plow and weed fields, walk days or weeks to reach places you have to go, simply because there were no other means of transportation.

It also reveals the excitement and astonishment of learning to read and write, steal, beg, go hungry, and to see and experience, for the first time, novelties such as a train, a road, a movie. It shows how the vagaries of highly specific and unpredictable circumstances, even if unprecedented, can lead someone in one direction rather than another totally opposite one, regardless of the transaction circuits which might be operating and supposedly dictating the overall direction of a life. It also reveals the plasticity of social arrangements that might otherwise come across as rather fixed and deterministic, if they are visible at all in the macro landscape.

His story shows how quickly one's position can fall from the top of a hierarchy to the bottom, and then ascend again to the top many years later—all within the time span of an individual life. And it displays, in full view, how protracted civil litigation in various regional and national courts can consume so much time, energy, money, and goodwill, and thereby disrupt the normal flow of family life and kinship ties. Under stressful circumstances, these ties may become fraught with disputes and rows, whether these arise from legal tangles or more quotidian insults hurled from the rooftops.

His narrative also exhibits how the mixture of respect and fear found in Tarali attitudes toward Tibetans is much more complicated and nuanced than first appears, in which considerably more is involved than simple assessments of whether their "status" is higher or lower, and there are plenty of examples of both: high lamas, bandits, wise and just political leaders, or just traveling companions along the trails of northwest Nepal. It shows also how the sacredness and purity of the domestic hearth can be used politically, with accusations (involving me, to some extent) of eating socially contaminated (*jutho*, Nepali) food. Even in the matter of mortality, we hear how death suddenly and profoundly affects lives of the living in unexpected ways, and how even the prospect of death threatens the lives of those who will survive it. We also hear how rituals associated with death are carried out and what cultural assumptions they entail. My data on death from the earlier period were limited by the curious fact that during my year there, no one, at least no adult, died.

In addition, Chandra Man's story contains odd bits of information I just did not otherwise hear about previously, such as the eruption of a child's second teeth marking the age when he needs to begin observing caste rules, which is when Chandra Man felt he had to obey certain restrictions from which he had previously felt free. This is clearly an example that would have characterized the others too, but I just had not heard about that particular point before. That is, one goes through a learning period during childhood about the social system before one is expected to observe the rules that govern it. Again, probably any child anywhere goes through this experience in some way or another, but the Tarali cultural particulars are revealed here.

I also learned more specifically about the male preference for trading rather than agricultural work, because the latter is so much physically harder (though neither is easy). Similarly, I confronted the belief, illustrated poignantly in his mother's case, that the many difficulties we experience in this life are due not to errors of judgment or inadequate mental abilities or even malevolent intentions, whether one's own or those of one's enemies, but to bad deeds in a former life. Their repercussions continue to hover over us and cannot be escaped. As generalizations, none of these phenomena are new in South Asia and elsewhere. Furthermore, they are already widely known, but pinning them to specific cases shows how they work themselves into and through the failures and triumphs that routine, daily struggle yields in ordinary life.

Chandra Man also relates, revealingly, how he learned about how his own society worked, almost the way an anthropologist would. He did so by doing "fieldwork" among the fellow Nepalis he met and lived with after he had left his own village, the first time as a young child. For example, he discovered where he stood in the wider caste hierarchy operating in the generally Hindu world outside Tichurong, even though he already knew about untouchability from living with Damais (tailors) in Tarang, and Kamis (carpenters) in nearby Riwa village. Living below castes who regarded his as inferior was a new and jolting experience. Socially, he had always outranked anyone different from him, but no longer.

More than anything else, his story shows how a young child, even an orphan from a disadvantaged background, can—if he is clever, quick, talented, ambitious, smart, charming, and, one might add, lucky enough[30]—successfully make his way, against all odds, in an exotic and

---

[30] A Nepali might say that Chandra Man was *bhagyemani* (lucky), in the sense that his fate, over which he had no control (inscribed on his forehead by a deity a few days after birth), determined his life course. In fact, Chandra Man's mother made the opposite of just this point (i.e., that he was unlucky), to explain one of his naughtier episodes. Such post factum justifications are considered to have less predictive power than judgements guided by astrological calculations.

hostile environment. His tactics involved everything from ingeniously approaching the king of Nepal as a child (and currying favor with him by singing and dancing in front of him), to stealing money from his desperate and hardworking mother, and to resorting to the shame of begging, when he was on the verge of starvation, on the streets of Kathmandu. After running away from schools and teachers at an early age, the ultimately triumphant tactic he chose was to study hard, which resulted in achieving great success nationally, and even internationally, in the academic world.

Dealing with the impending death of a very sick person through bribery—offering them money or food to stay alive in order to avoid the sadness one would feel if they die—is a technique he learned about when his mother used it on him while he was a patient in a Kathmandu hospital. Thus, in addition to learning about the outside world, his socialization as a Tarali continued even in Kathmandu, so far away from home. Chandra Man relates that the conditions of the Kathmandu hospital in which he stayed for a month and which were very rudimentary in those days seemed, to use his own terms, "like heaven" in comparison to the chaotic and harsh life he had been living on the streets of Kathmandu.

As just one example of the poverty of that life, over the course of more than two fairly peripatetic years in Kathmandu, he and his mother never once rode the public bus anywhere, simply because they could not afford to do so. They walked wherever they needed to go, no matter how far the distance or how tired they might have been at the end of a long work day. Indeed, his mother not only walked everywhere, but she dealt with impending starvation by working as a coolie, carrying heavy loads of rice many miles, which is the only kind of work for which she was qualified other than crude and rudimentary household chores.

This, then, is the story of Chandra Man Rokaya, the first resident of Tarang, and indeed of Tichurong, to break away from life in his natal village and find his way first to Jumla, to the streets of Kathmandu, later to high school near Kathmandu, then to an Indian university, employment in the Agricultural Development Bank of Nepal, and finally to further studies in Australia.

Introducing him as Chandra Man implies a straightforward procedure which is deceptively simple. As is the case with other names in Tarang, Chandra Man's name is fraught with cultural complexity.

When he first went to Kathmandu with his mother as a young child, friends he made there of course wanted to know his name. He answered with the name by which he was known in his village, Pema, a Tibetan unisex name meaning lotus, as in the mantra "Om Mane Padme (or Pema) Hum," which is commonly translated as "Hail to the Jewel in the Lotus." They teased him and called him a Tibetan, which he very much resented. They made little rhymes out of it, such as "Bhote tote" (nonsense syllables).

Later, when he went to Pharping Boarding School, he was careful not to tell anyone his name was Pema. When he saw the King, he said his name was Chandra Man, so that's the name he used at Pharping. Also at Pharping he gave Magar as his last name (Chandra Man Magar is the name under which I came to know him as a student in Class 8), because he thought no one would recognize or understand Rokaya. Later he decided there might be more than one Chandra Man Magar with whom he could be confused, so after that he began calling himself Chandra Man Rokaya (his clan name, like Budha and Gharti), which is the name that stuck for the rest of his life.

What follows is Chandra Man's story of his life, told in his own words. It is, in a way, an ethnographically unfair presentation in that he has the luxury of including all sorts of details (and excluding others) that Bhim, Sukar, Lank Man, Bisara, and Dhanu did not record. What I write of the others is what I was able to get them to talk about in the process of answering my questions. But had they written their own stories the way Chandra Man did, without a lot of prompting, they might have included other information or expanded on what I did learn, which would have made a different book. From my point of view, it would have been a better book, but there comes a time when you have to go with what you have. Thus, what I have to some extent depends on the luck of the draw—whom I happened to meet and talk with, where, when, and under what circumstances. I had waited forty-four years to do so, which I thought was enough.

❖   ❖   ❖   ❖   ❖

Beginning: Eight Years Old

A court case brought suffering to my mother and my sister and caused the death of my father. That was the beginning of this story and all that happened to me, beginning when I was eight years old.

My great grandfather Sundayo, my father's father's father, was the richest man in the village. He had many sheep and goats and many storage pits full of grain. He had a big house and many valuable possessions of other kinds, such as gold for making ornaments. My family had so many fields I once asked my paternal uncle Birka how Sundayo collected all these fields. My uncle laughed and told me this story. "Sundayo was very, very strong, and his wife was very strong, too. When they went to the fields with their plow and ox, they would plow wherever they liked, and the owner of the field would come there and ask, 'Why are you plowing here?' Then there would be a great wrestling, you see. Sundayo and his wife always won, and from that day on kept the field."[31]

In their time Sundayo's two sons Lamakyap, a bachelor, and Dhai Singh, my father's father, also had the village's largest number of sheep and goats. Lamakyap was a good shepherd. He loved his sheep and goats very much and was ready to sacrifice his life for them, too. But he was a very hot-tempered fellow. When he was shepherding his flock, a weak sheep might fall behind. Then he roared with anger and would abuse the sheep. "Come, why are you here? Your friends have gone on!" The dumb sheep, how could it understand him? Lamakyap would take out his kukri and cut! At once the sheep would die.

There must be some other interesting stories about my ancestors, but before now I was not interested in learning them. All these things were not in my mind. Now I wish I knew more about what my father was like and what my grandfather did and what my father did.

My grandfather Dhai Singh had two sons, Jokhia, my father, and my father's younger brother, Birka. When Dhai Singh and his wife died,

---

[31] It is likely that Chandra Man's description here refers to the fact that much hill land was publicly owned and lay fallow. Peasants were welcome to transform this "wasteland" into farms, thereby benefitting not only the peasants but the government also, by way of increased land rent income. Of course, sometimes peasants could have fought over who would cultivate a particular plot of land, resulting in the struggle Chandra Man describes between his great grandfather and others.

my father, who was a bachelor then, went on living in the big family house with his uncle Lamakyap, and with his younger brother Birka and Birka's wife Lorni.

One day my father and Birka went to herd sheep. Lamakyap stayed behind to guard the house, because Lorni was going to be away that day. When my father and Birka returned they found the housed burned to the ground. Lamakyap was severely injured. His neck had been cut by a kukri. The thief had entered the house, attacked Lamakyap, and then set the house on fire. He was never caught. Lamakyap soon died, so that day Birka and my father lost their uncle, their house, and many valuables.

Lorni, though, had not lost everything in the robbery. She was wealthy and could supply money enough to rebuild the house. While it was being built, all three went to live in a room provided by an orphan girl in her house. The girl's father had died when she was seven and her mother when she was eleven. That same year her only brother also died so none of her close family was living. She was very much alone.

According to the custom of our village, when a family has a son or sons to inherit most of the family property, the daughters, when they marry, then go to live in their husbands' houses. But when there is no son, one of the daughters, when she marries, stays at home and the husband moves to her house. He becomes a kind of "male bride."[32] The daughter and her "bride-husband" have a right to an only son's share of the family's property.

When the orphan girl's brother died, her paternal uncle began making arrangements to have her marry her father's sister's grandson. With him as her bride-husband her land would be kept among her paternal relatives. She had agreed to this and was about to marry when my father and the others moved into the room she provided them. She and my father fell in love. It is customary in our village for a boy to marry a cousin, if possible, and preferably a father's sister's daughter or a mother's brother's daughter. For example, Lorni is Birka's father's sister's daughter. My father had several cousins he could have married, but he did not like them as much as he did the orphan girl. So in spite of the arrangement already made, he and the orphan girl decided to marry. That is how the orphan girl became my mother.

---

[32]   This is the *gharjwai* referred to in Chapter 3.

When she married my father, he became her bride-husband. Still my mother's uncle attacked her as if she weren't an orphan with no brother, and as if my father at the time had a house. He said, "You went to his house so you and your husband shouldn't have all the fields and valuables you would have had if you had married according to my arrangements. You will get only what we will give you as a dowry."

At the same time my father's younger brother, Birka, and his wife Lorni were saying, "Well, since you went to her house as a 'bride' you will get only a dowry share." It is our custom that if a boy goes to a girl's house as a "bride" he gets a smaller inheritance than the equal share he would have had otherwise.

So, my mother's uncle was telling her she could not receive all her inheritance because she was a bride, and my father's brother was telling him he could not receive all his inheritance because he was a "bride." My father and mother were stuck in the middle of all this. What to do?

I don't understand all that happened. I was very young or maybe unborn then. But I know this was my father's situation. He tried first to get the full share due my mother and him as her "bride-husband," and took his case to the government regional court in Jumla, a number of days' walk to the west. But my mother's uncle and his supporters were able to persuade this court that my father was not a "bride-husband." So the court ruled that my mother had gone to his house, though how she would have done this when at the time he had no house I don't know. All my mother could claim was what her relatives would give her as dowry, and they gave her the house she was living in, plus a few very small fields.

It's the second case, between my father and his brother, that changed my life, caused my father's death, and brought so much suffering to my mother and my sister. Birka was saying my father was a "bride-husband" and was claiming that even if he wasn't, and wanted to claim a full half of what he and Birka had inherited, he wouldn't be able to. According to Birka this was because my father had borrowed a lot of money from Birka and Birka had accepted my father's best fields as repayment. The argument wasn't so much over these fields, though. It was over my father's claim to his full share of those that remained. There were many more than the dowry portion Birka was willing to give him.[33]

---

[33] This dispute over land ownership is a good illustration of how the contingencies of everyday life complicate and modify the formal rules of inheritance and property rights that anthropologists traditionally attempt to discover and codify.

During my childhood and before, Tibetans were very influential in our region. For settlement of disputes we often went to a very powerful Tibetan living to the north in a Tibetan village of Upper Dolpa. We felt he would make a just decision. My father and Birka agreed to take their dispute to this man. My uncle insisted that my father had gone to live with his wife as a "bride" and my father insisted this wasn't true. As proof he argued that according to the Jumla court my mother had come to him as a bride and that was why she had forfeited land to her paternal relatives. The Tibetan decided in favor of my father, and at that time Birka agreed with the decision. But Birka was never really satisfied and kept urging my father to press another case against my mother's relatives. Finally he said he wouldn't accept the decision because a Tibetan settlement wasn't the law of the land, so he took his case back to the Nepali government court in Jumla. Having to fight this case led to my father's death.

My mother told me that soon after my birth (on April 13, 1946) my father left her and when I was five or six he came into our lives again. He died when I was seven, so I didn't have more than two years of contact with him. I don't know how old he was and never thought to ask.

When he came back to live with us, my little sister had been born, and before her a baby brother who died when he was only a few days old. From this time I remember my father beating me black and blue with his foot, kicking me. I don't remember why, but I must have done something wrong. That was the only beating I remember him ever giving me.

I remember my father best when he returned from working on this new case in Jumla. No decision had been made, and the officials had said, "Come back after a month or six weeks and we will settle this case." As he was returning he fell ill with a fever. Between our village and Jumla there's a very high pass. The area near the top is frozen and covered with snow during much of the year. He was crossing a frozen stream there. Maybe because he was sick he wasn't too careful, and he slipped and fell through the ice. The ice was so sharp it nearly cut off his little toe. He didn't lose his toe just then, but later it fell off.

When my father came home that time he brought me a very nice pair of shoes, and I was very, very happy. I was beyond myself with joy. They were made of very soft yellow leather, without laces but with heels and toes. They were my first pair of shoes. I immediately put them on and went down to the village spring to show them off. I walked in the mud and water there. By the next day the thin leather had dried and cracked, so I wore them for only one day, and after that they were useless. But they showed my father surely loved me.

I've heard that the Jumla court finally decided in my father's favor, but that the papers were destroyed in a fire. I doubt that my father knew how the case had been settled before he died.

I'll always have in my mind's eye what my father looked like. He continually was smiling and was very healthy, strong, and good-looking. He had a black mole on his cheek with a bunch of long hair growing out of it, and he had a long moustache. He always wore a black Nepali cap and was smart in appearance. He had a very likeable personality and was clever and wise. One could not help but love him. He was one of the four village headmen, and nowadays everyone praises his deeds. Villagers tell me I look like my father, that my smile and my looks and habits are as his were.

After my father came back from Jumla he was sick, but at first it wasn't too serious. His disease was just beginning. My mother and father used to sit in the sunshine on the roof of our house. One day they were at work spinning wool for making blankets, and I was sent to collect sweet buckwheat leaves. We eat them as a side dish. I was returning in the late afternoon with a small basket of leaves on my back and a tumpline across my forehead. My parents were laughing at me. My father started clapping when I came near. "Oh bravo, bravo! My dear son is coming with a basket of greens." I put my basket down and hugged and kissed him. He said, "Now my dear son will show us a dance. Ya! Ya!" He started clapping and I danced. This often happened when I returned from the fields with food I'd been sent to collect. My father, you see, was famous as a dancer, and as a singer too. Some men give this up when they marry and some don't. My father kept on singing and dancing, though never in my presence. But he did help me learn to dance by encouraging me in this way. My mother never danced because women in our village are called bad names if they do.

I was never afraid of my father, but I was afraid of some Tibetans. I was told this kind of people were homeless, landless wanderers. They carried swords and guns. They would kill people and loot the wealth of the village. I remember when I saw such people for the first time. Two other boys and I were playing on the roof of a house when we happened to see three or four Tibetans who wore long swords at their waist and a long coat that covered most of their body. They wore Tibetan boots and had long hair. Half their foreheads were covered with hair. When we saw them we were thinking they must be robbers, and we ran down into the house as fast as we could.

That night I had a dream about them. They were teasing me with their swords and at last they caught me and chopped me up into pieces. But my body parts and my head came back together and in the dream I was not feeling hurt at all. I was just very afraid and kept saying, "What will happen? What will happen?" Then those fellows changed into black puppies and ran away.

I was always afraid of robber Tibetans after that, and of beggar Tibetans too. Our parents didn't help us. They would say, "If you do bad things and if you disobey and if you cry, the robber and beggar Tibetans will come and take you away." Then sometimes they would say, "Meow, meow," pretending to call them. At night if we wanted to go out they would say, "Don't go out. The beggar and robber Tibetans are hungry and they will catch you and chop off your head."

Of course we were also afraid of dangerous spirits. In the forest or wherever they lived I used to run bending my head down and not breathing. Not breathing at all. I didn't look from side to side, just down, because if I looked from side to side I might see something. I never saw or heard even one of them, but I was afraid I might because I heard many things about them from my villagers. They have different shapes. Some assume the shape of monkeys or apes, hairy with long manes and long teeth, big teeth sticking down. Sometimes they look like goats, very powerful goats, great big ones.

One night when my father had grown quite weak we had another encounter with Tibetans. We had taken our supper and were about to sleep. My father lay on the ground and my mother was sitting near him rubbing his feet. My father was resting his head on one hand, and with his other hand he was counting the beads in his rosary while saying a Buddhist prayer. I was sitting there beside him. All of a sudden two Tibetans rushed into our house and without our permission pulled down our goat hair blankets from where they were hanging, scattered them in the dust, and sat on them. They began abusing my father, saying many things I didn't understand and so cannot remember. One of the Tibetans was a soldier and the other was something like a headman. They came from the village Tarap. The headman ordered the soldier to tie my father up. The soldier got up with a rope in his hand and at once jumped toward my father, and in doing so put one of his dirty long boots on our sacred fireplace.

This made my mother very angry. She cried and wept and fought with the soldier until he went back and took his seat without tying up my father. Then my mother rushed out the door and cried out to the men in the next house. They woke up, and some of them went to inform one of our headmen. Others came into our house and requested the Tibetans not to tie up my father. Finally a headman came with his wife and others. They advised my father and mother to offer the Tibetans food, a half rupee, and, as a token of respect, a white scarf. My mother kept refusing to do this, but all the others forced her to, so she prepared rice and meat. But as she was serving them she kept muttering angrily like this: "My poor husband is sick and although he is sick they have come here to give us trouble. They are cheating us and insulting us and instead of taking revenge we give them food!" By doing this she cursed the food, and they could have died from eating it. What else could she do? We had no weapons. My people were very simple. They were peaceful people, very hardworking and intelligent in trade but not in politics. They weren't bold and couldn't speak boldly to others and put them down with speech. They never carried weapons which could harm people, like swords or knives or guns. They never gave others trouble. The Tibetans who came that night finally left. I don't know whether they were pleased or still angry.[34]

Besides the Tibetans to the north, those who gave us trouble were the Jumlis to the west, and Mykotis and Pun Magars to the south. I heard the Puns used to give us a lot of trouble, but I don't know what they did. I myself was never afraid of them or the Mykotis. I was only afraid of the Jumlis and Tibetans.

After the trouble with the Tibetans that night my father became very sick. He grew weaker and weaker and was unable to go back to the court in Jumla to hear its decision. My mother was very sad and very anxious. Perhaps she was thinking about her future life and what

---

[34] Chandra Man's graphic description of Tibetans provides a glimpse, from a child's point of view, of the classic conflict between settled farmers and nomads. It also illustrates, however, the ambiguity of these relations: powerful, wise men who help settle disputes by making just decisions, or thieves and murderers who threaten villagers, including children, or even friends who are good traveling companions.

would happen if my father died. She kept weeping and saying, "Don't go and leave us. What can I do for my son and daughter? Both will be like daughters.[35] Don't go, don't go." My uncle Birka and aunty Lorni never came to see him.

One day I went to my maternal uncle's house next door just a few steps from our house. He sent me to work in his fields. When I came back at night and was about to take my dinner with him and his family, they told me, "Don't take salt." When I heard this I felt that . . . I felt that . . . I can't explain in words, you see, but it was as if I fell from a high tree. I immediately went to my house and saw my mother and many men weeping in the room outside our center room. My mother was lying there and weeping, crying in pain. She prayed to God, appealing to God, "Oh, what have you done to us?" And to my father, "Oh, where have you gone, my husband? What shall I do?" She was crying so.

I began to weep, but I was just weeping. There was a great hurt in my heart, but I didn't say anything. I just kept weeping.

The next day at the time of the funeral my little sister and I both went to a neighbor's house. My little sister was only about two years old, and we were told we should be afraid of the corpse. When the funeral procession began we went up on the roof of the house to watch it. I don't know what my sister felt, but I felt nothing then. I was just seeing the many men, a huge crowd going after my father. They took him to one of our fields, burned the corpse there and dug a grave. We have a very big river, the Bheri, near our village, but we believe it is better to burn the body in the fields than to throw it in the river. We only throw a corpse in the river when the fields are so dry there is danger of fire.

That day I didn't eat salt, and I had to have all my hair shaved off. I don't know whether my uncle shaved his head or not, but he was supposed to. My sister may have eaten salt because she was very small and innocent, but none of the other close relatives were supposed to eat it.

All that day and during the following days people came to give us consolation. Some came from very far away. Some offered one or five rupees. Some brought a wooden container of beer. But we had to

---

[35] She refers here to the fact that daughters possess none of the prerogatives that sons do, such as ownership of wealth, including inheritance of land, as well as political clout, physical strength in case of fights, and general high status. She later plaintively tells Chandra Man, when she has caught him stealing money from her, that her daughter is a much better person, and wonders "Why couldn't God have given me her as a son and you as a daughter?"

provide most of what they ate. If we had had dried mutton we would have added that to the lentils, but we had no special food like that.

Before my father's death I think he was farming what was left of the half share he inherited from his father, plus the few fields that belonged to my mother. But right after his death my mother told me that my uncle and aunty began to plow all my father's fields, leaving for us only the few that belonged to my mother as part of her dowry. Now the situation was very serious, because my father wasn't there to defend us, and I was too young to help.

About two or three months after my father's death my mother decided to go north to where the Tibetan who decided cases lived. I think she must have been guided by some man in this, and must have heard about the fire in Jumla, meaning there was no proof now of how that case had been decided.

One day my mother told me she had decided we must go early the next day. We wouldn't let my little sister know about our leaving because she was very small, and if she knew she would try to follow us and call my mother back.

That night all three of us slept in a neighbor's house. Early in the morning my mother just pinched me and I got up. My sister was sleeping soundly. My mother must have made plans with the people there to take care of her while we were gone. A family from the Tibetan side was going our way. My mother knew them well and we traveled together. The moon was shining when we left the village.

We had to carry our bedding with us and enough food to go and come back. The trail was very difficult. We had to cross many rivers, and my mother carried me across them on her shoulders. It seemed to me then that the river was not flowing, but that we were going fast up, up, up. I was surprised.

At last we got to the village of Nawang where the powerful Tibetan lived. I don't know how many days we stayed there, two or three maybe. But one thing I can't forget. I was a little joker when I was a small boy. I used to tease everybody whether he was a great man or a small man, it didn't matter. And I was teasing that very fellow, you see, the one who was going to decide our case. I was teasing him with the signs I made with my eyes and my mouth. One day I was playing in a stream near his house. I was alone. I was enjoying it very much. I was making a bridge and playing on the bank in the mud, throwing the mud into the water.

All at once that old fellow came toward me with a big stone. "You are always teasing me. Now I am going to kill you!" I thought he was really going to kill me. I was so afraid of him I ran without knowing where I was running. I jumped from one field to another field and fell and ran.

All the rest of the day I stayed hiding in one place. When evening fell I went up to his house and peeped through his door. They were just saying, "Where has the boy gone?" and the old man was laughing. "When I did like this" and he waved his arm in the air "he ran away." The old woman was saying, "You shouldn't have frightened him. Now we don't know where he has gone." She came out to look for me and saw me standing near the door. "Oh! Why are you afraid of him? He was just playing with you. Come in, come in." She held the door open and I went in very shyly. They gave me a cup of tea, the kind they drink with salt and butter and roasted barley flour. Although I had been in a very miserable condition all day, I wasn't feeling it any more.

I was always happy in those days, running here and there. I had no worries and never asked my mother what was going on with our case. I just ate my food and ran out to play. So I don't know how the case was settled, but it couldn't have satisfied my mother. She must have had the same trouble with my uncle and aunty as my father did when he went to the Tibetan man. She soon decided she would have to go to the court in Jumla herself.

My mother and I left for Jumla just as we did when we left for the Tibetan side, going over to a neighbor's house in the evening and leaving very early in the morning without telling my sister. My mother had made plans for her to stay with people in two houses of her closest relatives. They were to take care of her turn by turn. They also looked after a cow and calf we owned jointly with one of the village families. And since there was no man in our house to work our fields, we leased them out, on a half-and-half shared basis.

On this trip my mother was always asking which man in Jumla was clever or shrewd, and who was also a good man. I think someone told my mother to go to the man she eventually went to. His name was Swananda and he lived in Pipalgaon. He was a senior clerk, a *raita*. He acted like a lawyer and wrote what had to be written. By caste he was a Thakuri, the highest section in the high-ranking Warrior group. We stayed at his place, in his cowshed. My work was to look after his horse and his buffaloes, and my mother's work was to take mules from his cowshed to the fields. Also she hulled his rice and carried manure to his fields. I saw too that she gave him the multicolored blankets our people trade and sometimes to please him she gave him the whole leg of a goat or a sheep. People were coming and going from our village, and she must have asked them to bring these things.

One day my mother announced, "From tomorrow you must study with the two sons of Swananda." I was very happy because I had seen that these two boys and the son of a Thakuri from Humla were studying and learning to read. I could watch them but hadn't been allowed to read with them. I had seen a person reading a letter in my village. There were four or five village men who could read. There was no school in our village, and they had learned from a guru in Dunai, the main town in our region, or from the old men in our village who had learned from other old men.

After my mother had announced this plan, I was just waiting for the next day, and at last the next day came. My guru sat there in front of me. In a metal tray I put a rupee and some rice, some red powder, and my book. Then I put the tray down in front of him. I touched my forehead to his feet and said something in praise of God. Then he began to teach me the prayer of Saraswati, Goddess of Learning. He recited it in Nepali, and I repeated the words after him. That is how I became his pupil.

That was the start of my education. We studied with the guru in the daytime and in the evenings. I studied so hard at first that I didn't notice whether or not I had gotten hungry.

We pupils each had bamboo pens. One evening one of the boys lost his pen, we didn't know where. But when the boy put it to our guru that he had lost his pen, the guru immediately suspected me. He said to me, "You have taken his pen." I replied, "I have my own pen. Why should I take his pen? I didn't take it." But he didn't believe me and said, "You must have taken it." At that I was very angry, but within myself. He was superior. We were under him, and I didn't dare talk back. He could beat and kick us, so I was afraid. From then on I was always trying to convince him that I wasn't a thief.

Sometimes I went to this teacher and asked him to tell me what a word meant. But I never dared ask him about the word more than once. I was afraid he might abuse me. I was thinking like this.

The other boys never treated me like a fellow student. They were just letting me come and not noticing me. They were thinking I was far below them, that my clothes were dirty and torn. They were ahead of me because I was just learning the alphabet, and they were already beginning to read. Also I wasn't learning much because I had to spend time herding Swananda's buffaloes and horse, taking the buffaloes to one place and the horse to another. They continually insulted me by treating me as a very low caste person, just as we treat a Damai, a member of the Tailor caste in our village. They used very harsh, shocking words to me: "cow-eater," "ass," "drunkard." They called me a Bhotia, the word for Tibetan, meaning they didn't want to sit near me or take food from me or play with me. In my village we play with low caste children until we get our second teeth. Until then we trust each other as equals. It's only after we get our second teeth that we aren't supposed to eat or play together. They were treating me as if we all had our second teeth.

I had learned about caste from the behavior of my parents. Chetris, members of another section of the Warrior caste, used to come to our village from Jumla or Dunai. We had to give them food. Some accepted cooked food from us, but others used to cook their food themselves. I remember a Chetri who used to cook his chapatis at the same fireplace we were using. But I noticed he didn't use the iron dish we use for cooking chapatis until he cleaned it with some oil he had brought. From the beginning I learned not to offer a Brahman food we had cooked. I also learned that Kamis, members of the Metalworker caste, and Damais (Tailors), were lower than me, while Brahmans, Chetris, and Thakuris were higher. My villagers told me Tibetans were lower than we were, but I was feeling that they and the other castes were all the same. It wouldn't cause harm to a Chetri if I touched him, and it wouldn't harm me if I took food from the hand of a Kami.

But when I was in Jumla I had to change my mind about that. Jumlis were much stricter than my villagers about touching and accepting food. If Chetris from Jumla go to a Kami village, even though they don't touch a Kami, when they come back they sprinkle their body with water, so as to purify it. In Jumla we were living with Thakuris as part of their household. We could take cooked food from their hands, but they would never take it from ours. They made me feel that I was very much lower than they were. This was the first time I felt that way. I never felt I was a very low person before.

I don't know how long we stayed in Jumla. My mother was always trying to please the *raita*. To win a case you must find a good organizer and speaker, someone who can present your case well to the court. In those days you had to pay a lot of money to get your case presented well. Besides the fine blankets and the meat, I know my mother gave him a lot of wealth, including a pair of gold earrings. I don't know how much money they were worth. My mother thought he must have kept the blankets and earrings for himself and didn't use them for winning the case. Whatever he did the result wasn't good.

One day I was far away from Swananda's house, grazing his buffaloes in the midst of the forest. It was about noon. My mother suddenly came running. She was out of breath but at once began berating me. "You unlucky fellow. You father-eating fellow." She grabbed my hand and we hurried back to the courtroom. On the way I understood that we had lost the case. I kept trying to please my mother, but I couldn't find any words to do so. We reached the courtroom. Many men were standing around. At once my mother unwound the *patuka* wrapped around her waist and threw it over a big beam. One end she tied around her neck. She cried out, "I am dying in the name of Swananda. I couldn't get any justice here, so I am dying in the name of Justice." I was thinking my mother was really dying. I was bewildered. What to do and what not to do? But some men came and stopped her.

So now my mother had lost the case, and also had to pay money to the court. I don't know why she lost the case, but I do know that my uncle and aunty had more gold earrings, more blankets, and more money to spend in Jumla than my mother did.

Next we learned that my mother had to spend two or four months in jail. I still don't know why. The jail was a bad place. It was a very old sort of jail, with dark earthen floors and no windows. It was very damp, not comfortable at all. In the room where we stayed there was one other woman. We each cooked our food in different corners. Then the room filled up with smoke. During the day my mother could go about in the compound but couldn't go out the gate. I was free to go in and out of the compound. At night we had to be in our room and the guard locked the door. One night I cried to go out to the latrine. They wouldn't let me out so I had to go in a corner of the room.

Finally one day the guard came, unlocked the door and said we were free to go home. My mother picked up the few belongings we had left and we hurried out the compound gate and along the trail to our village. We never wanted to see Jumla again.

In jail my mother was always remembering my sister and saying, "My daughter, my daughter, what has happened to my little daughter?" And now her sorrow came again. I couldn't understand her sadness. I was too young. I was always going my own way, thinking how when I reached home my friends would come and ask me what I did, and I was thinking how I would boast. I would tell them many things about Jumla, and would wear my Nepali cap. In our village if a person puts on a Nepali cap he is considered a great man or a headman. So I was thinking this way.

When we reached our village I remember especially my little sister. When she saw my mother she at once fell upon her and embraced her. My mother was embracing her too. My sister was crying very hard, and I don't know if she was weeping from the joy of seeing my mother or from sadness over the unhappy days which she had passed. I remember how dirty she was. In places her skin was black with layers of dirt. She had sore eyes and a runny nose, which she had wiped sidewise with her hand. On her cheeks there were cracks from the cold. I took her hand and I remember the smell. It was salty from her tears maybe.

My mother must have been upset to see my sister in such a condition. She had left her in the care of her close relatives, who were not poor. According to custom everywhere they should have taken good care of her. When a person requests a relative to take care of a child they should be responsible. My sister's face and clothing showed that nobody had looked after her very much.

I don't know how my uncle and aunty felt, but four houses of close relatives on my father's side and four on my mother's were always kind to my mother and were always pitying her. They were very sad when they heard she had had to stay in jail and had lost all her money and jewelry and her court case too. Their eyes filled with tears and they invited us turn by turn to eat in their houses. My sister and I would usually go to bed early, but they kept talking a long time into the night about the court case and my mother's sad condition. When my mother talked with these relatives she always talked about me. "I have this son. If he were not alive, I would give up; this case, all this trouble. My daughter and I would have no fear at all. I could support both of us and then she will be married and will be supported by her husband. But what will happen to this son? If I do not fight there will be nothing for him."

What my mother was saying is true. She could easily have supported herself with the rights she had to her house and to her few fields. They would have been enough for her and my sister until my sister married and was supported by her husband. But like all my villagers she worried about the future of her son and wanted to earn and be clever for him.

At this time my mother was about thirty-five years old. She was young enough to remarry but she never spoke of this. Our relatives also never suggested it. Though in her younger days, in her happy time, I was told she was the most beautiful woman in the village, now when this calamity fell upon her, she was pale and very thin. She didn't have any rings on her fingers and no necklace around her neck. Mostly our women wear gold earrings and silver bracelets. But she wore none. She left her blouse open so it didn't hide her chest. She tied some of her hair back but let the sides come down. She didn't care, you see. Women who are happy take care of themselves. She always seemed sad.

I worked with my mother in the fields. One thing I learned from her has been very useful to me: she taught me to do the work of a boy and the work of a girl, too. To work in the fields, except for plowing and tilling, is considered to be work for a girl. But I was helping my mother with all the different kinds of work. I was her right hand. We planted, and after the plants matured we harvested together. I even hulled rice with the pole pestle and winnowed it. I also used to bring water home from the tap and went to the forest to collect wood.

One of my most troublesome jobs was shepherding. When we needed manure for our fields we borrowed cattle, and I had to keep them on the right field during the day. At night I brought them home to our cattle shed so we could collect the dung.

When it was time to graze the cattle in the forest I went there with the other boys, and we collected the cattle from every house. In the forest the big boys used to become like bosses and send the little boys after the cattle that strayed away. We were afraid of those boys. They were big and it is our custom that when there is a job for either a big boy or a small one, then the small boy should be the one to do it. I was one of the small boys.

In the evening we brought the cattle to a very large field where each boy without any help is supposed to separate out his own cattle. I would set aside a corner of the field for my cattle and would begin by taking one of them there. Then I would go for another one, but always when I brought the second the first would be gone. This gave me a lot of trouble and caused me to weep and curse. Usually the older boys separated their cattle first and when one of mine would begin to follow their cattle back to the village I would have to run and bring it back. If I didn't, then it would spend the night in someone else's cattle shed and we would lose all the dung from that cow.

Oh, I faced so much trouble. Sometimes my young bulls would chase after a heifer in heat. They'd all follow, and it is very difficult to get them back because the heifer runs away and they chase after her. When I would run after them, I would lose all the rest of my cattle. They would be on their way to the village. Sometimes I didn't have a single cow or bull. How to show my face to my mother? I was afraid of what she would do. So on those nights I would go to a friend's house and stay there. Sometimes when my mother found me she would say in a sweet voice, "Why are you staying here? Don't you have a house? Let's go. Aren't you hungry?" I'd think this time she isn't angry with me. But when we got home she'd pick up a stick and beat me and I'd be cursing the cattle that made me get such blows. She'd abuse me, and as an example tell me about herself. "When I was a seven-year-old girl I could shepherd the cattle and bring them home. Now you are much older and a boy and you can't bring even one cow." On such nights my mother couldn't go out and bring our cattle to our cattle shed because she didn't know where they were staying. All the dung was lost. I had such days many times.

We had to collect a lot of wood to store for winter, and I would be sent out to help get it. Sometimes I'd return with a big bundle and hide it in the cattle shed. I'd go in the house and say, "Mother, please forgive me. I couldn't bring any wood because I was tired and fell asleep." She'd be very angry and be about to beat me when I'd shout, "Be careful! Let's look outside once." We'd go out and when I showed her the big bundle she'd be very happy. I was never afraid of my mother when I hadn't made a mistake, and I sometimes would joke with her. Other boys would never joke with their mothers. I was the one who was the joker. In the weeding season when the sun is very bright and hot I used to go to the fields with my sister. We used to sleep sometimes and didn't finish weeding the field. But when we came home I lied and told my mother we had finished. Then I'd be afraid of my sister, that she'd tell my mother the truth. If we quarreled over a piece of meat or some sweet thing she'd say,

"May I tell? May I tell?" She'd talk like this and I'd become silent and let her have the thing. My mother would find out about this cheating when harvest time came. She'd see all the weeds. But even though they didn't help the crop, she wouldn't be so angry with us then.

Of all the boys I had the hardest life. They didn't have to weed or cook. The other boys had to shepherd and get fuel and sometimes they helped with the harvest. But they didn't have to work continuously. Sometimes for harvesting my mother left so early in the morning I was sleepy all the way to the fields. I'd wish I had a father or brother to take me on trading trips.

The other boys never made fun of me because I had to work so hard, and big men and women used to admire me in front of my mother. They'd tell her she had a really good son. My mother used to say, "He is my right hand and if he weren't, I wouldn't have any food in my mouth."

The Trip to Kathmandu

About a year after we got back from Jumla I came to know that my mother was planning to continue the fight with my uncle and aunty. She knew she was right, but the Jumla people wanted too much money. So she was thinking, "I must go to Kathmandu. The King lives there. He must be sincere so I think it is sure I will get justice there. Kathmandu will be the place where water and milk are separated."

Except for her gold earrings, which she gave to the *raita* in Jumla, my mother still had some precious ornaments. She sold these to relatives. I don't know how many there were. I don't know how much money she collected, but all at once she was ready to go.

My sister was about four or five years old, and to leave her we did the same thing we had done before. We went to sleep in a house belonging to a relative of my mother and left while my sister was still asleep. My mother once more asked some of her relatives to look after her.

Again we had to go to Jumla. My mother had heard that a magistrate there, an assessor (*bichari*, Nepali), was taking a big group of people to Kathmandu. My mother knew him, and I know he always felt pity for her.

The trail to Jumla was hard for me. When I was getting tired my mother would tell me about this place called Kathmandu, even though she had never been there. She said, "We will ride there in a very long house which is running." I was just thinking and wondering, "It must be a really big house. Its legs must be very strong and thick, and it must have a very big moustache and very big eyes." I was thinking like this, you see, and I used to forget all the difficulties, all the troubles. That was the first time I'd heard about the train.

When we got to Jumla we went to the *bichari*, joined his group, and left for Kathmandu. But we couldn't always be with the party. They were all men and at night slept in tents they brought with them. We went to villages and asked to stay in one of the houses there.

I was a little boy, eight years old, and my mother was an old widow, so everybody was very kind to us. It's natural when you're a stranger and stay in someone else's house for them to ask, "Where are you going?" and "Where are you from?" and if you say, "I am going here," then they say, "Why are you going there?" It's natural, you see. So everybody was asking my mother questions and she was explaining, "I have a great enemy and he is giving me trouble. I fought here and I fought there. I couldn't get any justice, so I am going to Kathmandu. That's the place where I hope I get justice." My mother was describing her troubles and sorrows and at the same time she was telling them about me. "What is my son going to do?" and she would start to weep. When they heard about our miserable condition most of the women's eyes would fill with tears. In some places we didn't have to cook food. They provided it and some gave us two or three meals of flour for eating on the way. So we passed the nights that way.

The days were very hard, and we were on the go continuously. We didn't have any rest days. I was a small boy, but I carried our food in a small basket on my back. Sometimes I was so tired I was crying and my mother would encourage me. She would tell me, "When we reach Kathmandu I'll buy you shoes or new clothes." Sometimes she used to tell me interesting stories, and in this way we travelled together. We also gossiped sometimes and sometimes we were laughing. Sometimes when I was whining, "I can't, I can't," my mother would agree with me and we would sit down. But I was not supposed to rest long, and after a little while she again would urge me to go on. Sometimes we were with the *bichari*'s fifteen porters and sometimes we were with him. Sometimes we were ahead, sometimes behind, and sometimes we were apart from everyone. But my mother and I were always together.

One day we came to a dense forest. When we were crossing through it we were just gossiping when three men approached and one of them cried out, "Hey, where are you going?" My mother immediately answered, "Oh, we are going to Nepalganj, and our friends and porters are just behind us." When they heard this the three men turned away. When I heard their cry, at first I thought it was a ghost. I was afraid. When I saw they were men I was relieved. But I noticed my mother was weeping. I asked her why and she told me, "See what your father has done to me. Why did he leave us?" She was blaming her fate on my father and God. Mostly our women are not allowed to go alone very far from our villages. But now she was traveling without a husband or any grown man, only with a very small son. So she was telling me all her troubles and telling me they were thieves. When I heard they were thieves I was very afraid. She said if she hadn't answered as she did, they might have done some harm to us. After that day we never parted from the porters.

After about fifteen or sixteen days, we reached Nepalganj. We stayed in a large house with all the *bichari*'s group. Nepalganj was the biggest town I'd ever seen, and it was the first time I'd ever seen a car. I was so surprised to see it going that I wondered, "What to say? What words to say?" I'd never seen anything go so fast. It was a jeep, a green jeep. I can remember the color, and I also remember I didn't like the smell of its exhaust.

We stayed in Nepalganj about three days, and my mother was telling me, "Don't go outside, because it's such a big town you might lose your way." But I was so curious to see the town and all the new things that I escaped from her and went to see what was there. I was wandering about and looking at the buildings, big shops, and many glittering things. I was thinking I was in a new world, in heaven. All these things were new to me, things I had never seen before. The houses were very different from our houses, and the roads! I saw this hard-surfaced road and I was thinking, "Oh, they have such a road here. If we could only have such a surface on the roofs of our houses at the time of harvest, all our crops and grain would not get mixed with dust and dirt. How good it would be if it were on my house!"

I didn't notice where my steps were taking me, and I reached near a very big pond the people had made. In the middle of it there was a white marble statue, and from the back of its head was coming water, a fountain of water. Nowadays I would recognize the statue as Mahadev, Lord Shiva. I was wondering how water came from his head, so I crossed to the statue on a bridge. I looked at it a long time and then was bending over the railing and looking down at the pond water. I was imagining if I fell in what would happen to my mother. She would weep very much. I was thinking like this and began to return.

It was quite late and I had lost the way. What to do?[36] All around me looked the same. That road seemed like this road, and this road seemed like that road, and if I saw a building here it looked just like the building there, all white and red in color.

One thing I forgot to tell you. I don't know whether I should tell you or not. I am very different now from what I was then, in my boyhood. I was a very funny boy, making fun of everybody—a joker. Since Nepalganj was a very big town I thought the shopkeepers must be very rich, so I began to dance for one of them, and he gave me a pice. Then I thought, I'm getting money, so I went on dancing from one shop to another, dancing and singing the way I did in my village for my friends. In this way I collected many pice, about half a rupee.

I decided to follow a street, whichever way it led me. Fortunately it was the right way. When I came to a well, I knew it was near our house because the day before I'd come here and drunk water, and washed my face and feet.

My mother had been worrying about me until she saw me. At first she was very happy, but then she was scolding me, telling me, "I'm taking trouble for you and you are always disobeying." To please her I gave her the pice I'd begged. She was very surprised and then was happy again.

It was time to take the train to the Indian town of Gorakhpur, and from there to Raxaul on the border between the two countries. "Now," my mother said, "we will ride in the house that is running." When I heard this I was very excited. We went to the station about noon and when I saw the train I was thinking it couldn't be the same thing my mother had told me about. Where were its legs? To me it looked like some kind of huge snake, and I was very surprised to see so many people coming out of it.

My mother had bought the tickets, and we were just waiting in the footpath for the train to empty. My mother was holding my hand

---

[36] This is one of almost countless examples of the frequent Nepali plaint: *ke garne?* (what to do?) mentioned earlier.

very tightly. Suddenly the train signaled WHOOO! and everyone went rushing to its rooms. We also rushed, and my mother and I were separated but went into the same room. I never had such trouble. I was small and was under many men. I began to cry. Then a man helped me. He caught me and lifted me up onto the shelf that could be let down over the lower seat. I was happy then and forgot all the trouble I'd had.

I was feeling very comfortable the first night. I remember once when the train stopped and I looked out the window. It seemed to me the trees and fields were moving and we were still. The second day I remember stopping at a station. There was a huge crowd. Some were crying out, "Hot tea, hot tea!" Others were selling peanuts or bananas. Whatever I saw I asked my mother to buy, but she just bought me a banana. That was the first time I'd eaten one. I'd eaten peanuts, though, in Jumla. That day all we had to eat was bananas. Nothing else at all. By noon it was hot, and I was very thirsty. I was begging my mother for water and she was always saying, "How can I give you water here? You must be patient." I couldn't bear the thirst. When the train stopped I wanted to escape from my mother, but she was always reminding me not to go outside. The train only stopped for a short time and she was afraid I'd miss it.

But the next time the train stopped I quickly moved to the door and escaped from my mother. She was crying out from the window. But I ran and found a well. The water wasn't sweet. It tasted very bad and it was hot. I drank very much of it, but it didn't satisfy my thirst. I came running back again and my mother criticized me. Later when she was sitting and talking with the men in the room, they were saying I was very alert and smart.

At first I was very happy on the train, but after the second day I began to hate it. My head was aching and I was always thirsty.

Finally we came to Raxaul and we all rested there for a day. We ate in a hotel and that day I would have had enough food in the morning and in the evening, except for one thing. I will never forget what happened. Mostly our friends from Jumla were Chetri and Thakuri. There wasn't room enough for everyone to eat at the same time, so they took their lunch and supper first. We noticed that before they ate they took off their caps and shirts and put on clean dhotis. Nowadays these castes aren't as strict about this. But it is hard for them to give it up, and many in the hilly regions where people aren't educated still do it. We had noticed they were doing it in Jumla.

When our friends had finished, our turn to eat came, and we decided we must pretend we weren't lower than they were. So I took off my cap and shirt and my mother took off her blouse and we both sat on small, low stools. But when I began to eat I couldn't help laughing. Each time I'd begin to laugh my mother looked at me with big eyes and kept saying, "Be quiet." But I couldn't help laughing. I couldn't eat and laugh too, so I couldn't eat very much, not as much as I wanted. It was the same at supper. We did the same with our clothing, and again I couldn't help laughing.

I didn't like Raxaul. I was happy in Nepalganj because I was walking in a new world, but in Raxaul I was bored. I was smelling very bad smells and the water didn't taste sweet. I was too hot and felt lost in the noise of the trains and factories. I didn't like the huge buildings and their shining metal roofs.

When it was time to leave the next day, I asked my mother if we could walk, but she said we had to go on a train. I was sad, and when we came to the station I climbed on the train with my head bending down and when it started I didn't want to look out. Instead I wanted to sleep and forget my headache, all the noise, and the way the train swayed. I remember I slept on my mother's lap.

When the train stopped at the next station, my mother bought me some bananas, peanuts and a biscuit. But I had lost my appetite and ate only the bananas. My body felt heavy and I wasn't feeling well. I lay down across her lap again until we reached Amlekhganj. Then my mother woke me up and told me we had finished the train part of our trip.

Next we had to go by bus. At the bus station we took our lunch— some bread and some curried vegetables. They were delicious, but I was still feeling the swaying of the train and even though I was on the ground it seemed to me the trees and fields were moving, the way they did sometimes on the train.

After a while we got on the bus. This was my first bus ride, and it affected me very badly, worse than the train. The road was unsurfaced, so the bus bounced up and down. The bad fumes from the bus gave me a headache, and after a few minutes I began vomiting. There might have

been many good and beautiful things worth seeing, but I didn't feel
that anything was good. I was thinking that this period was the worst
time of my life. Tears were falling from my eyes, and I kept vomiting,
vomiting. I don't know whether my mother and the others were sick. I
wasn't seeing anything.

At last we reached Thankot, near Kathmandu.[37] It was dark when
we got off the bus there. We stayed at a hotel, and the people we were
traveling with and my mother told me we didn't have to ride the bus
anymore. I ate a little rice and went to bed early. The next morning I was
feeling much better, but when I learned we had to ride the bus again,
from Thankot to Kathmandu, I was very sad, and angry too. My happy
face turned gloomy and I said to my mother, "You told me we didn't
have to ride in the bus anymore." My mother was suddenly angry and
she threatened me: "You are always giving me trouble so I'm going to
leave you here alone." Although she may have been just frightening me,
I thought she meant what she said. So I agreed to ride the bus, and at last
we reached Kathmandu.

Kathmandu

Now our friends went their own way, leaving my mother and me all alone
under the large pipal tree in the Chetrapati section of Kathmandu. I was
feeling so unwell I didn't care what happened to us. But my mother was
weeping. This was the first time we had been in Kathmandu. Everything
was unfamiliar. We didn't know where to go or where not to go, and
we didn't know what to do or what not to do. My mother was blaming
her fate, murmuring that in her first life she must have done a very bad
deed. But her sadness and worrying and weeping didn't affect me. I was
just trying to sleep.

After some time a smart-looking, long-mustached man appeared. He
wore a black coat and a black Nepali cap. He came from a village near
Jumla. I wasn't happy to see him because I thought he would help us and
we'd have to move and go somewhere. I was so tired and unwell I didn't

---

[37] This is the version in Hitchock's notes; my notes relate that they walked the final
stretch to Thankot from Bhimphedi. Since the trip to Kathmandu would have
taken place about 1954 or 1955, and the road (called the Tribhuvan Rajpat) was
not completed till 1956, it seems more likely that Chandra Man and his mother
would have walked from Bhimpedi. I cannot otherwise account for the different
versions, unless buses started plying the road when it was not yet finished.

want to move. The man asked my mother why she was weeping, and she told him about all her suffering and sorrow. She said this was the first time she'd been in Kathmandu. In our village we believe Kathmandu is the largest city in the world and that if anyone gets lost there he'll never find his way out. It would be like being in the midst of a jungle.

My mother told this man my father had had a ritual friend, a Bhotia, who used to come and share our house in the winter when it was too cold to stay in his own village in Upper Dolpa. His name was Budhiman Subha.[38] Some of the Bhotias living north of our village regard him as their king and are afraid of him. She asked the man to take us to Budhiman's house. He was very sad when he heard my mother's story and led us to Budhiman's house, which was near the Snow View Hotel. Budhiman was sitting at one of the windows. He was the fattest man I'd ever seen. His head was very big and his neck was like a pillar. I was frightened by him.

When my mother told Budhiman why she had come he didn't appear to be very sympathetic, but he ordered his servant to take us to a section of the city near Thamel, where Budhiman had turned an old palace into a wool warehouse and workplace. It also provided rooms where the Tibetans who worked there cleaning the wool could live. It was winter when we came, so there was a lot of wool and many Tibetans at work cleaning it. We could see that Budhiman was a very rich wool contractor. His servant showed us to a room of our own where we could live and cook.

I didn't feel anything particular about Kathmandu. I'd already seen big buildings, hard-surfaced roads and autos. I'd so frightened my mother in Nepalganj that I wasn't allowed to go out, so I didn't see other things that would have been new to me. My mother had a job cleaning wool, and I was given the same work.[39]

In April 1955, two or three months after we came to Kathmandu, His Majesty Tribhuvan died in Switzerland, and my mother and I got a chance to see his corpse. We went to the airport where there was a huge crowd. All the men were glum and some were weeping. I saw the corpse as it was carried from the plane. It was followed by some officials

---

[38] According to my notes the man was Laliman Sikba, a Serchand from Thakkhola, but the name Budhiman Subha sounds more correct to me. I may have misspelled the name in my notes.

[39] Chandra Man told me he received 50 or 75 pice per day for cleaning the wool.

who threw money into the crowd. I picked up two or three rupees but my mother forced me to throw them away because we believe it is bad to take money that is scattered behind a corpse. If we take the money we will have to pay twice or thrice the amount on some occasion in the next life.

The corpse was being carried by four Brahmans who had shaved their heads and were wearing white dhotis. We couldn't see the face of the King. The whole body was covered with flowers and the likeness of a huge snake.

The royal burning ghat is at Pashupatinath along the Bagmati River. We went there and watched from the opposite bank. We saw a very large group of soldiers walking in front of the corpse and another large group following behind. Some men were arranging the sandalwood for the funeral pyre, and I saw three or four tins of ghee.

People in my village told me that as soon as a king dies he is reborn. With my whole soul and body I was bent on seeing this peculiar thing. I kept on watching and I kept on watching, but I couldn't see anything except smoke and ashes. After I watched for a long time and saw nothing, I thought the King probably was reborn in his palace. My villagers also told me that to become a king a person has to climb up a very steep mountain along a path of slippery stones, like those in a river. He has to go down the other side using the same kind of path, and without ropes or any other kind of help. When I couldn't see the King's soul being reborn I began to think my villagers' beliefs about a king's soul and about the slippery stones might be wrong.

One day it happened that Budhiman's clerk took all the people who were working for Budhiman to a movie. We all went. I had heard the words *cinema* and *movie* but didn't know what I was going to see. There was a big hall and we sat in chairs. I was thinking that as soon as the hall was full a dancer and drummer would appear, the same as in my village. After a little while the door was shut. Everyone was silent. It became very dark and at once the movie began. I can't remember all the story but I remember something that impressed me very much. It was raining in a jungle and there were tigers and men shooting at them. I was terribly frightened. I thought everything was real. The rain would reach us and the tigers would jump out and catch us, or we might be hit by a bullet. But suddenly the rain stopped and the tigers were dead.

Now, this movie affected me very much. It was very bad for me.

From this moment I converted myself from good to bad. Before seeing the movie I didn't need any money. I was satisfied with just the food I was getting in the morning and in the evening. But after I had seen it I was always trying my best to steal money from my mother so I could see a movie again. I was very bad. From that day I began watching to find out where she kept her money. We had no boxes she could keep it in, and one day I discovered she kept it all tied up in a piece of cloth which she carried in one of the folds of her *patuka*. So it was difficult to steal money from her in the daytime. At night, though, while I was pretending to sleep I noticed that when she unwrapped her waistband she took the small bundle of money out. Then she undid the cloth it was in and put just the money under her pillow.

My mother and I slept together. One night around midnight I wasn't sleeping. I was keeping awake with the thought of getting the money and was watching to see whether my mother slept or not. When I was sure she was asleep I put my hand slowly, slowly under her pillow. But her head was pressing on the money, making it very difficult to get. I began trying to move her away a little farther, but not with my hand. I started to groan and turn this side and that side, and at last her head moved a little and I got the money. I was afraid to take all of it, so I picked out one note. It was ten rupees. Then I rolled up the money again and put it back just the way it had been. I don't know when I went to sleep, but the next morning I woke up with new zeal. With so much happiness I lost my appetite and began planning how to escape from my mother.

We were all working in the palace's large courtyard, which was surrounded by a high wall. People came and went through a big gate in the wall. I pretended I had to go to the latrine and got through the gate that way. As soon as I was outside I started running as fast as I could to the same movie house. I used the ten rupee note to get a ticket and was walking away when the man called me back. "Here, take your money." I don't know if he kept some of it or not. I didn't know what class the ticket was, if it was first or second or third. So I entered the door I'd entered with my mother and sat there. I wanted the movie to start right away, but the room didn't fill and I thought, "Why are the people not coming quickly?" I was half losing patience with the movie and half frightened over the money I'd taken. At last it began. It was the same movie I'd seen before, but this time I wasn't as happy with it, or as frightened by it.

After the movie I took the money to a hotel and spent it on delicious food. I bought cooked meat and all the sweet things the hotel was selling that day.

From this day on I could only think of how I could steal money from my mother to go to the movies and the hotel. My poor mother didn't know I was stealing because I always put the rest of the money back where I'd found it, and when she woke up in the morning she put it back in the folds of her waistband. I didn't wear a waistband and didn't have any pockets. I wore Nepali trousers and a long shirt. When money was left over from the movie and the hotel, I kept it in the hole at the top of my trousers where the cord for holding them up comes out.

Sometime later, I don't know how long, the work of cleaning the wool was finished. Budhiman said, "This palace has been taken by another man, so you will have to move out."

There were places where my mother could stay, but she wanted a place that wouldn't give her a bad reputation. She was afraid this would happen if she lived with a group of women, and also they might influence her to be bad. When she found a gentle Newar man with a good family she appealed to him to let her stay in his house, not too far from the palace where we'd been working. He was a good, simple man and she fell at his feet. "I want to stay with you and your family. I don't mind working and will serve you as much as I can."

The old man gave us the downstairs of his house, two small dark rooms. One was the kitchen, separated from the other by a broken door. The kitchen room was very, very damp, like the bank of a river. It had no window; the other room had the main entrance from the outside and also a window. But only a small portion of the floor had been cemented. We used this room as our sleeping room. The woman of the house gave us three mattresses made of jute sacks stuffed with straw. For bedding we also had two goat skins we had brought with us from our village. Our rent was six or seven rupees a month.[40]

The day after we moved to this house my mother decided to enroll me in a school. We both went to a bookshop to buy me a copybook. To pay the shopkeeper my mother unwound some of her waistband and took out her money. I was trembling. Now she was going to find out about me and the money. What to do? What to do? When she counted

---

[40]   This would have been about 50 cents; in 1968 I paid $4 (an exorbitant amount) monthly rent for a large room in a Tarang house.

her money, she didn't say anything, but she looked at me with big round eyes, and I knew she knew about me and would punish me when we got home.

She bought the book and we left the shop. Neither of us spoke any word on the way home. But there she caught me by the hair and beat me severely. I couldn't speak any words, but after a few minutes my tears and weeping came.

The owner of the house and his wife came running and asked about what had happened. My mother was weeping. "I'm taking so much trouble for this boy and he never obeys me. For him I left my little daughter and sold my jewelry, and for him I left my village and came here to try to get justice. Now when I go to get him a copybook I find he has stolen ten rupees." The house owners weren't very angry with me and instead of scolding me they turned against my mother. "He is too young to know what he's done. These days young boys do things like this. You are in a foreign country. You are both father and mother to this boy. He is your only son and the only friend you have here, and you are his only friend. You shouldn't be treating him like this. You should try to remind and teach him in a good way."

The next day my mother took me to a tutor. She said she didn't have money to pay him but promised that if he would teach me she'd wash his dishes. The man agreed.

I didn't stay with the tutor that day and remember something that happened when we got home. My mother put the fingers of one hand on my forehead and with her other hand held me up by my clothing. She was furious and pushed my head back very hard. "If you don't read and if you disobey me I will leave you. I will commit suicide. So be careful."

My mother wanted me to go to the tutor because in our village a man who knows the Nepali alphabet is considered the equivalent of a lawyer or physician. If he's studied for two months he becomes wise. When my mother pressed her fingers on my forehead I was thinking to myself that I wouldn't deceive her again and would work hard and learn.

After our midday meal that day my mother went out looking for work. I wasn't allowed to go out. My mother locked the door to our rooms from the outside.

My mother found work with a big merchant whose shop was in Chetrapati, across from the resting place where we sat when we first came to Kathmandu. She worked as a coolie, like the many men and women who came there to carry loads of hulled and unhulled rice. They didn't have to carry the weight the merchant said they ought to carry. They could adjust their load according to their capacity and were paid by the weight and the distance it had to be carried.

I was weeping in the evening when my mother got home. She might have felt pity on me, because the next morning before she left for work she bribed me. "My dear son, if you will work hard and learn from the tutor I'll buy you new shoes and a new shirt and feed you good food."

It was difficult for me to understand the tutor. So while he kept on talking my mind was wandering elsewhere. I was thinking about how I felt when my mother and I were in the bookstore, and about how I felt on the way home and at home when she beat me. Suddenly the tutor noticed I wasn't listening to him and he called out, "Child! Child!" Then he went on talking for about an hour, I think. After that he marked in my book and said, "You must learn this by heart," and I went home.

I walked with great pride, and when I was near our door I called out, "Mother, I learned! I learned! I went to the tutor and I learned!" I was trying my best to tell her I was a good boy. I was quite happy and she also was quite happy.

After we had eaten our main morning meal, our "lunch," she and I went to her job. When we got to the paddy merchant's shop in Chetrapati, she asked the merchant, who knew how to read and write, to teach me. That way I wouldn't have to be with her while she carried loads.

I had learned half the alphabet in Jumla, and now I was being taught the other half. I was listening to him and for a few days I was doing quite well.

Usually when we got up in the morning we ate nothing. My mother went to work carrying loads and I went to the tutor. Whoever came back first cooked our lunch.

Kathmandu is where I learned to cook what we ate for lunch. Sometimes we had broken, cheap rice. Mostly we had ground corn. It was very hard to stir, but I learned how. As our single side dish we had a vegetable spiced with chilies ground up with salt. When we had chapatis as the main dish we didn't have a vegetable side dish. With chapatis we only had the mixture of chilies and salt.

After eating, my mother went to her dishwashing job, and I stayed at home. When she came back we went to the paddy merchant's, and while my mother carried loads I studied with him. In this way, going to the tutor in the morning and the merchant in the afternoon, I learned all the consonants, all thirty-four of them.

After a few days I wanted to play with the boys and girls of my neighborhood, so in the morning I was leaving my house but not going to the tutor's house. I was playing instead. After lunch I was forced to go with my mother, but in the morning I could deceive her easily.

Soon my mother found out what I was doing because the tutor saw her and asked, "What happened to your son? Is he ill or what?" My mother might have been too astonished to answer, but when she got home she was furious and beat me severely. She caught hold of my hair and pulled me this way and that. With her fist she hit me hard on my back between my shoulders. She slapped my cheeks and pinched me and hit me with a stick. She was so angry she didn't care if I died. Nobody came to separate us. I was crying and folding my hands. Without any words I was praying to her to stop and within myself was promising not to deceive her anymore and make her sad. I was sorry and felt pity for her.

After this my mother decided she would guard me and take me with her in the morning, so I stopped going to the tutor. She begged the merchant to keep on teaching me and to make me a good man. "I am taking all this trouble and if he's not a good man there's not any meaning in it."

Nowadays I can't remember what I learned with the morning tutor. I might not have learned anything because I was only there a few days. I learned more from the merchant because he was guarding me and forcing me to learn. Even though my mind was often outside with the new friends I was making or was at the movies, I at least had to sit in front of him with my head bent looking at the book. In spite of this I liked him very much because he fed me.

During those days when I was doing quite well with the merchant my mother loved me very much. She was working every day. She didn't take any days off. It isn't the kind of work usually done on Saturdays, but she and all the other porters too were trying to carry as often as they could. Sometimes they got a rest when nobody came to buy and there was no paddy to carry. Sometimes from the shop I saw my mother and other porters quarrelling. Suppose there is only one load of paddy and everyone is rushing to get it. Who is supposed to get it?

Nowadays I think my mother often must have been very tired, and sometimes she must have been hungry. I remember especially how she wept when she thought of my little sister because she was so very young. My mother would keep saying, "Oh, my daughter. Oh, my daughter." I can remember now how she felt, but at that time I wasn't concerned about her sorrows and feelings. I was always following my own way. I never was worried about the future or whether or not we had food to eat that day, or whether we would have food the next morning. We always did have food, though when we had rice it was the cheapest kind, rice of poor quality, with the grains broken. Sometimes we had chapatis and sometimes ground millet. We always had a vegetable cooked in ghee, but only one, not two or three.

From the beginning of our stay in their house, my mother was helping our house host and hostess, bringing their water from the public tap, washing their dishes, and being a guard when they were away. This having a *chowkidar* (house guard, Nepali) they liked very much. I used to carry things for our host when he went to his glue shop in Asantole. He was very kind to us. When my mother was in need he helped her sometimes with money, and he advised her about her court case.

I remember that once or twice my mother took me and went to the gate of the King's palace, where she had cried out asking for justice. We never saw the King. My mother kept telling me that if she saw him coming in his car, to get justice she would lie down in front of it. She often went to the high court of justice, and she would ask, "When is my case coming up?" They would tell her to go back and wait. She had a lawyer and would go and wash his clothes. I don't remember whether or not she also gave him money.

Under this program I couldn't go to the movies. In the morning the theater wasn't open, and in the afternoon I had to go with my mother to the merchant's shop. But I was always wondering how I could escape from studying with the merchant. I had a great desire to see the movies and to play with friends.

After I stole the ten rupees from my mother she hid her money somewhere else. At first I didn't know where. But one day I happened to see that she was hiding it in a bag with all our clothes and was hanging the bag with a rope from the roof. Now I was happy and began thinking how I could take some more money and have a good time.

One day I went with her as usual to the merchant's shop. She went her own way and I was left there to study. Right away I asked the merchant for permission to go to the latrine. He allowed me to go, and as soon as I got outside I ran home.

I took ten rupees and went to the movie theater. The picture I saw was about God, and it affected me very much. There was a war, and men were shooting and killing each other. One of the dead men, through the power of God, came back to life. I was very astonished. At that time I still was thinking the movie was real and was wondering how it was possible to wake a dead man. I couldn't understand the Hindi language but was enjoying myself anyway.

After the picture was over I wanted to see it again. So when all the people left the theater I stayed there, and when the next showing started I still was sitting in the same seat. The checker came and went on checking everyone's ticket. At last he came to me and found I was watching the movie with a ticket from the first showing. He slapped me and twisted my ear. Then he pulled me by the ear to the door and threw me out. With what was left of the money I went to the hotel and had some good things to eat. I had spent all the ten rupees.

Now when I was finished with the movie, the hotel, the good things to eat, and all the ten rupees, I was about to go home. But I was afraid. I was trembling. What should I do? What should I say to my mother? Perhaps by now she'd know what I had done. She might have checked the money bag and found out that ten rupees was missing. How could I go home? I was sure my mother would beat me. So I decided I wouldn't go home. I had already eaten and my stomach was full, and I just roamed the streets. When night fell I got into a taxi that was parked with three or four others and slept there.

When I got up in the morning I was feeling cold. Now what to do? I had no money and no food and nobody to give me these things. So I went home.

Instead of abusing me my mother was very sad. She knew all these things—that I stole the ten rupees and had run away from my teacher. She said she had been very worried about me and had wept until the middle of the night. In the morning when I got home she wasn't weeping, but her voice sounded like she was weeping. "Son, I am taking trouble for you. We have no parents here, no fields, and no great sum of money. And you are stealing from the little money we have and are spending ten rupees in one day. I am carrying loads from here to there to support you and you never have had to fast. If I hadn't been feeding you, then yes, you must do like this. You must steal money. But I am giving you food. Why are you doing this? At first a thief steals from his own house. After that he gradually becomes bolder and bolder. He tries to steal from other houses and has to go to jail." She was telling me these things and I was bowing my head.

That day after lunch she left me at home alone. Without a word she took all the money from the bag and went out. She said nothing about going with her to the merchant's. From that day my studying with the merchant ended.

After a week she enrolled me in a school. I went there and studied very seriously at first. Her words had made an impression on me. But after a few days at the school I forgot her advice and her severe beatings. I left school and began to roam about and do as I pleased.

As soon as I joined the school I had many friends, and some of them weren't going to school regularly. One day I went with some of them to swim in a pond and nearly drowned. I saw a small boy with water coming to his waist. He was smaller than me so I thought the water wasn't deep and jumped in. But the water where I jumped in was over my head. One of my friends had to grab hold of my hair and pull me out.

I was enjoying myself with these boys, and the master didn't care if some of us weren't attending regularly. So my poor mother didn't know I wasn't going to school. In the evening and in the morning I was bragging that I was a good boy and was continuously going to school. I didn't like to study, but I pretended to read, and it seemed to me my mother was very pleased. I would be pretending to read and would order her, "Bring me water!" as if I were an important man, so she would go on thinking I was working hard and she could be proud of me.

I don't remember how many days passed with my acting like this or how my mother came to know that for many days I hadn't been in school. She didn't beat me, but she seemed very tired of advising me. She said, "You unlucky fellow. You'll never be an educated man. It isn't written on your forehead." From then on I didn't have to pretend I was going to school anymore. I was free.

One afternoon my mother sent me to the merchant's house to get ten rupees. I came to know then that she had deposited all her money with him. As soon as I got the money I began dreaming about the movies and the hotel's delicious sweets and chicken.

I think now that I wasn't a bad boy but my environment wasn't good. My new wants made me a thief. The movies and the hotel were always attracting me. Whenever I got any money the only thing I wanted was to go to these two places.

So that afternoon, even though I knew it was wrong, I went to enjoy the movie and eat some delicious food at the hotel. Then I came back to our house. My mother had prepared supper. When she asked me for the money I lied to her. "I couldn't meet the merchant because there were a lot of women with children waiting there to see him. The women had a cock and didn't want to commit the sin of killing it themselves. So I killed it for them. They gave me the head and told me to stay and take supper with them. I ate there so I'm not hungry."

I couldn't tell if she was feeling happy with me or not. She didn't say anything. But the next day or the day after I don't know exactly what happened, but I can imagine that she went to that merchant for the money. She told him that she had sent me but that I couldn't see him and that I had killed a cock for the women and had eaten there. I imagine he got very angry and told her all about me. Anyway I was in our house when she suddenly entered. She caught hold of my hair and said a very bad word in our language, which means "you black sheep of the family" (*tyanan*, Kaike). She pulled me by my hair all the way to the merchant's house. It was about a half hour's walk and with her free hand she was beating me all the way.

She showed me to the merchant and he began abusing me. "You scoundrel fellow, your mother is carrying loads and suffering so much for you and you are doing this to her." To my mother he was saying, "You foolish woman, you shouldn't be taking all this trouble for him. You should better go home and enjoy yourself and not care about his future. I think this son will never give you happiness and will never become good. If he was my son I would already have killed him." By then many men were staring down at us from their windows. My mother was blaming her fate. "This all is punishment for bad deeds in my first life." I was just bending my head and crying because of the beating. But I can't say I felt ashamed. I was thinking that considering that I was a very young boy, what I had done wasn't so very bad.

At home again she began preparing my meal. All the while she was cooking she stayed very angry. She kept murmuring and abusing me. Sometimes she compared me with my little sister. "Why hadn't this black

sheep of the family died as soon as he was born? How glad I would be."
Or she would say, "My daughter is far superior to you. Why couldn't
God have given me her as a son and you as a daughter?"

Sometimes she would remind me of our enemy. "There may be a
rumor in our village that we are doing well in Kathmandu, when as a
matter of fact you are stealing from your mother, and aren't studying.
Instead of wanting to be a good boy and wanting to take revenge on our
enemy you are making our enemy laugh at us."

When it came time to serve me my food she just threw it on the
tray. "Here, take your THOM." There is no word in English or Nepali
like this word we have in our language. It means even if this is sweet
food, if one addresses it in this manner it is insulting food and you are
despising the person you give it to. She was murmuring and a very
strange thing happened. "Oh, God," she suddenly cried. "Oh, God,
take my life. I don't want to live in the world any longer with this
son. What wrong did I do that you are punishing me so?" She was
beating herself on her breast when suddenly she fainted and fell over
backwards.

When I saw this I was very much afraid. I jumped up and put my
hand on her stomach to see whether she was dead or not, and I put my
hand in front of her mouth. It seemed to me she had died and I was
terribly afraid. I could see all my future. "If she dies what will happen
to me? Where will I go and who is going to keep me? How will I be
able to get back to my village?" All these fears for my future swept over
me and I rushed from the room. Outside I grabbed a big stone and fell
over backwards on the ground. I was beating my chest with the stone.
It means I was terribly sorry and also terribly afraid. I was crying, "My
mother died, my mother died, and I also want to die."

The house host and his wife came and asked me what was the
trouble. I was weeping and telling them my mother was dead and I also
wanted to die. I was beyond my senses and even though I was hitting
myself very hard with the stone I wasn't feeling it. It may seem I didn't
care about my mother, the way I was disobeying her and not worrying
about her, but inside, in my mind, I loved her very much, you see. I
realized, too, when I thought she was dead, that she was the only person
in the world who was helping me. Many neighbors had gathered and I
thought they all would hate me and beat me and kick me.

The house hostess had gone in to check on my mother. I don't know whether my mother was pretending or not, but she got up at once. It was a wonderful thing to see her standing, a very wonderful feeling.

My mother didn't go to work that day, and the next day she decided that since I had no work to do and wasn't going to school, she would take me with her wherever she went and I would carry as much paddy as I could. So when my mother got paddy to carry and there was some for me, I carried a load of about thirty pounds. In this way we passed one or two months. It was difficult, and when my mother had to carry eleven or twelve miles from here to there and there was nothing for me to carry I was bored. I had to go with her without any pay and take all the trouble in vain. My mother realized this, and she knew I was out of money. She knew the merchant who was keeping her money wouldn't give me any of it. Since no money was stored in the house she thought I wouldn't be able to steal the way I did before. So finally she set me free. In the early morning and in the evening I was with my mother. But the rest of the day I was free to swim, or play in the street, or roam in the bazaar.

Many things happened on the street in front of my house. I fought with many boys, and sometimes I used to dance. We played marbles and hop scotch, throwing a stone into rooms drawn on the ground and hopping from room to room. We also played at taking prisoners in a game from India.

Two young, very beautiful and sweet girls were living nearby, and I loved them with a very pure love, as sisters. They were the same age as I was but they wore good clothes. I always wished to please them and to make them love me. But they were always teasing me and treating me the way the daughter and son of a rich man treat a beggar. They were always calling me a bad name: "cow-eating Tibetan." I usually didn't answer. But when I got farther away from them I used to say to myself, "If God would only give me the power to make them wonder at me and admire me. I wish I had a horse and a cap and boots and a good jacket. I would ride in front of them and look down at them and they would be so surprised." I was always wishing so, and in my mind I'd imitate the man on the horse. These two little girls affected me very much. I used to comb my hair and wash my clothes, trying to make them shine.

Once during Holi I was coming to my house and the two little girls were nearby with some other children. They had guns that shot colored water. I was afraid. I knew they would shoot colored water on me if I crossed near them. They were telling me, "Be careful. Be careful." I at once climbed the big wall that runs along our road, and I ran down the back side of it until I got to my house.

When we had been in Kathmandu for about a year and a half there was a big celebration for the King's coronation, and I saw many big men. Some were riding elephants and some were on horseback. Some were in carts drawn by horses and some were riding in decorated automobiles. All the fine-looking carts attracted me, and I was thinking that if God changed me into one of those fellows who were riding in the carts and changed him into me, how much I would enjoy that.

As I was thinking so, the carts passed me, and I saw other things too. There was an old woman coming by, very bent over. She couldn't stand up straight. Many people noticed her and were talking about her. I heard that she was one hundred years old, and that was why she was allowed to walk in front of the King and to worship him by scattering rice and flowers she carried in a silver pot. Behind her came a marching band followed by a huge crowd of militiamen who were dressed in white and red and carried guns on their shoulders. Many elephants began passing by, and at last I saw the King and Queen on their elephant. It was carrying them seated on a throne. The King was wearing a white jacket with a high collar, and he also wore a large medal made of green stone. Both the King and Queen wore their crowns and had on dark spectacles.

When I saw the King I thought of my villagers' story about the slippery mountain and how the King was chosen. I scolded them and myself. "We were wrong. We were so wrong! The King is chosen by seeing who can ride such a great elephant or other huge animal, and whoever does that wears such a good jacket and puts on those dark spectacles."

Some army officers were walking after the King, and one of them was scattering coins. When I saw this I was thinking that whoever wanted to be King also had to be a very wealthy man and be able to provide all this money for scattering to the people when he passed by. I was thinking this, and was thinking how lucky I was to see all this and find out that what I had learned in my village about how the King was chosen was wrong. I was proud to think that when I got back to my village I would be the one to tell everyone the true method.

The officer continued throwing money. Many men were racing each other to get it, and I ran after them. It was very difficult for me to penetrate that crowd. I had no shoes, and sometimes my feet got stepped on. But I was so attracted by the money I didn't care. And also, you see, there was a fight of hands, only hands. If one man got a coin, another man would try his best to take it from his fingers. When I got a coin another fellow unfolded my hand and took it away. I was so disappointed and angry with that man! But I went on trying because that officer kept on throwing more money every few steps. I kept on following the huge crowd. Finally I was clever and got two half rupee coins. As soon as I got one I put it in my mouth so nobody could take it from me, and as soon as I got the next one I put it too in my mouth.

Night was falling and the procession was ending with a turn around the Kathmandu parade ground. Then it broke up into sections. The King's section included the officer who was throwing money, and I followed it as far as the palace gates. When the King went inside the officer stopped throwing money.

I went home feeling very proud of myself, thinking how my mother would pat me on the back and say, "Well done! Well done!" With this feeling I reached home in no time. I showed my mother the money, and she was proud of me. Then she said, "You are very wise and very clever and very courageous, but at the same time you are a scoundrel."

One day my mother gave me a half rupee and sent me to buy kerosene. I went with that 50 pice coin, but I bought only 25 pice worth of kerosene. That was too small an amount, and I thought, "Surely she will know it isn't 50 pice worth." So I went to the tap and mixed the kerosene with water. I didn't know the mixture wouldn't burn. When I brought it to my mother, she put some in her little lamp. It wouldn't burn, and she was blaming the shopkeeper. She tried twice or thrice and still it wouldn't burn. I said the shopkeeper must be a very bad man, and I would go tomorrow and scold him. My mother didn't want to go to that shop again, and she never found out. Oh, I am always ashamed when I think of those days!

I was idle, with no work to do. So one day my house hostess advised my mother to give me something to do. She told my mother she would give me some work that would benefit her as well as me, and she set me up with a little stand. She gave me ten or fifteen packages of cigarettes, plus chocolates, nuts, and biscuits. She put all these things on a winnowing tray and gave me a stool to put it on. I made a long paper rope that burned slowly so that a man could light his cigarette. Then she told me this cigarette is worth this price, and this chocolate is worth this price, and this nut is worth such and such a price.

Now that I knew I was going to be a shopkeeper, I was very pleased. I said, "Oh, you needn't teach me. I know all about this." My mother and my house hostess were laughing. It seemed they were pleased with me.

I took all the things and set up my shop on the corner of our street where I thought a lot of customers would come. I stayed there for about an hour waiting for even a single man to come. Eventually a few men came, sometimes for one cigarette, sometimes for a packet, and some men bought a few nuts. For a little while I was happy, but soon I was bored. The sun was hot, and I began dreaming about the movies. I decided to run away from that place and to sell my things cheap. I mean, like give them away. I checked to see if my house hostess was out of sight, and whether anyone else was looking. I picked up all the things except the stool and ran as fast as I could to the movie house. There was a huge crowd. I don't remember what I charged for my things, but it must have been little, because it only took half an hour to sell them. I forget how much money I had in total, but there was enough to pay for my ticket and to have some left over to spend at a hotel.

After the movie and the hotel the same feelings of fear came over me. Where should I go now? Then I remembered the taxi stand I had gone to before, and went there to sleep. I was happy because I wasn't hungry, only cold.

The next morning I had nowhere to turn but home. Oh ho! That house host and hostess were really angry with me. They didn't beat me, but said they were going to kick me and my mother out of the house. They were abusing me. They used all kinds of bad words, but I didn't reply. I just stood there bowing my head down. My mother also didn't speak. She was a very wonderful woman, you see. She could get very angry with me and beat me, but if anyone else tried to beat me, she would say, "No, nobody can touch him. He is my only son. He is my diamond." My mother promised to pay back the money. Then after a little while she beat me very hard the same way she did before, using a stick and grabbing me by my hair.

The next day she decided to get me a job washing dishes in a hotel. I didn't like the job at all, but I was forced to take it. At noon the dishwashers had lunch. At tiffin we got only a cup of tea, and then we worked until midnight before we got our supper. It was good food, not delicious, but enough. I don't know how many days I worked there, but I lost patience. When I didn't have the job and was free, I could play with my friends. Now I couldn't do that, so one day I ran away from the hotel. All morning long I visited my friends and went to the pond to swim, and in the evening I finally went to my mother. She asked me, "Why have you come home early?" I said, "If you don't want to feed me, I won't eat, but I don't want to do that work." She said, "Then I can't go on feeding you. The money we brought from home is almost gone, and these days I'm not finding many opportunities to carry loads. If you don't work it will be very difficult to support ourselves."

Our Most Miserable Days

Now that we were almost out of the money we had brought with us to Kathmandu, our most miserable days began. One day when I hadn't had enough to eat I decided to beg in the street. I didn't want my mother to know because I knew begging was a bad thing. I believed she would beat me severely if she knew. So I did it secretly.

I started by begging money, not food. It was difficult for me to do. I didn't know what to say and I felt ashamed. Sometimes men discouraged me. "You are handsome and you can work. You don't have to beg."

At one of the most popular Kathmandu temples, Machendranath, I saw that many beggars were sitting in a row outside it. They were begging for rice and pice given them by passersby who came there to worship. I quietly joined the line. I must have seemed like a beggar because my clothes weren't clean. But those beggars possessed patience, and I wasn't a patient man. To collect one pound of rice or one rupee's worth of pice they had to wait a whole day. Many men who came to worship were only throwing two or three grains of rice, and some gave nothing. I didn't like that way of begging, so I got up and left and began begging money on the street. I would ask a man for one pice. Some were kind to me, but others would abuse me. "Look at this fellow. He is quite young and strong and he is begging." They would say, "Why don't you work? Go away! Go away!"

I used to get a half-rupee sometimes. But that wasn't enough for the movies or the hotel. It was only enough for chocolate. I had no concern about tomorrow and used to spend whatever money I got each day.

At last my mother came to know I was begging. One day my first tutor saw me begging. I was very ashamed and sure he would report me to my mother. I was very afraid to appear before her. But that night she neither beat me nor scolded me. She told me this: "That is not so bad, my son," and she repeated the Nepali proverb: "If we beg we get money, if we steal we get kicks."[41] Then she added, "It is all right if you beg, but if you collect a lot of money, please, son, save it."

When we began thinking we might run out of the money my mother used when she had to spend more than she earned and realized we might starve, my mother asked me to beg for rice. The next day I went out early in the morning and began to beg for rice house to house. This way I was able to beg about two pounds of rice. Then I went to the shops and begged for vegetables. Some gave me a few potatoes, and some gave onions and some chilies. This was work that benefitted both of us, my mother and me. When I was going home with these things I felt very proud and promised my mother not to do bad things that would trouble her and make her sad.

During these days when we had to get food by begging I used to tell my mother that women were also begging at the temple. I suggested we both go there to beg, and finally she agreed to go with me. We went very early so as to catch all the people who go there early to worship, and also so my mother would have time afterwards to try and find carrying work.

I guided her to a place in the line at Machendranath, and we both sat down in front of our spread blanket. My mother wasn't used to begging and was quite ashamed. We sat there about three hours that day and only got one pound of rice. That was less than I got by myself begging from house to house. I liked to roam about when begging, but my mother never would go with me. So on days when she came we went to the temple and sat separate from the others. We really weren't beggars. I think some people could see this, and they took pity on us and gave us more than they gave the others.

One day when we were begging at the temple my mother saw some men who knew us and she was very ashamed. After that she never

---

[41] I was unable to find the Nepali equivalent for this proverb.

begged any more. I did all the begging. I would go to the same places every three or four days. Some gave me food even when my carrying bag was already half full. Many would advise me. "Come to my house and work and if you are an orphan come to the Paropakar High School for orphans." Some men took me to a hotel and fed me. I was very grateful.

Begging for food didn't give me enough money to go to the movies and the hotel. What to do? Now I will tell you how sick these two things—the movies and the hotel—had made me. I decided to steal our iron pot, the pot we used for preparing spiced vegetables. I carried it under my shirt and went to the bazaar. I had to keep moving from shop to shop because at each place there were some who said, "Oh, don't buy that. He has stolen it from someone's house. After you buy it the owner is sure to come and will be angry with you for buying it." I kept saying my mother ordered me to sell it because we were out of money, but no one believed me. Finally I sold it to a hill man who passed by carrying a basket of wood on his back.

As soon as I got the money I ran to the movie house. I can remember that movie very well. It was called *Hari-Hara Mahadev* (Shiva as both destroyer and creator). I didn't know the meaning then but did know some people repeated that name when taking a bath.

That movie was especially interesting to me, because it was about a small boy like me who was the son of Mahadev. He was in a great fight with long-mustached giants, the enemies of Mahadev. They had terrible faces. They went "Ha-ha-ha!" and wind, and sometimes fire, came from their mouths. Oh ho! I saw that some men had such power. I felt a great pity for that small boy and was angry with the giants who tried to harm him with their wind and flames.

The giants commanded a huge army, and Mahadev's son stood alone. They all started towards him, but before they could reach him his father, who had a large snake around his neck, came and stood behind him. Mahadev held his hand over his son's head, blessing him. Nowadays I know the boy prayed to his father and then became very strong. He was able to kill many men just by waving his arms. He didn't have any sword.

When I saw the power of the boy I was very affected. I thought if I could be like him how I would punish my uncle and aunty. I was thinking such thoughts.

In this movie, after only a few minutes Mahadev's son killed the whole army. Just one great giant was left. When the giant moved to attack him, the boy ran between his legs and the giant fell down. The boy jumped on his back, turned him over, and punched him so hard the giant fainted and was half dead. Then this small boy just clapped his hands and the huge figure became very small, so small the boy could hold him in one hand. He just circled his hand around his head and threw the giant away. The corpse landed before his parents, Mahadev and Parbati, and that was the end of the movie.

It was quite dark when I got home. I didn't have to fear my mother that night. The pot I had stolen was new and she had hidden it away out of sight. But the next day when I got home she already was there and had discovered the pot was gone. She had a stick and gave me the severest beating I'd ever had from her. At the end she pushed and kicked me out of the house and said, "I don't ever want to see your face," and shut the door.

Outside I wept and I wept. I was crying for help, but no one came, not even the house hostess. She had heard me in trouble for my bad deeds too many times before. That night I slept in a taxi.

The next morning I was thinking that if my mother wouldn't support me I would support myself by begging or some other means. I had changed, you see, from the way I was when we first came to Kathmandu, when I slept with my hand always on my mother's stomach, afraid that suddenly she might die and leave me alone.

I had heard that helpless orphans, and old men and old women, would get support from the King if they went to his palace gate and cried for help. So I went there and began to weep. The gate guard asked me, "What happened to you? Why have you come here?" I lied, "My mother died yesterday and I don't know anyone in Kathmandu. I came here to beg for rice." I went on weeping and other guards came. They believed me and went like this: "Tsk, tsk, tut, tut." I lied in such a way it was like real, you see.

Some of the guards began asking me questions—"How did your mother die?" and "Who carried her away?"—such questions. I told them my mother had been sick for three days. "Yesterday she died and two dark-skinned men came and carried her away." They believed me and reported my case to the King. I got rice enough for two days. I had no way to cook it, so I sold it and spent the money on sweets and bread.

On the third day when I returned to the palace gate, by chance a man who knew my mother and me was there on some business with the palace. As soon as I saw him I hid my face with my shawl. But one of the guards who knew about my situation began talking with him about me. The man said, "Where is he?" The guard pointed at me and I was forced to show my face. "This one? This one? Why, I saw his mother carrying a load of rice just this morning. He must have done something wrong and angered her. He isn't telling the truth."

Now the guard began to yell at me. "This isn't a game. This isn't a playground. You could be shot for bringing this false case before the King. You'd better run off right now!"

So I left the gate and decided to go and beg at the temple. After an hour I had only a handful of rice and a few pice. I decided to try the bazaar, but that day only a few men gave me pice. I began to realize it was going to be very difficult to get enough money to support myself. That day was the first when I didn't have a full stomach, and I began remembering my mother and the place in our house where we ate.

The next day my mother and the man who recognized me at the palace gate were out searching for me, and found me near the large Kathmandu tank called Rani Pokhari. My mother didn't say a word, but the man reminded me of all she was doing for me, and added, "She is offering you a full stomach in the morning and in the evening, and always is trying to make you a wise and a good man." When I heard his words I felt very ashamed. I hated myself.

My mother was weeping when we reached home. She embraced me and kissed me. "You must swear that from today onwards you won't give me trouble and won't do these things that make me sad. Swear, my son." Our custom when we swear is to bite the person we are promising on the arm or shoulder or cheek. I bit my mother's arm and swore, "From this day on I will be a good boy and won't do much bad things again."

Although my mother encouraged me to beg for food because we often needed the extra, she had to tell me to stop. This was because of our neighbors. When they criticized her for allowing me to beg, she at first denied I was doing it. Eventually, even though I tried to do it secretly, they all knew and persuaded my mother it was shameful. If we didn't give it up it would mean we belonged to a very low caste. We were too proud to accept that. We knew we were higher, and from that day we stopped begging.

Now that I had promised not to steal or to beg and to be a good boy, I felt a little restricted. My wish to see movies and go to the hotel was still there, but I had no way of getting money. What I did to see movies was try and slip in without a ticket at the same time a lot of people were entering. Sometimes I was able to get into one of the four movie houses I knew about and sometimes I was able to see the whole picture. When I got caught by a checker he usually just twisted my ear and kicked me out. But some also gave me a beating. One locked me up for a long time in the movie house latrine.

When about two years in Kathmandu had passed I fell very seriously ill. I lost my appetite, and my mother told me I had a very high fever. When we were asleep together she would wake up and tell me I was very, very hot. She was afraid I might die. "If you die how will I show my face in our village? What will have been the use of my troubles and suffering?"

She didn't know what to do for me, or what medicine to buy, and for about a week I lay in our dark room, alone most of the day. Then the morning tutor, I think it was, advised her to take me to Bir Hospital, the government hospital. She didn't know anything about hospitals, but as soon as she got this advice, she carried me there on her back.

In the crowded waiting room she laid me down on one of the long benches, and we waited for the doctor for at least two hours. He had many sick people to see ahead of me. When he finally came he put those things in his ears and pressed my chest with a disk that was connected to them. I had heard that in hospitals many men are cut open. When he pressed that disk on my chest I thought this is what he was going to do to me. I was very afraid. After a few minutes the doctor told my mother I was admitted. After some time two men came and carried me away to a room with a lot of other sick people, each in his own bed. The beds had sheets and a red blanket. They put me in one of them.

That was my first time to be in a bed like that. I had never slept in sheets before. Although I was very sick, I was thinking Kathmandu was like heaven. It had rooms for sick people and they had beautiful beds with blankets and sheets to sleep in.

Late in the afternoon my mother could come to see me and could stay for about an hour. She always asked, "How are you? How are you feeling?" I always replied, "I am the same. The same as yesterday and the day before." Then she would repeat, "Son, do not die," and she would tell me all the good things she would get me. The same plea is used in our village when a loved one is dying. "Don't die. I will give you a lot of money. I will give you sweet food and new clothing." They are bribing the loved person not to die. In the same way my mother was bribing me. And in our village the sick man may say, "I don't want to eat. I don't want to eat. I've lost my appetite." Then those who love him will plead, "You should take this food with our love. If you don't take it, how will you stay alive? If you die, think what will happen to our faces, and what will happen to our eyes. Do you want to keep us wearing our gloomy faces, always weeping? If you love us, you must take this food. No one can live without food." When the sick person hears these pleas he closes his eyes and even though he doesn't like the food, he tries very hard to swallow it. I did the same for my mother when she pleaded. She wasn't allowed to offer me anything but milk for seven days. But after that I could eat biscuits, and she always brought me some.

In the hospital I kept thinking I was in the King's fairyland. I knew the big room and all the fine blankets must have been very expensive. I was going over in my mind what I'd tell my villagers when I went home. I would tell them that in Kathmandu I had tanks to swim in, four different movie houses, and many, many other things to enjoy, and when I fell ill, I had a nice comfortable bed with sheets and red blankets. I would tell them I was living like a king.

My disease was typhoid. When my mother heard it was a very dangerous disease she lost patience with the doctor. Whenever she came she would plead with him to save her only son and would keep telling him how much she had suffered for him. One day when she was there the wife of the King's next younger brother[42] came to the hospital. She and her party, which included her children, were walking from one patient to the next. When my turn came and they stopped by my bed, she asked my mother why she was weeping. She told the Princess all her troubles and said, "If he dies I will drown myself in Rani Pokhari."

Unlike the King, the Princess wore plain untinted spectacles and was the fattest woman I'd ever seen. I was frightened by her because of her size, but also because I remembered how whenever high officials came to our village they used to give us trouble. If we refused to give them food they would beat us. They would tie a headman's hands behind

---

[42]   This would have been Princep Rajya Laxmi Devi, wife of Prince Himalaya.

his back, make him squat, and tie his neck to a stick placed behind his knees, and then would kick and beat him from behind. I was thinking that here in Kathmandu a member of the King's family might also give trouble to poor people.

But the Princess listened to my mother and called the doctor. She talked with him, but I couldn't hear what they were saying. As soon as she had left the room the man next to me said I was a very lucky fellow. She had granted me one hundred rupees. Right away I forgot about my sickness and was thinking my mother would keep it and when I got well I would use it to buy new clothing. I didn't think of the movies and the hotel. I was thinking how the new clothes and new shoes would astonish those two girls.

I heard the other patients talking among themselves. "He is a lucky fellow. Her Highness checked everyone, but nobody else got anything." I was feeling very proud, thinking I must be special and different.

I soon learned I wasn't to get the one hundred rupees in cash. Her Highness had given the money to the doctor for medicine. Knowing that made me less happy and less proud.

The pills the money bought were long with rounded ends and were covered with a thin layer of plastic. Some were yellow, some were green, and some were red. I had to take them once or twice a day, and they acted so quickly that after ten days I was feeling well. Now whenever I see Her Highness I hold my hands palm to palm and lift them high, thinking she had given me new life.

There was a piece of paper behind my cot about my sickness. When I had recovered quite a lot, the doctor had written there, "One-third food." But my appetite was improving so quickly that I wasn't satisfied with that amount. I was ashamed to tell the doctor, so when my mother came I explained to her I wasn't getting enough food.

When she saw the doctor she told him I wanted more food. The doctor berated her, saying, "We don't need you to tell us what we should do. He only needs this much food. Are you thinking that food is what will cure your son?" My mother was silent, and I was unhappy to see her sad face.

After a week I was given half food, but still wasn't satisfied. I always was looking for my mother and hoping she would come with biscuits. When she brought oranges too I was happy from my legs to my top.

When I had to leave the hospital after about a month, I was thinking if only I could have had enough food, how good everything else was. In the hospital I had a servant to cook my food, and if I wanted water a servant would bring it to me. If I didn't get so hungry, I'd ask God to let me stay there always.

I left the hospital when we had been in Kathmandu two years, and were beginning our third winter. It was during this third winter, when I no longer was allowed to beg, that we had difficulty getting enough food. I remember my mother getting up early every day to go out and find work. I lay in bed and was warm. From there I could see out the window. The fog was thick and freezing water dripped from the window frame. To keep myself warm when I got up I put hot coals in a clay pot and held it close to my body.

My task was to cook our late morning meal, and my mother was very pleased with me for doing this. She used to hold my chin and shake it. She would say, "So long as you are good you needn't worry about your food and clothing. I will support you even if I have to starve myself and go naked. Together we will take revenge on our enemies."

I remember noticing this third winter how changed in appearance my mother was. Her eyes were large and wide apart, and her nose was small and narrow. She looked healthy and her eyes were bright when we first came to Kathmandu, and I remember at that time our house hostess telling me she was a very beautiful woman. Now after two years of hardship her cheeks were sunken and her cheek bones stood out. Her eyes had lost their brightness and her skin was pale. I still often slept with my hand on her stomach, and I could feel her ribs sticking out, just skin and bones.

One day when I was still asleep my mother suddenly came into the room and put her hand on my face. This is an insult, especially when you say a word from our language at the same time. It means, "You are a bad person and bring misfortune upon us." My mother added, "You have ashes on your forehead," which means that the person's fate written there is no good at all.

I was taken by surprise and checked back to see whether I'd done anything wrong. I couldn't think of anything and my mother was so angry I didn't dare ask. She began packing our goat skins and our clothing into a sack, and I thought we were going to move. When she had finished packing, she caught me by the hand and said, "Come, you unlucky fellow" and pulled me along with her out of the house. She walked so fast I had to run to keep up with her. As she went she was murmuring, "If I don't find justice here in the King's place either, I'll kill myself." As soon as I heard this I remembered Jumla and thought she must have heard we had lost the case. This time I thought she might really commit suicide, and I was very fearful.

When we reached the courthouse she acted just as she had in Jumla. She cried out that she was going to kill herself in the names of the judges, and threw herself on the ground. I was so frightened I wept and felt as if a huge piece of wood had been thrust into my chest.

A number of officials came to where she was lying. Some tried to console her, others abused her. They said, "Woman, you are a fool. You didn't understand what we said. We told you that you weren't defeated but you had to wait. You are always in a hurry. We are working on your case."

My mother wasn't at all afraid of them. She stood up and said again how she had tried for justice in Bhot and Jumla and had come here in a final attempt. She repeated her threat of suicide, and added, "Then you can do whatever you wish with my orphaned son. He stands before you." A policeman came and separated us from the judges, and we returned home.

Nowadays I'm thinking some officer of the court had come to tell her to go to the courthouse. There she learned that she had to wait some more. She was so angry and disappointed because she had already waited two years.

Settlement and Return

One day in early spring my mother came into our house and said to me, "Your good uncle, that cheating, cunning fellow, has come. You must try your best to meet him and learn his thoughts and desires." She was sending me to be her Central Intelligence Department man.

I knew that when hill people came to Kathmandu they usually gathered on the large, grassy parade ground, the Tundikhel, in the middle of the city. In those days there were many narrow footpaths crossing it and a beautiful big tree in the center. Under this tree there was a large sitting platform and on it were statues of soldiers. They were in uniform, wearing caps and carrying packs. Near the platform and along the paths people had set up small stands like the one the house hostess had given me. Some advertised what they had to sell by playing windup gramophone records with singers on them. I wandered here and there on the parade ground looking for my uncle.

Eventually I saw a group of men dressed like our Tarakotis, people from my village or nearby villages. I noticed especially their yellow shoes, the kind that are made in Jumla. I didn't recognize them as persons I knew, but was sure they were Tarakotis, even though at first when I asked where they were from they said they were from eastern Nepal. Soon they realized I didn't believe them, and admitted they were from a Tarakoti village not far from mine.

When I told them I was from the Tarakoti village of Sahar Tara (the Nepali name for his village, Tarang in Kaike) they said, "Oh, are you the son of that woman?" When I told them I was, they said, "Your uncle has come here to see you, to meet you and take you away." Now I became very curious and in a hurry to meet him. I asked where he was, but they didn't know. They said he had been with them only a short time ago, but had left to visit somewhere, leaving behind his bag for them to watch. They told me to wait with them and he surely would be back. But I couldn't wait and ran off to hunt for him.

I found him in a small crowd that had gathered around a gramophone. Right away I went up to him and greeted him, but not respectfully. No, proudly and regally. If I had wished to greet him with respect, I would have bent down before him and touched his foot, then lifted that hand to my forehead. Next I would have taken his right hand, palm up, and lifted it to my forehead. Instead I stood before him and gave him a soldier's salute. To my mind I was insulting him. He didn't seem to notice, though, and embraced me. He suggested we return to the parade ground and talk together on the platform beneath the big tree.

Right away when we got there he said my mother and I were fools to have come to Kathmandu. "You left your little sister without making arrangements for her proper care, and your house and your fields are being ruined."

I answered, "Yes, we are fools, and we came to Kathmandu to enjoy ourselves, just like tourists. Not because we were in trouble and had to come."

We talked some more like this. I was trying to impress him. I wanted him to think I was an educated boy and could take revenge on him for causing us so much trouble.

Mostly my uncle just laughed, but at the same time I think he was proud of me. You see, we were talking Nepali. That was very important. I was pretending I'd forgotten our own language. In our village only educated people spoke Nepali, and I was speaking it very fast. He was expert in Nepali and could understand me very easily.

He wanted to know where we were staying. I gave him our address in Thamel, and he said he also was staying in Thamel. I told him I'd show him how to find our place and was hoping on the way he'd take me to a hotel for some tea and some sweet things. He'd just arrived in Kathmandu so I knew he had plenty of money. But he didn't offer to buy me anything, and he didn't come with me all the way to our house. But when we separated he said, "We are going to compromise this case, and we will be reconciled." Hearing that made me feel happy beyond description.

My uncle never came to our house, but soon after I met him, he and my mother must have met, possibly at his place. After about a week had passed my mother took me with her early in the morning to my uncle's place. Some Pun Magars from Bhuji Khola were present. The Bhuji Khola is a river valley about five days' walk to the south of our village. With them was one of the Pun headmen who had much influence in the region and was generally spoken of as "Umrao Mukhiya" (i.e., the headman whose ancestor was a local military and administrative official in the late eighteenth and early nineteenth centuries when Nepal was emerging as a nation, a title now only honorary). When we got there my uncle went out and bought a goat's head. We all had a feast for our main morning meal.

After we had eaten, the men discussed the case. From what was said I think they must have heard that my mother was going to win, and to save more time and expense they wanted to work out among themselves a settlement and reconciliation between her and my uncle. To make my mother more ready to settle that way my uncle described my little sister's sad condition. He said my mother's people were taking such bad care of her that he had brought her to his house. He described her health as so poor my mother thought he was preparing her to find out that my sister had died. He denied this, and to prove he was telling the truth, according to our custom, he bit my mother's arm.

I was aware of what was going on as they talked, but I wasn't listening closely. I was dreaming instead of what it would be like to get back to our village. I was a little homesick, you see. I was thinking about how much my villagers would admire me, and I would boast about all the things I'd done and seen while living so long in Kathmandu. I was thinking too of the new clothing and the new shoes I would buy, and of presents for my sister.

That night I kept asking my mother, "When will we be going? When will we be going?" She said it would be in less than a month and immediately I asked her, "Then we must buy some new clothing and new shoes?" She answered by imitating me in a very high, whiny voice. "We must buy new clothing and new shoes, mother." Then in her normal voice she said, "New clothing and new shoes! To go home with these things you have to have saved. Have you saved any money? Of course you have, haven't you, and you've been a good boy, too, and always went to school and never stole anything."

I was so sad I started to weep. After a while my mother took pity on me and said, "I'll buy you one item of new clothing, but I don't have enough money for shoes. You'll have to beg your uncle for those. But you must approach him humbly."

I had a different plan. I thought I could frighten him. He already thought I was educated, and after our first discussion I'd tried to make him more certain that I was. A few times when I knew he would see me I had pretended I was on the way to school. I had borrowed a very thick arithmetic book from one of my friends and added two of my own. I put on my Nepali cap, slanted it to one side, and marched past looking very serious.

So when I went to ask him for money I stood before him with my arms folded and spoke in a very serious way. I pretended I was speaking for my mother too. "We are taking pity on you. We were going to win the case, but in the meantime you came and wanted to compromise. If we agree to compromise, we'll be going back to our village, and I'll have to have a pair of shoes." My uncle was smiling all the time, especially when I said, "If you don't agree then we won't agree with you." Nowadays I'm thinking he wasn't very frightened. But he did say he'd buy me a new pair of shoes.

Soon our day to start home was fixed. My mother and my uncle had gone to court and obtained a paper describing their reconciliation. One copy was given to my uncle and another to my mother.

I was feeling a mixture of happiness and sadness. I was sad because my life in Kathmandu was very, very wonderful. Thinking of it now I realize I haven't told half the good things that happened to me. One of the best things I've forgotten to tell you was my happiness over finding a little dog, though it's also one of the sad things.

One day when I was begging from shops in the busy Asantole market I happened to see a small puppy. From my childhood until this day whenever I see a small puppy I long with my whole soul to catch him and embrace him. This little puppy was just running here and there with its tail curving up over its back. It was walking very nicely, as if it were dancing. I liked it very, very much. I looked here and there to see if anybody was caring for it and saw no one who might have been the owner. So I caught it and carried it home with me.

In the evening when my mother came home from work and saw the puppy she scolded me. She said, "To support us you have to beg and yet you bring home a puppy as if you were a very rich fellow. So now it's up to you to feed him. Go and pick out the rice from the pot in the storeroom. Go and pick out some lentils too." She was angry but then began laughing a little too, and began teasing me. When I said I'd feed him half my own share, she said, "I'll keep watching to see how you feed him when your stomach's only half full. I'll be watching like this." And she opened her eyes very wide.

My mother let me keep the puppy. Sometimes at night it slept with me. It had very small sharp teeth and sometimes used to bite me here and there, but not so it hurt. I loved it very much, and wherever I went it used to come with me.

One day when I was playing marbles with my friends in the road near our house, a red automobile came along very fast. It blew its horn at us. We moved to one side but the puppy, who was with us, didn't get out of the way and the automobile drove over him and he was dead. I was so sad I didn't have words to express it. I was so angry with the driver I'd have thrown stones at him if he came that way again.

When my mother told me we'd be leaving Kathmandu in only two more days I decided to visit all the familiar places. When I went to the movie houses and the hotel I wanted to see a movie and eat delicious things, but I had no money. So in a soundless voice I said to those places, and to other places I was sad to leave, "Good-bye, I am leaving all of you and perhaps I will not see you again." My mother wasn't sad to leave.

She was homesick and wanted very much to see my sister. When she told our host and hostess she wasn't really satisfied with the court case settlement, they told her, "Be satisfied with what you got. You say you have a little daughter in your house. Remember her."

When we were saying good-bye to our host and hostess, my mother called them her father and mother. She said, "You gave us shelter in our time of need, and gave us food."

The night before we were going to leave we went to the place where my uncle was staying and spent the night there. He woke us very early in the morning, and we went to the bus station. Only a few people were on the streets and the city was very quiet. The only light came from the street lights. I was reaching up in my mind and touching them. "This is my last time to see you. At home I will have nothing like you, only our smoky pitch pine tapers."[43]

At last the bus came. It started, and for a few minutes I wasn't feeling well. I mean, my body was feeling well but my mind was very sad. But after a few minutes my mind as well as my body was swaying. Again I started to vomit. I hadn't been on a bus since we came from our village. My mother and I always walked everywhere in Kathmandu. We never took the bus. I hated them, and they cost money, which we couldn't afford.

I can't remember much about the trip home. But it was nearly the same: bus, train, and then by foot the rest of the way. It was a little different, though, because we crossed the border between India and Nepal to the east of Nepalganj, at Bhairawa. We walked from there to the market town of Butwal and on north and west to the Bhuji valley. The Bhuji valley was where the Umrao Mukhiya lived, and we stayed there with him for a time. The route after that is high and sometimes difficult. We were happy to have a chance to rest.

One thing I remember, the most important thing. In Gorakhpur the train stopped for two or three hours. It was lunchtime and we could get off. I saw ten or twelve tall black fellows carrying toys in big baskets on their heads. I wanted very much to take one of the toys to my sister.

---

[43] There are no windows (at least no windows with glass) in Tarang houses, so that even in the middle of a sunny day artificial light is needed to find anything. Nowadays some people have flashlights, but the traditional source of light was a short piece of sap-filled pine wood, which would light up as soon as it was lit and provide a strong light for several minutes.

What to do? I had no money and didn't dare ask my mother because she already had told me we didn't have any money for toys or other things to take home. I didn't want to ask my uncle either. Even though he had bought me a pair of shoes I was still acting proud before him, and didn't think it was a good idea to ask him for money.

So I decided to steal a toy. I walked until one of the men put down the stool he was carrying and set his big basket on top of it. Four or five people came and were standing around him. I kept checking his eyes while he talked with them. When he wasn't looking in my direction I took out one of his toys and turned it over and over in my hand, as if I was wondering whether to buy it. I checked his eyes again and as soon as I saw him looking away I tucked it into my shirt and walked away.

The toy was a pretty little girl doll made of plastic. It was colored very nicely. When I joined my mother and uncle I showed it to them and told them I stole it because I wanted to take it to my little sister. They didn't scold me.

The trail we were taking to my village crossed a high pass. When we reached the end of the pass we were high above my village and the other villages of the Tarakot area. Some, like our village, were on the steep hillside rising beneath us from our side of the Bheri river, and some were on the opposite hillside. Looking down I could see the forest where I used to collect wood and the fields where I used to try and keep the village cattle. As I saw these things, and the river where we boys used to go with our tiffin and to take baths, I felt I was finding again some precious things that had been lost to me for a long time.

At Home Again in Tarang

We had to live off our relatives until our own new crop had grown. We had relatives in Pali and Kani, and would spend some time with them, too. I had to do all the work, since my sister was small. Three or four years passed. My mother should have had an operation in Kathmandu, but we had no money for it. I went with Nandra Lal's father to help him in his trade, carrying half his load and half someone else's. My mother died one month after I left, but they didn't tell me until I got home.

Two days before I reached home I had a dream about food being prepared after a funeral, and I dreamed that my mother was very thin and ill-looking. At the resting spot at the top of the village I couldn't see anyone on my roof. I was worried, and asked why there seemed to be no one there. I was told my mother doesn't know we're expected today and is probably working in the fields somewhere.

Coming on down the hill I was prevented from going to my own house, and didn't find out about my mother's death until I entered a friend's house and was told, "Dear brother, don't be sad." I understood immediately what had happened, and wept. They took me inside and offered me some honey and other food. I stayed there three or four days, but then my sister and I moved back to our house. We were afraid to stay alone, so we stayed with Raji Man, whose mother was a friend of my mother, but we cooked our own food.

I took care of all the rituals associated with death, including one year later distributing cooked rice to everyone.

Before her death, I didn't pay too much attention to my mother's instructions, but afterwards I was very conscious of what she had said: "Keep the reputation of your famous father; work hard, and you'll have a good time in the future; and if I die, don't lose our wealth, so don't gamble." I deposited all my wealth in Raji Man's house for safekeeping.

I went on cultivating, plowing for other people, hauling firewood. After the harvest, I again went trading with Raji Man and helped take care of his horses. On this trip I was twelve years old, and I felt that God was with me.

Near Baglung, the King had come on tour, and they showed a documentary film. I went to see it, but I had already seen it in Kathmandu.

The next day I left, but stopped after a couple of miles to see the King, who was also leaving. I saw two men I knew—one military, one a *badahakim* (governor). I wanted to speak to the King about my tough life and ask for a job. In Tarang big men beat and bullied orphans. I told Raji Man I would sell sweaters and blankets to these Kathmandu men and ran away. After twenty or thirty steps I fell to the ground, murmuring, "God, I am leaving." By this trickery I escaped from my trading companions from home.

But the procession had gotten ahead of me, and I didn't know the way, so I followed footprints, but took a wrong turn. I went some way before I realized my mistake. The sun had already set, so rather than retrace my steps, I took a shortcut through the jungle, where I met a man with a horse. I told him my plan to see the King, and the man told me to go to his house and work for him. I didn't say anything, but laughed inside since I could just as easily return home and do that kind of work.

I reached the royal campground when it was dark. I didn't know what tent the King was in, so I decided to wait till morning. To get food, I went in front of the military men and began weeping, telling them I'd lost my parents, and they gave me food and shelter.

In the morning, the guard would not allow me to go into the King's tent, so I crawled in under the back side. Tulsi Giri was sitting by a fire, and I went up to him and said I wanted to see the King.[44] He said something, and the gatekeeper came in and grabbed me and threw me out. I was discouraged, but waited around till noon when the party set out for Gulmi. I saw the King but couldn't get through the crowd around him. I followed the procession and caught hold of the tail of the last horse, and gradually hauled myself forward along the trail. The military men warned me that I would get kicked by the horse, but I didn't even answer.

The King stopped on a plateau for breakfast. The military formed a circle around him. When the King approached, I got scared and my voice became faint. The King didn't hear, but smiled at me and asked the ADC what I had said. The police came and grabbed me.

That night's camp was on the bank of a river. I was given tea and an egg. My mother had told me that if I hung back on the trail I would be kidnapped, taken to someone's house, fed, killed, and used for oil. So now I was afraid when they fed me, but that night I heard the military men talking about me—that the King would take me to Kathmandu and send me to school. Now I was happy and not scared anymore. I went to bed, but couldn't sleep. I made up some *bhakha* (songs from my village) and the next day I danced and sang for the King. I was offered a horse to ride the next day, but I didn't know how to ride, so I often rode on the back of a servant. From Dang, the King returned to Kathmandu by air, and I followed by train. I lived with the military for about six months in the Chinese Embassy.[45] Later, at Pharping Boarding School, I used to dance for the King on his annual visit.

---

[44] Tulsi Giri was a senior minister in the Congress government of the 1950s and prime minister off and on in the 1960s and 1970s.

[45] The building to which Chandra Man refers was at that time a private dwelling of the commander-in-chief of the Royal Nepal Army. It became the Chinese Embassy much later.

Into the Larger World

At Pharping I entered Class 6, but I was weak, and the headmaster told me to go to a school in Kathmandu. I wept, because I had developed a love for the place. An English teacher asked me some questions that I couldn't answer, and he said I was unfit for Class 6. I said I would work very hard if they would just give me a chance, so they let me stay. The medium was English at that time; even though I failed English and Geography, they were willing to promote me, but I decided to stay in Class 6 another year to get a firmer foundation. The next year was easy, and from then on I was first in my class, and in Class 8 I was first in the entire school, finishing with a score of 728 out of 800. In Class 10, the final year, I stood first in the half-yearly exam, but at the end I didn't attend class for a month because of anxiety and disputes with the headmaster, and I stood only third.

I was the monitor in all my classes and had to control the students. Once I beat a favorite of the headmaster, who then gave me the nickname Bear. I wrote a poem that I read before the school, the central point of which was that one should not judge the character of a man from the outside only; all my friends clapped at this, but I don't know whether the headmaster got the point or not.

I stayed for a month at the school during the winter vacation to study for the SLC. I asked the headmaster to arrange a house for me in Kathmandu, but he didn't do it. But a rich man from Nepalganj, with several houses and a mill there, had two sons at Pharping whom I had helped. He offered me money sometimes and invited me for Dasai, but I refused. But he let me stay in his house while I was studying for the SLC exam.

I had to apply to the King for money and received Rs. 100; this wasn't really enough to travel home on, but I had a little extra, so I bought things for myself and my sister. I went to Pokhara and hired a porter. While I was walking on the trail towards home I ran out of money, but villagers along the way helped me. My sister, who had been staying with my uncle, Birka, had come as far as Baglung, so we came home together, and moved into our own home.

I had to cultivate my fields, so I went to the villagers to collect manure, and to borrow a plow and oxen. They wanted me to be the schoolmaster, but I said I had to work, so the panchayat decided to pay me Rs. 200 plus food and labor for my fields. Sometimes I used the pupils to help in the fields, and I would teach them while we worked. Other people did their own work first, and only after that would they help me. I got very tired and sore plowing, since I hadn't done any work like that for seven years.

I tried to guide the village in development. I said I would teach a class about panchayat, but those who came quit after a week, saying they were too old. I offered to teach without pay and tried to get younger people. I told them they were wasting their time just roaming around the village at night, that it was bad for their health, but they didn't follow my advice.

I was asked to run for the office of *pradhan panch* (mayor) in an election. I made up a platform about forest conservation, opening a night school, etc. Then I found out that two friends were also running, so I withdrew; the winner asked me to be secretary.

We made rules about animals going into fields with crops in them (Rs. 5 fine). We collected Rs. 5,000 to renovate the *dharamsala* (a shelter for pilgrims), and we planned to improve the trail to Tupa. We made a new water hole for the animals, repaired the tap, and put brass heads on the waterspouts. We had government help, and an overseer guided us and designed it.

Meanwhile, I got the results of the SLC–First Division, and ranked fourteen or fifteen in the entire country. Haimendorf had arrived, and he advised me to continue my education and to come to Pokhara with them, and he would help with finances. By the time I reached Pokhara they had left. In Kathmandu I was told that Hitchcock wanted to see me. He had sent me a wire in Dunai asking me to come to Kathmandu, after he had heard about me from Haimendorf. I had left before the wire arrived, and I had planned for further study, but I had about three to four months before the next session began, so I agreed to help Hitchcock for that time. He said they would help me come to America if I worked with them for a year in Tarang, but I had already decided to continue my studies in India.

Then Hitchcock became ill and our project had to be abandoned. We worked for two or three months in Kathmandu, first on ethnography, but then on my life history. I still wanted to go to America, but I vacillated and in the end decided instead to go to India to study. I studied Agriculture at the university in Nainital, and at the end of the first year scored 62% (58% is enough for First Division). I still wanted to go to America, and was never sure I had made the right decision in not taking Hitchock's offer.

Rumors were started that I had taken Hitchcock's *jutho*,[46] so I called a meeting of everyone in the village, but only a few people came. If I were proven guilty of taking *jutho*, my wife and I would have been outcasted, and so would my in-laws. There's no belief that a Brahman can purify someone. The rumors seemed to die down after a while.

During my year back in Tarang I had married Paljum, not by the usual procedure—capture—but by leaving early in the morning and taking her across the river to Pali village for a few days. Marrying by a process other than capture had never been done before, and people thought we were very odd. Then we came back and feasted the villagers in the traditional way.

After graduating from the university in Nainital with a major in Agriculture, I continued my studies in Agra. After that I became a section officer in the Agricultural Development Bank in Kathmandu, a job that lasted for thirteen years. I could have continued and progressed farther at the bank, but I decided to enter politics instead. This meant that I lost the pension I would have received if I had served for a full eighteen years. I tried for the nomination of the Congress Party to contest the election to be the representative from Dolpa, but I did not receive the nomination. Instead, Kabu Budha, from Gomba, was nominated, and he won the nomination and the election. After I lost, I helped Kabu in his campaign to be the candidate, then helped him in his election.

Before that, the bank sent me for three years to The University of New England in Armidale, in New South Wales, Australia, where I received my MA. By the time I left for Australia, my wife and I had two sons, and then a daughter after I returned. My younger sister married a man from Tupa and therefore went to live in his house there, but they did not have any children.

❖　❖　❖　❖　❖

---

[46]   In this context, *"jutho"* refers to partially eaten food on a plate; as leftovers, it has come into contact with someone else's bodily substance (saliva) and therefore would transmit that person's essence to anyone who might eat it. As a foreigner, Hitchcock would be considered of low rank, and therefore no one would eat his *jutho*. It is acceptable for someone of lower rank to eat the *jutho* of someone of higher rank, but not the reverse.

Chandra Man died in 2000 CE (BS 2057), of jaundice. A doctor had incorrectly diagnosed his condition as tuberculosis, and by the time he realized his diagnosis was mistaken, it was too late to halt the progression of the disease. His wife, Paljum, and their two sons and daughter subsequently remained in Kathmandu, traveling occasionally to Tarang. One of his sons has since died, and his daughter now lives in England with her husband, a 12 Magarant Magar who serves in the British army.

I saw Chandra Man perhaps two or three times, briefly, in Kathmandu, in the years before he died. This was long before I developed an interest in the present study (or restudy), so I lost the opportunity to talk more with him about the many things he could have told me about his own life, and about Tarang life as he had experienced it as an adult. The information he provided to bring his life history up to date I obtained from him during the original fieldwork in the late 1960s, when he was visiting the village during a vacation period from the university where he was studying agriculture, in Nainital, in the Indian Himalayas just west of Nepal.

Chandra Man Rokaya, 1946-2000.

Time Line for Chandra Man Rokaya

1946   Born (BS 2003) in Tarang

1952   Walks to Jumla with his mother to fight the court case

1954   Travels to Kathmandu with his mother to continue fighting the legal case

1958   Meets and charms King Mahendra on his tour of west Nepal

1963   As a student in Class 8 at Pharping Boarding School, meets Fisher, who is teaching his English class

1966   Meets anthropologists von Fürer-Haimendorf and Hitchcock

1968   Marries Paljum

1970   Works with Fisher in Tarang during vacation from Nainital University, India

ca. 1972 After receiving his BA from Nainital, pursues further agricultural studies in Agra

1974   Works as section officer at the Agricultural Development Bank in Kathmandu

1978   Receives MA degree after three years of study at The University of New England in Armidale, New South Wales, Australia

1989   Resigns from the Agricultural Development Bank to enter Tichurong politics (unsuccessfully)

1990   Works for Action Aid (British NGO) in Kathmandu

1993   Retires from Action Aid

2000   Dies in Kathmandu

10

Conclusions

A book such as this one does not require a grand finale or other rhetorical flourishes with which to conclude. However, it does need to specify the relevance of the Tarali story for Nepal more generally, and to clarify why what has been said is analytically important for anthropology more specifically. It stands as a testimonial to the collective lives of people in an obscure village in northwest Nepal as they have evolved over a period of forty-four sometimes quiet, sometimes tumultuous years, and those years are experienced quite differently according to the financial, educational, and kinship backgrounds of its citizens. One size rarely, if ever, fits all.

My accounting of it is neither comprehensive nor encyclopedic, nor does it provide closure to any number of issues arising in the contemporary development of Nepal and in theorizing in the current anthropological community. Rather, it is highly selective in choosing a few urban individuals, originally from the same village, who both represent other, similar individuals, and also contrast with those still living in the village. It purports to exemplify more expansive, sweeping analytical approaches, and to test them against the specific cases of a few individual lives about whom the book is principally concerned.

Presented as an old-fashioned anthropological trait list of the sort a government researcher might compile for the *bikas*-oriented bureaucracy that employs him or her, the novelties that I found occurring over a period of forty-four years in Tarang would include the following:

Electronic: solar collectors, cell phones, DVDs

Transportation: the Juphal airstrip, use of horses and mules, improved trails; partial construction of a new roadbed along the Bheri River that will eventually reach Tarang and proceed beyond it so that the people of Tichurong will eventually be able to travel by road to India and Tibet

Agriculture: introduction of fruit trees (apple and peach), harvesting of *yarsagumba*, honey as a crop, better protection for chickens

Politics: extortion by Maoists, participation in national elections, including Dhanu's victory as Dolpa's representative running on the UML (United Marxist-Leninist) ticket in the national Parliament

Education: expansion of village school to Grade 8, hiring of more teachers (one for each grade), construction of school buildings, including a modern toilet, increased enrollments

Fashion: women wearing tee shirts; men wearing slacks; women wearing smaller earrings and shorter *patukas*

Architecture: slight changes in painted house decorations (inside and outside), installation of cooking hearth chimney and window screens (the latter two, so far, in only one house)

Government presence: pay for teachers' salaries; registration of births; provision of rice ration, subsidized rice and salt; employment for roadbed construction; improved trails (e.g., to hot spring), improved hot spring facility; installation of two new water taps within the village

Health: construction of Ayurvedic facility

Ritual: modification of Chaite Bokne after the death of the *patum*; minor adjustments in ritual life, such as truncating of Saun Sankranti

Labor: hiring boys from distant villages as domestic servants (in four or five houses)

Conveniences: introduction of plastic five-gallon water jugs, replacing heavy brass jugs with smaller capacity; village shops located in village houses (three or four)

Culture: more intellectual interest in origins of Tarali culture, greater interest in, pride in, and promotion of Kaike language

Each of these items considered alone might seem insignificant, but taken together, they comprise an extensive, if modest, list. But in addition, these form more dense connections to, as well as sense of connectedness with, the larger world also, which plays a part in redefining a self, a locality, and an ethnicity. Collectively, they amount to subtle, but significant, lifestyle modifications. Some of these features are accessible to everyone, or at least all households, such as *yarsagumba* harvesting, change in diet due to fruit trees, better hot spring facility, a rice ration, even an occasional flight to Kathmandu. Others have been adopted only by one or only a few individuals, such as a hearth chimney, solar collectors, shops, honey as a crop, hired labor to help with routine household tasks, and use of mules as beasts of burden.

Innovations have been irregularly and inconsistently adopted. And yet there are patterns that run through some of the items in the list that affect everyone regardless of personal participation: *yarsagumba*, solar collectors, the "walking houses" that Chandra Man noticed, and the apple trees are some of them.

These instances of change in Tarang are small, incremental, sporadic, and, it might seem, in the larger scheme of things, inconsequential. Yet the significance of this study, including the agency-laden autobiography of CM Rokaya, lies in tracing the contours of change in the local order as much as in the larger scheme of things. Nothing in Tichurong approaches the vast changes in life that accompanied the restructuring of economic life by the carpet industry, *yarsagumba* notwithstanding.

Still, the discovery of *yarsagumba* brought about dramatic changes both in Kathmandu *and* in Tichurong. Since carpets are not woven in the village and agriculture is not practiced in Kathmandu, it is *yarsagumba* that ties the two communities together economically and helps retain traditional social ties among people living in disparate locations. Those living in the metropolis of Kathmandu have followed a new way of life. The lives of those back in the hinterland are not as visibly different, certainly not when they are still out performing backbreaking labor on those steep hillside fields, but if you've never seen a telephone, or picked an apple off a tree, or had access to water within the village, or had much of a discretionary income to dispose of, its innovations are sufficient unto the day.

Past and Present

But adding up the items on a trait list tells us nothing about the larger shape of life. They do not explain why life in Tarang seems much the way it did before: daily life lived publicly on rooftops where information, good and bad (expressed in heated arguments), is transmitted; hierarchical social structure divided into marriage classes and castes; lack of plumbing and usable electricity; persistence of traditional construction and architectural house styles; and a heavily agricultural economy that has remained unaffected by technological change in the means of production, even if work gathering *yarsagumba* cuts into total labor spent in the fields and results in smaller production of edible grain crops.

And yet, people go back and forth with some frequency between Kathmandu and Tarang. More important, regardless of the frequency of travel they feel at home in either place. Taralis still constitute a single ethnicity with an esoteric language (for the thousand or so who speak Kaike), bound together by continuing kinship and marriage ties, the latter almost exclusively between Tichurong partners. Unless someone is physically unable to travel, whoever lives in Kathmandu returns now and then to Tarang, and those in the village occasionally go to Kathmandu, whether on brief trips or for extended stays, whether for business, pilgrimage, or for family visits. Traffic flows in both directions. It may be tied to election cycles or *yarsagumba* harvesting or village rituals or marriages, but it occurs, if not regularly or predictably, at least frequently.

Framing the original ethnography in terms of transaction circuits seemed a sensible and analytically powerful way to approach it in the 1960s. In fact, I believe my efforts were more insightful and prescient than I thought they were when I recorded, formulated, and stated them. To my surprise, the different transactional backgrounds continue their influential contribution in helping explain the different routes Tarali lives have followed in the interim. Those most successful before have been followed by the most successful now, and that is to some extent because the transactional skills are always in play. The approach I suggested so long ago has not only withstood the tests of time, but it has continued to be crucial in the present. That approach omitted many nuances that needed to be added, to show how specific cases worked through these transactions, and the whole apparatus needed to be brought up to date. Now it has been. The nuances could be most clearly seen in the experiences of a few named, identifiable people who are demonstrating them by living them, rather than ciphers that impersonate them.

On the other hand—and this is a very significant caveat—the dramatic changes among a relatively small number of Taralis, mostly connected to each other through ties of kinship and marriage, while in some ways not surprising in view of their transactional backgrounds, are also not the only routes that could have led to these transformations. There are always viable alternatives for those who, if we can but find them, are able to counterbalance the advantages of those who seem to have selected their ancestors more carefully.

The telling, and compelling, counterexample here is that of Chandra Man, whose own life was not premised on any of the structural, kin, vocational, educational, or transactional advantages that several others discussed as examples in this book—Bhim, Sukar, Lank Man, Bisara, or Dhanu—enjoyed. Ironically, although his paternal ancestors had once played a dominant role and been a powerful presence in the village, Chandra Man himself grew up in harshly impoverished circumstances. His very detailed case shows how the many obstacles that stalked him unrelentingly in his early life could, against all odds, be overcome. The fact that through his tenacity he prevailed in the face of almost unimaginable adversity shows the futility of relying on grand, unitary, explanatory schemes (transactional or otherwise) to account for the sorts of successes he eventually effected. On the contrary, he seems to have singlehandedly refuted the analytic assumptions underlying the lives of all the others mentioned in the book.

Is this possible? It is possible, because no macro anthropological conceptual net is universally applicable, nor whatever its specifics was it ever meant to encompass all of social and cultural life. All analytical schemes are partial—they may account for many ethnographic facts, and the more the better, but they can never explain all of them. The broad generalizations still hold, and they are what give anthropology its cachet, but the wide-ranging anthropological analysis needs to allow for exceptions that prove the rule. Unless Chandra Man's case instantiates some still more universal, cultural principle that I have missed, his example does constitute such an inescapable exception.

This should not be construed as an assertion that Chandra Man's case is whimsical and somehow lies outside the range of common humanity. One might argue that more ordinary initiatives characterize the lives of all human beings. It is just that such initiatives do not usually result in the spectacular success that Chandra Man's did. Astounding as Chandra Man's experience was, it did not occur because of mystical, unaccountable, or incomprehensible forces operating in his life. Indeed, his existence would be quite unimaginable without two very key persons in his life: his mother and King Mahendra. His relationship with those two individuals, however, was fortuitous. They were determining of his success, and at the same time unavailable to the run-of-the-mill Tarali. History will not repeat itself here.

None of this should be construed as an attack on the myriad anthropological approaches, observations, and analyses that have been crafted over the history of the discipline, whether by my friends, colleagues, and predecessors, or in my own previous work. On the contrary, it endorses them, because it draws attention to the cases that escape the anthropologist's overall conceptual mesh, thus leading to alternative analyses that cut off such escapes. It states that anthropology must remain open to those elusive exceptions that belie the otherwise grandiose generalizations, and their epistemological underpinnings, which anthropologists spend so much time disputing among themselves.

In addition to the closing remarks above, one conclusion I draw, therefore, is that ultimately, all the social, economic, and cultural variables that are so undeniably important and are demanded to account for whatever regularities exist and whatever transformations have occurred in social and cultural life, wherever and whenever they take place on our planet, can be trumped by the exceptional individual. Those incomparable experiences have to be accounted for; they cannot be swept under the rug. The idiosyncratic factors accompanying whoever that person may be are not always obvious on the surface, as revealed in the researcher's questionnaires, surveys, tables, graphs, charts, and interviews, but they become unmistakable, and unavoidable, in the close reading of a single case.

Into the Future

I began this book wondering if my musings about the future, as I had imagined them in the late 1960s, would have any relation to whatever reality had transpired since then. I conclude that my expectations, stated as vaguely as they were, were more or less, though certainly not in every detail, on target.

As I wonder similarly about the future now, I have more to go on than I did before. As in other parts of Nepal, all sorts of things are happening—politically, economically, socially, legally, culturally, linguistically—all of which are taking place under the stimulating and fecund overhanging phenomenon of globalization. Road building continues unabated, including even in the hinterland of Dolpa. The road being built up the river from Dunai and points south reaches closer to Tarang every day. It will eventually continue on up the river through Inner Dolpa to the Tibetan border, facilitating the transportation, in and out of Tichurong, of products to and from the rest of the world.

That road will not pass through Tarang, perched high on the hillside above it. But if the road will not come to Tarang, Tarang will come to the road. Tarang has subdivided the flat area (*tarabagar*, Nepali) down by the river into parcels of land roughly 400 square feet, one for every house (eighty-eight) in the village. Any new landowner in this demarcated land, called Lingtu (*ling*, snow; *tu*, water, Kaike), will be free to do whatever he or she wishes with the land—cultivate it, graze animals on it, plant trees on it, and build a house (or a shop) on it. It could become another version of Dunai, with all its commerce but without all its government offices.

The basic idea is that the road will bring various opportunities—for example, the possibility of exporting fruit from apple and peach trees, not to mention facilitating export of *yarsagumba*, as well as providing services for tourism. Lank Man is participating in a plan in which the Agricultural Development Bank and the government are jointly investing in apple production in ten districts in Nepal, including Dolpa. They have already planted 4,500 trees in 5.4 hectares. There is no requirement for people to move to Lingtu, but if they do, Tarang faces the possibility of becoming a ghost town.

On the other hand, there has also been discussion for many years about building an airport above Tarang. Land above Samtiling, called Tolangya, was surveyed for such a facility in 1972, but political considerations prevailed and it was built in Juphal instead. If an airport were built, it would bring more activity to Tarang through a demand for tourism services, such as employment in portering and other assistance for trekkers, possibly including homestay opportunities in Tarang. Residency in Tarang would not preclude residence in Tolangya, or vice versa. People might commute between the two places.

More immediately, the Rs. 1,000 per-person per-season *yarsagumba* fee charged outsiders is currently being used by Tarang to subsidize the construction of toilets. Twenty or twenty-five have already been installed in fields near houses. Some are not being used as toilets, but for storage. As for action in cleaning up the pathways of the village, nothing has been done, not because of opposition, but simply because it is not recognized indigenously as a serious problem.

Predictions of the future are, of course, notoriously fraught with uncertainty of many kinds, ranging from political developments to acts of God. I would never have dreamed in the late 1960s of Nepal without a monarch; similarly, I now find it hard to imagine Nepal with a monarch. I would also never have imagined the series of earthquakes in 2015 that scared off Chinese *yarsagumba* buyers, resulting in sharply curtailed demand and lower prices in that industry. The earthquakes did not affect Tichurong, but they partially destroyed Bhim and Sukar's carpet weaving factory in Bhaktapur. The idea that the amenities of Kathmandu somehow provide a safer environment than that of Tichurong could not have been more mistaken. There was no safe haven over a broad swath of the mountains of Nepal, although the *yarsagumba* world has revived and the Bhaktapur carpet factory has been rebuilt.

Thus the repercussions were felt even in Tichurong, though it is far from where the quakes took place and wreaked their destruction. More ominously, geologists have predicted further earthquakes in the fairly near future that are expected to occur to the west of the locations of the 2015 quakes. Dolpa lies in their projected pathway. For Tichurongba (the people of Tichurong), in terms of seismic upheavals, the worst is probably yet to come.

All these questions are collectively left hanging, although probabilities could be attached to any particular one of them. The ultimate limit of prediction is perhaps this: how could anyone predict the coming of another Chandra Man, and the way a person of such intelligence and talents might affect any or all of these developments—in transportation, agriculture, trade, religion, politics, health, and education?

Unscientific Postscript

This book is the record of an anthropologist's attempts, which have evolved over forty-four years, to come to some sort of minimal intellectual terms with what has happened in Tarang and in Kathmandu, and to comprehend as much of it as I can with the anthropological tools at my disposal. It is a modest contribution towards an understanding of some of the changes that have taken place over the last few decades among people originating from the same stock—all still Taralis, but now divided into different orders and groups than previously. These changes could be summarized as a community that has been undergoing a process of social differentiation, economic specialization, and cultural stirring. It is a rising voice from parts of Nepal, in both the hinterland and its urban offshoots, that is not heard from often enough.

The extensive use of life histories, as I have attempted here, has required, and represents, an analytical approach that contrasts markedly with the one I had adopted in the 1960s. Here I have placed less emphasis on "systems" (as we had been taught to do at the University of Chicago) and more on specific people because of particular factors that have figured in their lives. I do not regard this as abdicating more conventional anthropological "society and culture" strategies, but rather as pursuing those strategies via a different tactic I was intellectually forced to take.

Rather than regarding individual Taralis as cultural zombies, I've come to believe that their success (or failure) can be understood only when the details of their particular, specific lives, which follow contours neither they (assuming they had been born by then) nor I could have dreamed of forty-four years earlier, are revealed. It is an argument, therefore, for utilizing life histories wherever and whenever we can, because they can illustrate how the course of individual lives may be predicted by general structural principles as well as fly in the face of them. They are a kind of litmus test of the large-scale analysis and generalizations that are the stuff in which most anthropology deals.

However, it is not only the Taralis who have changed over forty-four years. So has the anthropologist. I am not only older, but also, just possibly, although not incontestably, wiser. By now I have become interested in situations, some of them critical, that I did not pay much attention to the first time around, due to the limitations of my own experience of life at that young age: situations such as the manipulation of political power, the off-and-on feuding between families, and what lies hidden behind the "presentation of self in everyday life." I was on the alert for that "presentation of self" from beginning to end, but I didn't always understand or interpret it correctly. I also noticed aspects of village life that I simply missed the first time around, such as hierarchical relations based on factors other than membership in marriage classes, and how socialization of young children takes place in venues where it might not be expected.

Any account of individual lives should, therefore, for simple reasons of fairness, include an account of my own life, without which my account of their lives is one-sided. The people of Tarang have no doubt made their own assessment of me, as I have of them, but they are not given the opportunity to present it here, nor are they likely to do so anywhere else. My account therefore misses many details about me and my biases, limitations, difficulties, and the distinctions between what I thought I was doing and what I was actually doing that I failed to mention in the text. All this is in contrast to the ostensibly omniscient observer I spuriously posed as in the original book.

Although bits and pieces of my own life history have crept into the text here and there, unlike many anthropologists I do not entertain the self-deception that I am more interesting than the people I study. One way I try to keep this confessional mode in check is by attaching the following interview, entirely separate from my assessment of the people I was trying to understand.

The interview was conducted and published by my colleague, Gaurab KC. Being by nature very meticulous and painstaking, Gaurab revealed more about my past than any reader could reasonably find of interest. But for those curious about whatever information it might contain, and its relevance to the main body of work which precedes it, I offer it here. Presented as a document distinct from my narrative about what I found, or think I found, in the Tarali world some forty-four years after I first encountered it, I intend it as a kind of counterpoint to the life histories I recount above. If the Taralis have been heard from—one might even say exposed—reciprocity demands that I should be too.

It is a way of acknowledging, stating, and emphasizing that all life histories matter.

AN INTERVIEW WITH JAMES F. FISHER

Conducted by Gaurab KC
Studies in Nepal History and Society
2013

Western anthropologists began the systematic anthropological exploration of Nepal in the 1950s, most carrying out their fieldwork after Mahendra Bir Bikram Shah became King in 1955. Some of these explorers were established anthropologists while for others Nepal was the pristine field site for earning their Ph.D. degrees. The production of Nepal-related work significantly enhanced their academic credentials. Some Nepalis benefitted greatly by affiliating with these foreign scholars. This collaboration was a major impetus for institutionalizing the discipline in Nepal. Results of this cooperation significantly contributed not only to introducing Nepal and its culture to the world, but also to fostering the future of Nepali anthropology.

James F. Fisher belongs to the first generation of these anthropologists. He came to Nepal first as a Peace Corps volunteer in 1962. Since then he has produced a substantial amount of anthropological scholarship on Nepal, which he claims to be his *dosro ghar* (second home).

I seized the opportunity to interview Fisher when he came to Nepal to launch his book *At Home in the World: Globalization and the Peace Corps in Nepal* (2013). I had interviewed Fisher several times in 2011 while making a documentary film jointly with Sachin Ghimire on Dor Bahadur Bista. I went through Fisher's CV carefully and read many of his publications. Drawing upon these readings, I prepared a long set of interview questions. The main interview took place on 3 November 2013 in a house near Bhatbhateni in Kathamandu. It was recorded both on a tape recorder and on a computer, and its total duration was four hours and thirty-five minutes. I then transcribed the interview and sent it to Fisher. Numerous emails were sent back and forth between the two of us. Fisher devoted a significant amount of time to structuring and clarifying his responses to my questions.

I believe that many social science enthusiasts, in Nepal and elsewhere, will read with interest the life and work of an anthropologist who has contributed painstakingly to understanding Nepal. The readers will also obtain a glimpse of Nepal in the 1960s and the following decades, a slice of the disciplinary history of anthropology in Nepal, and other fascinating details of contemporary life in these pages.

Studies in Nepali History and Society 18(2): 329–388 December 2013

Gaurab (G): *To begin with, how would you like to introduce yourself?*

Fisher (F): How do I identify myself? Well, to begin with the obvious—I'm a seventy-three-year-old American male with children and grandchildren, but that hardly answers your question, since the same could be said of millions. My core identity is primarily tied up with my occupation, which is also, fortuitously, my avocation as an anthropologist. But I hadn't even heard of anthropology until my senior year in college. I was majoring in philosophy at that time, but

The author, James F. Fisher.

then I discovered anthropology and ended up coming to Nepal in the first Peace Corps group. I immediately became fascinated with the country and everything in it—the people, the food, music, landscape, religion, politics, education, social structure, kinship, family life, etc. Afterwards, I went to the University of Chicago for my Ph.D. in anthropology. Since then my whole life, my working life at least, has been involved with anthropology. I taught anthropology at Carleton College for almost forty years and before that at the University of Chicago, and also in Nepal and, most recently, Bhutan. So I would say my primary identification is as an anthropologist, but as a Nepal anthropologist, or let's say the Himalayas in general and specifically Nepal, because my entire life has been spent, either physically or metaphysically, in Nepal. By that I mean I am not always physically in the country, whether because I'm at Carleton or some other university or at meetings in different places, but even then I am thinking and talking about Nepal, and writing books and articles about Nepal. I am talking to people, whether students who want to know more about Nepal or colleagues in Nepal or elsewhere—but the subject matter is mostly Nepal. So I would say those two things—anthropology and Nepal—define me professionally.

G: *Many professional anthropologists have come from different backgrounds, and instead of introducing themselves as an anthropologist (though the majority do that) some also introduce themselves as social scientists or* *humanists or something else. Do you feel any hesitation about describing yourself as an anthropologist, or, contrarily, do you take pride in saying you are an anthropologist?*

F: I definitely am proud of the discipline and of its history, although it has been tormented in a way. It's been accused of being a 'handmaiden of colonialism' and all that. I understand this critique but I think it is misconstrued and false, and increasingly so. I am mostly proud of anthropology. I think what it does, what it contributes to the world, just in terms of understanding all of humanity, is unique and not available from any other discipline. What other discipline (e.g., Economics or Political Science) is based on and insists so relentlessly on the views and dignity of those which it studies? The answer is none, because those disciplines are intellectually imperialistic. Anthropology's insistence on the importance of the 'native point of view' defines it. That's what anthropology is all about. But also in practical matters such as development projects in Nepal, I think anthropology has much to contribute, has contributed to them, and will continue to do so, though there is always the temptation and danger of selling out to the big governmental and corporate money of development.

I don't distinguish really among the nationalities of anthropologists. None of us care whether we are Nepalis or American or English or Sri Lankan or German or Japanese or anything else. This is true for most scholars in Nepal, not just anthropologists, as can be easily seen from the selection of the annual Mahesh Chandra Regmi Lecturers who come from all over the world including, of course, Nepal. (I was hugely honored to be one of two Americans to give the lecture.) It's also true of the membership of ANHS (Association for Nepal and Himalayan Studies), the first Executive Committee of which I am the only surviving founding member. Mahendra Lawoti was our recent President, and Dor Bahadur Bista served as Honorary President of ANHS for several years.

One of the great things about anthropology in Nepal is the cooperation and mutual support and respect we hold towards each other without regard to nationalities. As anthropologists, we all speak the same language and work in the same way. This is equally true of our Nepali colleagues, so many of whom now are talented and highly trained and productive scholars. Of course professionally we disagree about all sorts of things, but not personally.

G: *It seems you are deterministically advocating for the discipline and forgetting bitter instances in its past. Many accusations against the discipline have been made, even by professional anthropologists. It's being charged, for example, that during the Vietnam War anthropologists were used by the American government as spies. Do you believe these allegations are misconstrued and false? If so, why have anthropologists been so frequently charged with these things?*

F: I think it's true that in the beginning anthropology had strong imperialistic overtones (this was somewhat true in Nepal too) and you are right that more recently, as in Vietnam, anthropologists have sometimes forgotten that their primary loyalty must always be to the mostly defenseless and powerless people they study. But I also think these are aberrations and anthropologists themselves have been the harshest critics of these missteps. I don't know of any discipline as self-critical as anthropology.

G: *Can you describe your educational journey in detail? Where, when, and what did you study for your B.A., Masters and Ph.D. degrees?*

F: I went to Princeton University for my undergraduate study, which I finished in 1962. While I was there I was always somewhat interested in philosophy—you know, questions about the meaning of life, the universe, and other such ultimately unanswerable mega-questions. I didn't have anything else particularly to major in so I majored in philosophy, but I was not entirely committed to it. I once visited my advisor's office. He was on the phone so I had to wait till he finished his phone conversation. On his desk I saw a booklet of the annual meeting of the philosophers, which listed the various papers that were being presented. I was flipping through it while he was on the phone, and I noticed one of the papers with the title "Is it now, now?" I thought, I can't contribute anything to that question. Years later, after becoming an anthropologist, I met one of my old philosophy professors again. I told him this story, and he said "Oh! No, no this is a very important philosophical question." And I can see how it is important. For instance, as soon as you say the word 'now,' it's already in the past. You can't say it about the future. So when is 'now'? Is it 'now,' now? Or is it ever 'now'? Even though I recognized that this is an intriguing question, I thought I could not resolve it, and I had better leave it to others to sort out.

Then the summer before my senior year I went to summer school at Harvard. I did this mainly because the U.S. economy was in very bad shape that year (1961), which made it difficult to find a job. Still lacking direction, I went there just to sample different courses but without any specific academic goal. I saw that they were giving an anthropology course. I had hardly heard of anthropology, although someone at Princeton had told me that they thought I would be a good anthropologist, even though I didn't have any idea what anthropology was. I enrolled in the course, taught by Douglas Oliver, (a prominent expert on Oceania who specialized in the South Pacific), and about five minutes into the first class I realized that I had found what I had been looking for all my life, but I hadn't known of its existence. Then I went back to Princeton and finished my philosophy major and applied to graduate school at the University of Chicago in anthropology, which accepted me.

At the same time President Kennedy was just starting the Peace Corps. They asked me if I wanted to work in a Peace Corps training camp in Puerto Rico during the summer after I graduated. I said, "Sure. That sounds like fun and I would like to do that." So I wrote them and then they wrote back and asked if I would be interested in being a Volunteer in a regular Peace Corps program. I was already accepted at Chicago so I said I didn't think I would be interested and said no. Just as an afterthought, I added that I would be interested if they had a program going to Nepal. I thought there was almost no chance whatsoever that that would be the case. I couldn't imagine that happening. But to my astonishment they wrote again and said, "Well, as a matter of fact, we do have a Peace Corps group going to Nepal."

Then I thought immediately that this would fulfill my dream because I had always been interested in the Himalayas after reading a novel by James Hilton called *Lost Horizon*. It's about a place called Shangri-La—that's where the English word comes from—a miraculous, enchanting, and idyllic place where everyone is kind, generous, and peaceful. The book doesn't say exactly where Shangri-La is but it seemed to be in Tibet or northern Nepal or somewhere in the Himalayas. I had always wanted to go there (the Himalayas, not Shangri-La, which was fictional), and this was my chance. So, I wrote to Chicago and they gave me a two-year extension. This is how I came to Nepal in 1962 and stayed till 1965, when I entered Chicago (which had granted me an additional third-year extension).

G: *Meanwhile you submitted your B.A. thesis at Princeton entitled "An Anthropological Approach to Ethics" (Fisher 1962). Did you have difficulties with your supervisor since instead of submitting a thesis in philosophy you wrote about anthropology?*

F: Yes, that's a very interesting question because that was my senior year, when I had discovered anthropology, but to graduate I had to finish in philosophy. So I was looking for some topic that would bridge those two disciplines. Now 'ethics' is considered to be a philosophical topic, not a subfield of anthropology. But I thought, ok, I will take ethics, a philosophical area, and try to treat it anthropologically. I did that basically by comparing two books by philosophers on the ethical systems of American Indian tribes. One book was *The Structure of a Moral Code*, on the Navajo, and the other was called *Hopi Ethics*, on the Hopi tribe. I wanted to see what the basic issues are, as anthropology has always promoted cultural relativism, the belief that every culture, and the ethical system it espouses, deserves to be understood in its own terms and not judged by the standards of other cultures. So I wanted to look at these two philosophical analyses of the ethics of those tribes. This is how I wrote my thesis. I don't think I was particularly successful, but it got me into the world of anthropology, and I enjoyed doing it. I'm not always a cultural relativist, though; taken to extremes, one could argue that female genital mutilation is the value of some cultures, and if people want to do that, who am I to say they shouldn't do it? There are good anthropological reasons why I disagree with that argument, so relativism itself is relative. Relativism is not a 'one size fits all' proposition; it has epistemological and ethical limits.

G: *Don't you think the concept of 'culture' itself is a problematic anthropological construction? Unlike following the Boasian trend, today's anthropologists compare, contrast, and divide the cultures, evoking reductionism, divisionism, and ethnocentrism.*

F: It is a minor irony that 'culture' is both the most fundamental concept at the core of anthropology as well as the most contested. Nevertheless, there is a consensus that culture, whether defined as a way of life, or, in a more circumscribed way, as systems of meanings and symbols, is what distinguishes us from other living creatures. It is the essence of our humanity. We may argue about how to study it— humanistically or scientifically, for example—but we agree that it is of central importance in achieving an understanding of humankind. It is a healthy sign that the definition of culture has evolved and continues to evolve. The last thing a growing, vibrant discipline needs is to know exactly what it is about.

G: *Again, instead of pursuing your Ph.D. in philosophy, why did you choose anthropology? Was it personal interest, or did someone inspire you?*

F: First of all, I had always been strongly interested in people; I was a 'people person,' as we sometimes say. I was just fundamentally curious about why people act, think, feel, and speak the way they do, especially acting, speaking, feeling, and thinking differently and cross-culturally. I became a total cultural determinist. Culture was the domain of anthropology, so it was a natural draw for me. Now, you can also study human affairs in philosophy, as the philosophers I wrote my thesis about did. I was talking about this issue one time with Clifford Geertz and he gave the same answer I had found. He had also studied philosophy in his undergraduate days and he said he found it unsatisfying and wanted to study real people as they live their down-to-earth daily lives, not just imaginary people philosophers sometimes create (such as might inhabit a planet we can't see because it's on the other side of the sun). I also wanted to understand real people by talking to them, living with them, sharing their lives, and getting to know why they were the way they were, and how they understood their lives. Anthropology attracted me because it was a profession in which I could do all that. Philosophy very rarely allows such activities.

G: *Can you explain this shift from philosophy to anthropology? Also, throw some light on how your philosophical orientation aided in anthropological exploration.*

F: Well, as far as this shift is concerned, I think once I discovered anthropology I thought, This is great, this is it. I lost some of my initial fascination with philosophy but not entirely. Even today, in retirement, I read about cosmological questions, not those posed by physics, such as when the Big Bang occurred, but philosophical questions, such as the one Heidegger raised about the universe when he asked, "Why is there something, rather than nothing?" For me, that's a fascinating question and I am interested in it in a very amateurish way.

Now, as far as philosophy helping anthropology, I give much credit to philosophy because I think what I learned from philosophy is how to think clearly, coherently, correctly, and critically, and to recognize ethnocentric mistakes of logic and judgment. It made me not just cautious but careful in what I am thinking about. Good anthropology requires a lot of thought and I would say philosophy helps me think about anthropological questions, whatever they are, more clearly than I would otherwise.

G: *When you submitted your thesis on an anthropological approach to ethics at Princeton, who were the dominant American anthropologists at that time?*

F: One reason I had not heard about anthropology till the summer before my senior year is that Princeton had no anthropology at that time. Oh, they had one anthropologist (Peter Kunstadter, a specialist in American Indians and Southeast Asia) in the Sociology Department, and I took some of his courses, but there was only that one person. So I was not very aware of what the total spectrum of anthropology was. I knew that Chicago was thought to be the best place but I knew of other places too, like Columbia, where Boas, Benedict, and Mead had been. Basically, I didn't know much more than what I read in my last year in college. This was only one year after A. L. Kroeber died; he was the first person to receive a Ph.D. in anthropology in America (under Boas, in 1901) and Margaret Mead was still a popular figure. I was simply not well informed at that time.

G: *In 1965 you began your graduate studies in anthropology at the University of Chicago. What was the training regime for anthropology graduate students? Who were your teachers? What did you read specifically about South Asia and Nepal?*

F: Chicago had the typical American four-field approach, which is quite different from the English or European model. There were two main tracks we all had to learn and each track had two components. One track was archaeology and physical anthropology. The other was social (or cultural) and linguistic anthropology. At an opening reception for new students each faculty member briefly introduced himself. (I use the male gender form because there were no female members of the faculty then.) Clifford Geertz said that he was either a social or a cultural anthropologist but he wasn't sure which because he didn't know what the difference between them was. After that first year we specialized in one or the other track.

It was a large and distinguished department, so our teachers, on the socio-cultural side, included Fred Eggan, Sol Tax, Clifford Geertz, Manning Nash, Melford Spiro, Tom Fallers, Paul Friedrich, and many others. The entire approach was less on specific cultural areas, such as South Asia or Africa, and more on general theoretical approaches regardless of what part of the world you were interested in. Chicago was very strong in South Asia, represented by McKim Marriott, Milton Singer, Nur Yalman, and Barney Cohn (plus many in other departments, such as A. K. Ramanujan in linguistics and in social thought). Chicago was very interdisciplinary with programs such as social thought that were not found elsewhere. As far as Nepal goes, I was the only one interested in it and in some ways I knew more than the faculty did, at least at the level of basic ethnography. My main influences in writing the dissertation were McKim Marriott and Manning Nash.

G: *Personally, who was your favorite anthropologist and what made you choose him/her as an inspiration?*

F: With so many talented faculty members around me it was hard to single out individuals, let alone others at other universities, or those from previous times. For example, I found much to learn from Malinowski, Boas, Radcliffe-Brown, even Tylor, although they were already dated. Among the living, I admired Eric Wolf and Fredrik Barth as well as those who taught me at Chicago, such as McKim Marriott, Manning Nash, and A. K. Ramanujan, who is the only person I've ever personally known whom I regard as an absolute genius.

The answer to your question changes over time. I would say most recently I have been influenced by Pierre Bourdieu and his theory of practice. Sometimes he is considered more sociologist than anthropologist but those labels are unimportant distractions. His idea of practice helps in the understanding of everyday questions and everyday lives which have always attracted me. Some are dazzled by Clifford Geertz's graceful literary prose, and he does write very well—perhaps *too* well since his style can overpower the reader and obscure flaws in his argument. I have always been enchanted by Lévi-Strauss but I can't say he influences me much because although I think what he writes about is fascinating, I also think it's more a product of his own brilliant mind rather than a product of the real world he supposedly is observing. But he's extremely imaginative and creative.

G: *When did you arrive in Nepal for the first time and for what purpose?*
F: I arrived in 1962 from Delhi in a DC3 twin-propeller airplane, also called a Dakota. It was the only kind of plane that could land in Nepal at that time. We had flown from New York to Delhi in a four-engine propeller-driven plane. That was a very long trip and it took us several more days to reach Nepal from Delhi because it was near the end of the monsoons. Two or three times we took off from the Delhi airport and were flying towards Nepal when we had to return to Delhi because of the monsoons. Finally we got through to Kathmandu on September 24th. There were seventy Peace Corps Volunteers in that first Peace Corps group. Our assignments were to serve here two years.

G: *Well, you mentioned in your recently published book,* At Home in The World: Globalization and the Peace Corps in Nepal *(Fisher 2013), how American people felt when they were recruited to Nepal, an admixture of zeal, anxiety, and fear. In your case how did you feel before leaving for Nepal and how did you feel after you arrived here?*
F: I've already mentioned how I felt before leaving, since I had always wanted to come to this part of the world. So the fact that I had this opportunity was simply thrilling. I couldn't believe that this was happening to me. That was before I started two months of Peace Corps training at George Washington University in Washington, D.C., and then one month in the mountains of Colorado. All this time we were basically learning about Nepal. We were studying Nepali language, listening to guest speakers, including the Ambassador in Washington, M. P. Koirala, and even President Kennedy at the White House, and so on. Everything that I learned enhanced and

increased my enthusiasm to come here. I was just dying to get here. In my case there was no fear or anxiety. I just wanted to get here as soon as possible.

My memory is that when we arrived here everything I experienced seemed quite wonderful. We stayed in the Royal Hotel, run by Boris, because that was the only hotel in town that could accommodate so many people. Actually, it was almost the only hotel in Kathmandu, regardless of size. We stayed there for a couple of weeks, as our classes continued. We met more Nepalis, and strolled around the bazaar and the temples. This was the first time any of us had seen these kinds of things. I can only say that my interest increased because I could actually see these temples and see the people selling fruits and vegetables, and see people carrying firewood from the hills around the valley, and I could practice a little bit of Nepali. I just had a wonderful feeling that this is the place where I had wanted to come, and here I was. So how could I be anything other than very happy?

G: *To be honest, did you really find this country, in your term, "wonderful"? Or did you find it godforsaken and boring?*

F: To some extent I was naïve. Sure, for me it was wonderful and exotic, but that can easily be construed as romanticism, which westerners need to avoid. Even on our Rs. 350/month salary, we were better off than most Nepalis. But "godforsaken and boring"? Not at all. Even now, after more than fifty years of visiting Nepal, it is an intensely exciting place not only experientially, but intellectually. Every time I come to Nepal, I discover new things—not trivial things, but important things about the culture that I should have known long ago. Intellectually, Nepal is a bottomless pit of complexity and cultural puzzles which keeps me alert and hopeful that I can contribute something to the understanding of it all.

G: *When you arrived was not long after King Mahendra seized political power by sidelining the dysfunctional Congress government and throwing some of the major political leaders into jail. Today many politicians and intellectuals believe that Mahendra strangled democracy. How were you oriented in the U.S. to Nepal's politics before your arrival in Nepal?*

F: We started training in June 1962, and arrived in Nepal in September. I must say that during our training program we knew that Mahendra had jailed the government; we knew that, but it wasn't presented in a very alarmist or threatening way. It wasn't emphasized. I think probably the American government didn't want to be on record as opposing the King or his government. They didn't want a lot of Americans running around Nepal who would be anti-King, even though the U.S. government was concerned that democracy had taken a step back—the American Ambassador told me that. But none of this had much effect on us. We were too busy trying to learn about how we would live in Nepal to worry about how the political system was working or not working.

G: *Why? Because monarchy as an institution is labeled as absolutist and autocratic today.*

F: I think to a large extent we were disenchanted with American politics. Even with the charismatic and idealistic young Kennedy, we were suspicious of politics as an activity and the corruption that came with it. Also, to some extent we were inclined to think that the political world in Nepal was so different from what we were used to that we were not competent to judge it. Unthinkingly, we were practicing a form of cultural relativism.

G: *How do you evaluate the Panchayat and the Mahendra era, his support towards anthropology and anthropologists? At that time in India anthropologists were not well perceived by nationalist Indians.*

F: Yes, that's undeniable. When I came to Nepal as an anthropologist in the late sixties, access to Nepal, getting a visa to stay in Nepal for a year, for example, all those things were easy to do. I don't know if Mahendra's idea was so specific that he thought he must have anthropologists on the northern border and therefore he would change his policy. More likely he just realized that Nepal needed to open up to the rest of the world; one way of doing that was to be receptive to foreigners or scholars who would have something to contribute to the country, as opposed to tourists, who could only contribute money. And, frankly, I think Mahendra was open to all this. It was certainly an open door policy, I would say, especially compared to India's policy. King Mahendra gave us Peace Corps Volunteers an audience at the end of our tours of duty in Nepal, whereas later on Indira Gandhi evicted the Peace Corps altogether from India. Ironically, Nepal changed, in a few very short years, from being one of the most closed and sealed off countries in the world, to being one of the most open and accessible.

G: *When you arrived as a member of the first Peace Corps group to Nepal you taught as an English teacher. Can you explain your experience, what you did, and how you contributed to teaching English in Nepal?*

F: My first assignment was in Bhaktapur, at Sri Padma High School. I was also assigned to Bhaktapur College, which was held in the same building where one of my students was Narayan Man, now also called Rohit, a prominent political leader. The college met from 6:00 to 10:00 in the morning, and high school from 10:30 to 2:30. So, I was doing both those jobs. I was given the syllabi they were supposed to be learning from. Now, keep in mind that I had no teaching experience. None of us did, which in retrospect seems like a scandal. They should have given us better training, but they didn't. So I took the book the students were assigned to read and tried to express it in simpler English. Some of the readings were quite difficult—for example, prose and poetry written in eighteenth-century English. It's not the English you hear on television or hear spoken nowadays. Whatever the assignment was, I would try to go over it line by line and explain it in my modern American English. They would sit there, seeming to pay attention, so after a while I would ask them if they understood what I was saying, or if they wanted me to repeat anything or explain anything. They would give me the affirmative shake of the head that they did understand (although I had no idea what that shake of the head meant then). I guess no one wanted to admit that they didn't understand it, or they were shy about saying anything, and furthermore they were not used to asking questions.

You ask what I contributed, and I am not sure I contributed anything substantial. I think the Nepali teacher would have done better, because he could have explained it all in Nepali. I taught in a similar way in Pharping Boarding school. If you want to hear English spoken with a modern American accent, then I suppose they got that at least, but otherwise I don't know that I really contributed very much. Maybe I contributed more in working with Nepali colleagues later, by helping edit their scholarship, when I emphasized that good, clear, written English is no one's first language.

G: *In 1964 you were also translator and advisor for educational policy and community development to Edmund Hillary. Can you explain in detail what that was all about?*

F: I still had remnants of this kind of Shangri-La notion and everything that I had heard about the Sherpas seemed too good to be true. They were Buddhist, they were peaceful, they were generous, and they didn't fight or go to war or anything like that. They were always portrayed as generous, unselfish, hospitable people. They were also far, far away in those days, when it took two weeks walk to reach them on foot—remote, just like Shangri-La. They were mountaineers, too, and I had always loved mountains and romanticized anyone lucky enough to live among them. I thought, if I can just go live among the Sherpas, maybe that would be more like the 'Shangri-La' Hilton had described. That seems absurd now, of course, but that's the idealistic and unrealistic way I approached it then. I think fundamentally I was interested in other ways of life, thinking that some must be better than my own (note my lack of cultural relativism here), and, if so, I wanted to find them.

Hillary came to Kathmandu early in 1964. That fall he would be leading an expedition to build three schools in East Nepal: one in Junbeshi, one in Chaurikharka, and one in Namche Bazaar. They needed staff, including teachers, equipment such as books, curriculum, and all those things. I wrote him a letter and said that I had two years of experience in teaching and education in Nepal, spoke Nepali, and could maybe help. When he read my letter he immediately agreed; after the expedition was over he told Peace Corps staff that I had been invaluable. The more I got to know him, the more I admired him, and my developing friendship with him influenced me profoundly. You don't share a tent with someone and not get to know him better. What most impressed me about him is that he treated everyone the same. Whether the Queen of England, a poor Sherpa, or me, he treated us all with the same respect.

I was finishing the Peace Corps in early June, and the expedition was to arrive in September, but he needed somebody to go up to Khumbu before then and make arrangements to build the schools, get the villagers organized to help in that, to buy land from farmers in Lukla to build the air strip there, which was also one of our projects, and generally assess how the schools were doing. So I spent the summer going around and talking to the teachers he had hired already, got to know them, and wrote a report on how I thought things were going, and also worked with a New Zealand mountaineer in the reconnaissance of Mt. Thamserku, another expedition objective. I also negotiated with a few local farmers in Lukla to buy some of their land and drew up the documents to make it legal. I spent four months up there.

Then in the fall the expedition arrived. Sir Ed was going to fly in a helicopter to Lukla to get the airstrip started. Meanwhile I had about 250 porter loads of materials for the school roofs, hammers, saws, nails and other things needed to build the schools, equipment to build the airstrip, and all that. So to get the other expedition members (about a dozen New Zealanders) and all those porter loads to Khumbu, he selected me to be the leader of the two-week approach march. I was in charge of the whole shebang, so that was all quite thrilling and exciting.

During my time in Solu-Khumbu my interest was in the schools primarily, and I was concerned about whether the schools would be disruptive to Sherpa life, partly because they spoke Sherpa and went to monastic schools of their own and became literate in Tibetan. They were Buddhist, and I thought if the schools we were building would represent simply Hindu culture and Nepali language, Sherpas might become disaffected from their own culture. Then I tried to work with and talk to lamas up there, suggesting that they also attend village schools so that they too would learn English and other modern subjects. That didn't happen, but the Sherpa schools eventually became the subject of my M.A. thesis (Fisher 1967). I did my Ph.D. fieldwork in Dolpa, but I returned to the Sherpas about ten years later, partly just to see old friends and be back in their area, with my family this time. I wondered if the schools had been disruptive, but I found that Lukla was causing even bigger changes. It was being used mainly by tourists, not by the clinic Hillary had built in the meantime. We built the airstrip to bring in medicines and to evacuate critically ill Sherpas, but instead thousands of tourists were coming in, so then I realized it wasn't education that was being disruptive, it was tourism—not necessarily disruptive, but inducing huge changes, let's say. Anyway that's how it all came out in my book on the Sherpas (Fisher 1990). I was grateful to Ed for writing a rather generous and positive foreword to my book which was, no doubt, instrumental in selling copies.

G: *Well, can you also describe the socio-political scenario of Kathmandu during the sixties?*

F: First of all, when we came in 1962 there were virtually no tourists; there were a few, but almost none. And there was a small American establishment—the Embassy, USAID, and a handful of missionaries. Other than that there weren't any Americans so there was no kind of American social life. There was a little bit in a sense. I remember the Ambassador invited all of us for Thanksgiving dinner at his house in Kamalkunj. I remember that we had been eating nothing but dàl-bhàt (pulse and rice). Back then I had gotten tired of it although now I consider dàl-bhàt an addiction. The Ambassador served us a very traditional meal with turkey, gravy, mashed potatoes, and pumpkin pie for dessert—"all the trimmings," as we say. It was just unbelievably delicious. I wouldn't call that social life because it was only one day, but it shows how strong the ties of culture can be. I was glad to have the opportunity to reconnect with my own culture, just as Nepalis do when they celebrate Dasai in the U.S.; sometimes they even kill a goat.

Regarding political life, we could see a lot of what was happening in the English press but we didn't really think about Nepali politics. We thought our job was to help the government help the nation to develop. I thought it wasn't our business really whether they should have the Panchayat system or monarchy or something else. We were just doing our jobs. We knew that there were politicians and that the King was an absolute monarch, but politically we were pretty naïve. Symptomatic of my cultural relativism of that time, I sort of liked the idea of an absolute monarch, that he was regarded by many as a deity. I thought (not very realistically) about how the system worked, and I compared it with the American system, where we had so much corruption and petty bickering among politicians (we still do). So we were kind of anti-political, or more accurately, anti-politician, I would say.

I became much more interested in politics later, when I got to know Tanka Prasad Acharya, the patriot and founder of the first democratic political party in Nepal. Conversations with him over several years, when I was writing a book, *Living Martyrs* (Fisher 1997), about him and his wife, severely challenged and changed my rather complacent and culturally relative views—naïve views, I would say now—of Nepali politics.

G: *From the very beginning of anthropology in Nepal, Nepal was portrayed as a Shangri-La, an exotic, virgin land, a land of mystery, a simple and traditional society, terra incognito, and so on. What do you say about these adjectives? Are they accurate or are they all anthropological constructions portraying mere romanticism?*

F: Well, if you said these adjectives were uttered by tourist agents I would say they just want to romanticize the whole country to attract tourists. If anthropologists say them, well—let's take 'terra incognita.' When I went to Dolpa I think I called it terra incognita because it was a valley where no outsider had stayed more than a few days. David Snellgrove had visited it once. Fürer-Haimendorf had passed through it, John Hitchcock had been there, similarly with Corneille Jest. So, I knew it existed, but no one had done extensive fieldwork there and certainly they didn't know about the relationships between that valley and Bhotias to the north and Nepali speakers to the south that I wrote about. So I wouldn't object to calling it terra incognita in that sense.

Other phrases, like 'land of mystery,' are excessively romantic and do turn Nepal into a fantasy land. If you don't take it too seriously that's one thing, but, for example, I wouldn't mind saying that America is a land of mystery too. There are a lot of things I don't understand about my own country. Fortunately anthropologists generally steer clear of such language. I don't want to romanticize Nepal, but Nepal is a very complicated place and you have to admit that there are, or were, places where very little was known. I would say Dolpa would qualify for being characterized that way. Not every place in Nepal, certainly, but I think part of my job as an anthropologist is to dispel this mystery and make it more 'terra cognita,' and that seems to me to be worthwhile for the country and for Nepalis, and for the world. I mean, we all deserve to know each other's countries, so why not Nepal?

G: *There are many places on the globe, so why did you choose Nepal as your pristine field site?*

F: As I've already said, I always wanted to see the Himalayas; seeing what life was like here for two years only whetted my appetite. I had grown up in America and I was restless and wanted to see the rest of the world. As for why Nepal rather than other places, again I suppose if there had been a Peace Corps program in Tibet I would have been interested in that too, but there wasn't. There wasn't anything in the Indian Himalayas or Pakistan, and Sikkim and Bhutan were closed to foreigners, so Nepal was really the only possibility.

G: *I don't understand why Hilton's book* Lost Horizon *dragged you towards Nepal.*

F: I don't remember exactly when I read this book but it was probably as a teenager in junior high school. The focal point is the fantasy land of Shangri-La, where life was not just good, but unimaginably (and impossibly) idyllic. Why wouldn't I, coming from a rather violent country (domestically and internationally), want to find such a serene and tranquil place? Well, I knew that Nepal lies somewhere in the Himalayas, and that was enough for me. What I didn't then realize is that the book is also full of imperialistic overtones, since the head lama of the monastery there was a European.

G: *In terms of coming to Nepal and writing about it, if I asked you which anthropological generation you belong to, what would you say, and why?*

F: Oh! Well, I guess the answer to that question would change over time, but as of now I would have to say I was in the first generation simply because there were so many who followed me, and very few before me. At the time I didn't think much about it, but in fact Fürer-Haimendorf, Hitchcock, and Jest had been in Nepal, even in Dolpa (and Berreman in the Indian Himalayas), so I thought of myself as the new kid on the block, more like second generation. But I was mainly just consumed by my own interest in the country and I didn't think about generations or anything like that. By now it's sort of the opposite, because there are so many anthropologists these days. I can't remember them or keep up with them, even those from my own country. Anyway, nowadays my answer would have to be first generation. I don't know when the big expansion began, maybe it was more in the eighties. I lose track of the decades but at least now, in 2013, there are huge numbers of anthropologists, all of them much younger than me, and they get younger all the time! Some of them are still graduate students, some of them have recently finished their Ph.D.'s, some are senior faculty members. I certainly can no longer claim to be a recent arrival here.

G: *Can you say something precisely about the early American anthropologi-cal research highway to Nepal?*

F: As I've mentioned, Berreman, near Dehra Dun, and Hitchcock in west Nepal, were probably the first. Robert Miller at Wisconsin wrote a little bit about Nepal, but not based on fieldwork. Leonhard Adam was a German but published an article on Nepal in *American Anthropologist* in the late 1930s. Following them there were other Americans of my generation, such as Mel Goldstein, who studied Tibetans, Joe Reinhard, who studied threatened peoples like the Kusunda and Raute, Ortner on Sherpas, and Messerschmidt on Gurungs, among others. After that, there were so many that it's not possible to list them.

G: *In one of your essays you write that "[t]he anthropological research there that had been hardly a trickle in the 1950s and a mere stream in the 1960s now appeared to be a roaring river threatening to overflow its banks" (Fisher 1985:104). If you look at the number of anthropologists during the period of the sixties through the seventies, there are relatively more British anthropologists and publications, compared to the number of Americans and their publications. Why is this? Was Nepal a lower priority for Americans, or was it a higher priority in England? Or something else?*

F: I think something else accounts for the odd fact that Britain, a relatively small country, early on out-produced Americans in Nepal Studies. In the beginning the British, heirs to a couple of hundred years' imperial experience in South Asia, had a head start on those from other countries with little background in South Asia, including the U.S. It took a while for the Americans to catch up.

G: *How do you compare your work with that of your other American counterparts like Hitchcock, Ortner, and Messerschmidt and also with other British anthropologists?*

F: I think the type of anthropological work one does largely depends on the type of department in the particular university a student attends. I believe Hitchcock had attended Cornell. Ortner and I were Chicago products, with its distinctive stance on anthropological approaches. Messerschmidt was from the University of Oregon. Mel Goldstein was from the University of Washington, while Joe Reinhard got his doctorate in Vienna. These different academic backgrounds to some extent determine differences in anthropological approach. One commonality is that, over time, we have all pursued a variety of interests and have made our findings available in a variety of publications.

G: *When you conducted your research in Nepal, most anthropological studies were taking place in the mountain regions. You also opted for the mountains. Was that the anthropological trend of the times, something like 'the higher the better,' or was it because of funding, or your supervisor's suggestion, or something else? Why, specifically, did you choose Dolpa as your locus of study?*

F: Advisors had nothing to do with it—they knew nothing about Nepal. Funding had nothing to do with it. It's more that, in general, going back to my original interest in coming to Nepal, I can't explain why exactly, but I was always fascinated by the mountains, and mountain climbing may have been part of it. (I discovered mountains and mountain climbing at the age of thirteen—the same year Hillary and Tenzing climbed Everest—at a summer camp in Colorado.) How people lived in these mountains was something nobody knew about. Everybody knows the mountains are here, but what actually is the effect of verticality on peoples' lives? That's what I was interested in. From a personal point of view I liked the climate; that doesn't mean that it wasn't bitterly cold during the harsh winters at high altitudes, but I would rather experience that than try to survive a hot summer in the Tarai. I think most anthropologists tend to think along these lines—that is, they want to go to a place where they think it is pleasant to live, or, if not pleasant, at least not too unpleasant. They might not admit it, but that's part of their rationale for doing fieldwork where they do it. Incidentally, sometimes during the freezing Minnesota winters I thought of doing fieldwork in the South Pacific, but I never did, because I had so many friends and colleagues in Nepal. I could not abandon my *dosro ghar.*

When I was deciding where to do my doctoral fieldwork, I knew it would be somewhere in Nepal, because I knew the language by that time. I was thinking about all this in Chicago, and I still was interested in the Sherpas, who struck me as exceptional (even though, having lived several months with them, I no longer thought their lives were idyllic!), but I also had noticed, on the expedition, contrasts among different Sherpa villages. For example, Namche Bazaar was oriented more towards business than agriculture; people there were thought to not cooperate very much and to quarrel and bicker a lot. Khumjung, on the other hand, was a more pastoral, agricultural, social sort of place. They had an annual festival called Dumje, when the whole village is feasted, conducted by turns, *pàlo pàlo*. So I thought, well, I could do a comparative study of dispute settlement in Namche and Khumjung. When people did have quarrels and arguments or fights, how would they settle or resolve them? Would there be differences in how they did this, and would such differences be tied to the economic base?

That was my idea when I left the U.S. and went to SOAS [School of Oriental and African Studies, in London]. I went mainly to learn Tibetan, because I needed that language, but I also wanted to meet Fürer-Haimendorf, get his advice, and so on. His reaction was, as he put it, "But I have already done the Sherpas. There is nothing left to say." He told me about this place in Dolpa that had an interesting language and interesting situation, and he told me he thought that would be a good place for me to go. So, in the end, I took his advice and that's how I ended up living for a year in Tichurong in Dolpa, instead of in Khumbu.

G: *So you became a student of Haimendorf and spent some time at SOAS. Can you tell more about it, or any unforgettable memories from SOAS?*

F: I was there for the first six months of 1968. I wasn't getting a degree or anything like that; I just took part in general SOAS activities. In addition to Haimendorf, Snellgrove was also there, but he didn't teach much and I learned almost no Tibetan. Do you want to hear some gossip about Haimendorf and Snellgrove?

G: *Yes, please go ahead.*

F: Well, Haimendorf and Snellgrove had a kind of competition or, more accurately, jealousy between them. This arose because they were both interested in Nepal, in Tibetan culture in general, and particularly in the Sherpas. The difference was that Haimendorf was an anthropologist while Snellgrove was a textual scholar. Haimendorf did not know Sherpa and did not know Nepali either. Snellgrove didn't know Sherpa but he did know Tibetan—that was his main claim to fame. But he didn't know Nepali. He found an intelligent and very talented young Sherpa monk named Pasang whom he brought back to London to help him translate things. At the same time, Haimendorf was writing his book on Sherpas, so he sat down with Pasang to go over some terms, spellings, and whatever questions he had that he couldn't figure out. Then in his book Haimendorf gave credit to Pasang for his help. Snellgrove considered Pasang to be his personal assistant, even his personal property, and thought Haimendorf had no right to talk to him. His attitude was, "What is Haimendorf doing with my man?" He thought, "I brought him here. It's my money. Pasang belongs to me."

So, when Haimendorf's book came out in 1964 (Fürer-Haimendorf 1964), Snellgrove wrote a review of it. It wasn't just critical; I would say it was snide and rather nasty. Now Snellgrove knew that I knew both of them, so he gave me a copy of his review and said, "Would you please pass this on to Professor Haimendorf?" That put me in an awkward position, in the middle, between them, as I was not taking any stand for or against either one of them. I was just a graduate student and very vulnerable and quite defenseless. Of course, when Haimendorf saw the review he was very, very angry. I think in retrospect that it was highly improper for Snellgrove to involve me in his vendetta against Haimendorf. We talk about blaming the messenger not the message, but fortunately Haimendorf didn't hold it against me, and we remained friends. It is a great pity that grownups, even academic grownups, sometimes act like children. The world of scholarship suffers because of it. Both Haimendorf and Snellgrove would have produced much better work if they had cooperated with each other. It wasn't just the Sherpas (or Dolpalis, I later discovered) who sometimes quarreled!

Also while in London I renewed an acquaintance with Malcolm Meerendonk, who I had met earlier in Nepal. He wrote what I still regard as the best pocket dictionary of Nepali.

Even more memorable, I met Sir Ralph Turner, who invited us to tea at his country house. I had an earlier connection with him, in that my principal at Pharping Boarding School was Dharanidhar Sharma Koirala, who was Turner's colleague and coworker on his monumental *Dictionary of the Nepali Language* (Turner 1931). Dharanidhar had been principal of the government high school in Darjeeling at the time. Dharanidhar told me Sir Ralph had asked him to be co-author of the

Dictionary, but he'd declined. I don't recall why. Perhaps it was just a matter of modesty on his part. I'll never forget Sir Ralph's study, with dozens of dictionaries of Indo-European languages open on long wooden stands. He was working on a massive comparative dictionary of Indo-European languages. His dedication to pure scholarship was an inspiration I've never forgotten. As for your question about generations, on second thought I would count Sir Ralph as the first generation (although he wasn't an anthropologist), Haimendorf and Hitchcock as the second generation, and me and others as the third.

G: *What specifically did you learn from Haimendorf during your short SOAS stay? Was it beneficial, and how do you evaluate him now?*

F: Haimendorf wasn't teaching any specific course while I was there, so I didn't sign up for anything that I could give or not give him credit for. I would say getting to know him was very pleasant and beneficial to me. We would meet socially and he would tell stories of the time he was in India, in the thirties, the time of the Raj, such as when he had dinner with the Viceroy; they ate on gold plates, and two bearers were assigned to each guest, to bring food, take away plates, etc. That world has long since disappeared. Well, as far as the Nepal side goes, you have to say he was a pioneer. He came here, and when you talk about terra incognita, I suppose that's what it was; there was not much known other than some Gurkha history. We knew that Gurungs, Rais, Magars, Limbus and others lived here, but that's about all—nothing about their daily life, nothing about the things anthropologists are interested in. He did that kind of exploratory research and deserves credit for it. If you look at his articles, they contained a lot of information. He was very productive.

Now, he did do intensive fieldwork on Sherpas, but he didn't know Sherpa (no foreigner does), or even Nepali. He needed Dor Bahadur Bista at his elbow, otherwise he would have understood nothing. So Dor Bahadur is the one who got the information and made it intelligible. Look at the literature on Sherpas since Haimendorf's 1964 book. I've counted some thirty books about Sherpas. But he always did have a European aristocratic and patrician air about him. For him, "natives" were to be studied and I don't think he could ever understand how they might be his intellectual equal. This bothered Dor Bahadur Bista, among others (Fisher 1996). And it bothered me.

Those thirty books contain lots of things Haimendorf just didn't know about or didn't ask about, or maybe he thought weren't important. He was an old style ethnographer, and I don't think he realized the depth of understanding that can be achieved in anthropology. Nevertheless, the rest of us stand on his shoulders. We might say, "Oh, he got this wrong. He got that wrong," but he was starting from scratch when there was virtually nothing for him to build on. He was the first man on the ground, and I can't take that away from him.

G: *Did you meet any other Nepali there and do you remember any discussions about Nepal?*

F: It seems strange now, but I don't recall any Nepalis around SOAS at that time. I'm sure there are many now.

G: *Did you meet T. W. Clark, the linguist who was an expert on Nepali, and did you take any Nepali classes with him?*

F: I did meet Clark, but for some reason he wasn't teaching any classes on Nepali. If he had, I would certainly have taken them. My Nepali can always stand improvement.

G: *Haimendorf had already worked a lot on Sherpas and other researchers have also researched them extensively. Why did you choose to write on them, as you did in your book* Sherpas: Reflections on Change in Himalayan Nepal *(Fisher 1990)?*

F: As I've mentioned, I had an initial, rather naïve fascination with the Sherpas. When I went back to the Sherpas in 1974 I was astonished at all the tourist flights going in and out of Lukla, which we had never expected. We built the airstrip to service the Sherpa hospital Hillary was going to build, but instead tourists overwhelmingly dominated the flights to Lukla. Not only were the Sherpa schools bringing change, but so were tourism and mountaineering. I thought this is the big story, even bigger than the schools. So I started working on that and I wrote an article about the tourists which came out in *Contributions to Nepalese Studies*, one of Tribhuvan University's (TU) journals (Fisher 1986a). By that time I already had two book chapters: one on the schools (which was my M.A. thesis) and the other on the tourists.

In the meantime I got interested in something called ethnographic futures. That was a strange development in anthropology, and it has never amounted to much, although I thought it was interesting. The basic idea was that most people plan for the short range, maybe for next year or at most a few years, when they plan for how to get a job, repair a roof, or buy a house. By contrast, the impetus behind ethnographic futures is to get people to think not just about the short-range, but for a longer period too, something like twenty-five years into the future, which people can imagine, but not one hundred years because that's too far into the future to be realistic. So I had the idea of applying this notion to the Sherpas. I talked to some Sherpas and asked them some questions. It wasn't very productive but it forced them to think about more than just climbing Mt. Everest. In twenty-five years they might not be able to climb, so then what would they do to earn money to live? They didn't think about such things much, so I asked them to think about their futures, and that became a chapter of the book. Then I needed a kind of introductory chapter for people who didn't know about Nepal or Sherpas, and I wrote a conclusion. So that was the book.

G: *Ok, then tell me how this book is new to the reader compared to the previous work done on Sherpas by Haimendorf and others?*

F: It's different first of all because I wrote about the cultural consequences of education. That had not been done before. There were magazine articles on tourism, but, again, I was the only one who had gathered data about tourism and included it in a book. So it was different in those ways. Certainly ethnographic futures research was totally different, so different that it has never been repeated and probably never will be repeated. In these ways it was new. Except for Haimendorf's book and a few others, mine was among the first.

G: *Unlike some predecessor social scientists or academicians, you asked Edmund Hillary to write a foreword to this book. Is that because he was a very popular individual in mountaineering, or was it more a kind of marketing strategy, or a way of paying respect to someone who had really contributed so much of his life to this community?*

F: I'd say all of the above, and in a way they amount to the same thing. Because he's a famous person, that contributes to marketing

(Everyone's heard of Sir Edmund Hillary, but who has heard of me?), and part of his fame comes from his post-Everest work with Sherpas. So, they all dovetail together.

G: *What was the thematic focus of your research for your Ph.D.?*

F: The thematic focus was that in the middle of Dolpa lived these people, Taralis, who were, first of all, tri-lingual. They spoke Nepali and Tibetan, but they also spoke their own language, Kaike, though only in three villages, about a thousand people altogether. This made them inter-lingual in the sense that they could talk to people on both sides of them (Nepali and Tibetan), who couldn't talk to each other. They were inter-cultural also, as they were aware of cultural systems and patterns of the Bhotias as well as of the Nepali Hindus, but they also had their own, local culture. They were inter-economic in the sense that they moved goods and services between those two polar ecological and cultural zones. They were interstitial in many ways. So, I didn't want to study them just as an isolated group, which is the way ethnicity is often studied in Nepal; I wanted to see how they were connected to the rest of their valley, the rest of Dolpa, the rest of west Nepal, the rest of all Nepal, and even India and Tibet, because their trade took them to these borders, and over them, as far as Calcutta. So that was my theme. I summed it up in my book by saying that salt and Buddhism flow down the river, rice and Hinduism move up the river, while modernism comes over the pass.

G: *Can you throw light on some of the major grants and fellowships you received for doing research in Nepal, including your doctoral research?*

F: When I came here to Nepal to do my Ph.D. fieldwork, that was under a Fulbright grant from 1968 to 1970. Then I had other National Science Foundation funds, and a Wenner Gren grant in 1974. When I came here to work with the anthropology/sociology department at TU from 1984 to 1986, that was also Fulbright, and I had a Social Science Research Council grant in 1988, and grants from the Smithsonian Institution, Ford Foundation, East-West Center, and other grants from my own college.

G: *Did you face any hurdle or inconvenience in doing your research in Nepal? If so, what was it?*

F: First of all, getting permission to go to the areas near the northern border was a hurdle. That's always been a problem for *bidesis* (foreigners), especially then, in the middle of the Cold War. Harka Gurung, one of the giants of social science in Nepal, helped me in this, pointing out the differences between the rules for Upper and Lower Dolpa. Second, you had to walk for two weeks from Pokhara to get there. I didn't really think of that as a problem at the time, though now I would, since it's a long and difficult trek. Once my wife and I were in Nepal I couldn't even discover whether I could find food in Dolpa, whether they would have enough surplus for me, or whether they didn't even have enough to feed themselves. I couldn't find anybody who knew. So what I did in Pokhara was to buy a year's supply of rice and dàl.

We packed that up in pony loads, and as it turned out we were both right and wrong: on the one hand, we didn't get enough in Pokhara to last for a year, but on the other, it didn't matter because as it happened we could get enough food in Dolpa to stay alive. There were no vegetables or fruit available, not to speak of little hard candies you can easily find in trailside shops elsewhere. It was not an easy place to live unless you had grown up there and were used to eating millet and buckwheat (it was too high and cold to grow rice). Even though I was willing to do it and wanted to do it, still I thought that as far as field conditions go, it was a pretty tough place to spend a year—with no R&R [Rest and Relaxation]!

Another obstacle was linguistic. I spoke some Nepali, and I tried to learn Tibetan in London, but unsuccessfully. Snellgrove basically had no interest whatever in teaching Tibetan; he only wanted to translate Tibetan texts. I wanted to learn the spoken language with a textbook I could work on by practicing with a tutor, or using language tapes, but there was nothing like that available at all. He was a professor at SOAS, but you know if I were an advanced Tibetan student he might have been interested in that, because I could have helped him on something he was doing, but otherwise he was not. So I came to Nepal without functional Tibetan.

And then Kaike of course was not known anywhere except in Tichurong, so I couldn't learn that in London or anywhere else. I faced the dilemma of whether I should take, maybe, three months or six months just to study Kaike or Tibetan, or both, or whether, since I already knew Nepali and the villagers knew Nepali (each of us was equally good, or equally bad), I should just start doing fieldwork in Nepali, getting information. I decided that since I didn't have all that much time, I thought if I just sit there learning Kaike and that's all I have to show for several months of fieldwork, and then leave, it's going to be a waste of time, since I would have no dissertation. I did end up with a two-thousand-word list of Kaike, so it's not that I didn't study the language, but I couldn't speak it much. So that was linguistically the problem; when the villagers were talking among themselves I couldn't understand what they were saying, which was a huge handicap, and I've always regretted not being better prepared linguistically. I would have had a much easier time of it in a Nepali-speaking village, but sometimes the most interesting option is also the most difficult.

Now, the final problem in this regard, I would say, is a problem that wasn't specifically related to Nepal, but I have always been hard of hearing, and I am completely deaf in one ear, which makes it hard even to understand English sometimes. By the way, Ruth Benedict had the same problem; she was deaf, and her deafness compromised her fieldwork to some extent. I've always been unusually sympathetic with her for that reason.

Language competence is not easily judged. On the one hand, I have passed for a native Nepali on the phone, where no one can see my alien features. Perhaps more relevantly, I worked in Dolpa for a year with no translator, although I might have done better work if I'd had one.

But all that's deceptive. It's true that I have a good accent, and at a superficial level I can chat casually and sound like a native speaker, but if the topic becomes at all complicated (or several people are talking rapidly at the same time) I am quickly lost. I can read haltingly, but high-level academic Nepali, such as that in the translation of my book, *Living Martyrs* (Jyuda Sahidharu), I find very difficult. Even Dor Bahadur once told me he preferred to talk anthropology in English, simply because the vocabulary is already there. I remember once at TU some of us faculty were sitting around after classes when an M.A. student approached us. Students could write their M.A. theses in either English or Nepali, and she had chosen Nepali. She asked us, how do you say 'social structure' in Nepali? We spent the rest of the afternoon debating her question.

I believe there are three levels of language competence. The first consists of virtually no knowledge of the language—this would apply especially to the earliest scholars. The second is people like me, who can sound more fluent than they really are, and whose reading skills are quite limited. I suspect this includes most foreign anthropologists. The third level is virtual native speaker proficiency, including reading ability. Virtually no foreign anthropologist (as opposed to a language specialist) ever reaches this level—perhaps one or two. I do try to keep up on relevant scholarship in Nepali, but I have to rely on help for that. I would be better off if I could read all that myself, but learning a language in your twenties makes that difficult, especially if you live in an English-speaking country, unlike Nepalis, usually upper caste and class, who often start studying English as young children and even attend English language schools, and of course they come by their Nepali naturally. It is a much easier process than what we foreigners have to go through at advanced ages. They sometimes say that foreigners have all the advantages. I wonder if they realize their good fortune? How I envy them.

You have to remember, though, that knowing the language is only part of it; you also have to know anthropology. After all, there are millions of Nepalis who speak much better Nepali than I ever will, but that doesn't make them anthropologists.

There is a paradox lurking here. Those with the least linguistic ability have been among the most productive scholars (such as Haimendorf and Hitchcock), while those whose linguistic ability is the most advanced often seem to be the least productive. Can it be that too much knowledge is a dangerous thing? I'm reminded that Edmund Leach said he was able to write his highly original, innovative *Political Systems of Highland Burma* book only because he had lost all his field notes. And it is well known that Lévi-Strauss, perhaps the most original and creative anthropologist of the twentieth century, did fieldwork of quite a low standard, partly because of his minimal linguistic competence in Brazilian languages.

G: *How do you compare the institutional and human resources available in Nepal and the U.S., as a graduate student?*

F: In general, the anthropology department of the University of Chicago was, and perhaps still is, the world's finest—a tremendous, cutting-edge faculty. The library is huge, including the South Asia library. I would say it has everything, including publications in Nepali; what doesn't it have? There was one problem at Chicago, though. They had everything one could wish for about anthropological theory, but nothing about methodology. When I came here I didn't know what to do, except to go someplace and do 'fieldwork,' whatever that was. I had a permit for this, and I had a portable typewriter, but I had no idea about how to do fieldwork.

Regarding Nepal, I would say, in terms of facilities and resources, it had almost nothing then. When I came here, besides Dor Bahadur, I knew Harka Gurung, who was always very kind and helpful. I probably wouldn't have made it to Dolpa without them. I had some kind of affiliation to get a visa, I think probably through the university, although in 1968 hardly any university existed, and certainly no sociology/anthropology department. So, I was pretty much on my own. When I think about it, it's kind of amazing, going to this godforsaken place of Dolpa. It was rough country to live in. I think the only support I had was through the Peace Corps, which forwarded my mail to Dolpa. They put it into the government *hulak* (postal) system so that was a help. That was all I had, but to get some mail every two or three months was better than nothing.

About the fieldwork, I had the impression that it is common practice to have a research assistant, so I should have one too. I advertised in the newspaper to find someone. A couple of people came by, and then this guy came who had an MA in geography. He was about my age, and I explained what I wanted to do. He sounded interested, so I said, "Ok, I'd like you to come and we will be there for a year." He said. "Fine," and then a couple of days before we were going to leave, he said he had to settle some of his affairs first. I said ok, and gave him money for the plane ticket and a couple of months advance for his salary, and urged him to catch up with me as soon as he could because I needed him. I never saw him again. You asked about hurdles? That was a hurdle.

G: *It is commonly thought that any anthropologist studying outside his/her own community should learn the language of the people being studied. In your case what was your experience in learning Nepali and Kaike?*

F: I had learned basic Nepali during Peace Corps training and then while living here. That was the only language I knew. Of course, I knew Kaike existed, as well as Tibetan. I had to choose between learning all three languages and trying to get substantive information. I chose to gather information because I thought I might never get any information if I did nothing but work on Kaike. Also, I was not a linguistic anthropologist. If I was, I should definitely have learned Kaike, but I wasn't. I thought, "Well, I'll somehow manage with Nepali." I didn't like not knowing Kaike (or Tibetan), but I thought I'll have to settle for that because I just didn't have the time, capacity, or resources to do anything more. Sure, ideally I would have learned Kaike and Tibetan, but we don't live in an ideal world. Sometimes we have to compromise, and this was one of those times.

G: *How did you travel from Kathmandu to Dolpa for your research?*
F: From Kathmandu we flew to Pokhara because there was no road then. In Pokhara we got supplies, including a year's supply of food. We needed eight Tibetan ponies to carry it there. We just started walking from the edge of Pokhara up to Baglung and from Baglung to Dhorpatan. In Dhorpatan the Tibetans in charge of the ponies said they could not go any further because we had to cross snow-covered passes. We found some other local people to carry loads the rest of the way. So, seven days to Dhorpatan and seven days to Tichurong, two weeks in all. Towards the end we had to cross two fifteen thousand foot passes and spend the night between the two passes. The problem with that was that if it snowed, we would be trapped between the passes where we were camping. We could be blocked from going either forward or backward. Luckily that didn't happen, but sometimes it does happen to the Tichurong people, who suffer from snow blindness because of it. Obviously I didn't want to turn around and go back to Pokhara, thirteen days behind us, so we took the risk. The next day we descended from the second pass, and I saw this village, with nice-looking fields and houses, and I thought that must be Tarang. When we reached it in the evening we found out that it wasn't Tarang, but another village, Gombatara. We were so tired after our knee-jarring descent from the pass that we spent the night in Gombatara. The next morning we moved on to Tarang, about an hour's walk away.

G: *What was your first reaction when you arrived in Dolpa, in terms of their acceptance of your research? Were you apprehensive about possible resistance, or culture shock?*

F: Not culture shock because I had been out in rural Nepal a lot and I knew to expect a different way of life. I would say at first I didn't think much about it because the people were friendly and hospitable. The first thing I needed to do was find a place to stay. There was one house that a woman had just rebuilt, because her old one had largely collapsed. She wanted five hundred rupees a month rent, and I offered her four hundred, which she accepted immediately. I also had a Sherpa with me, Changchu, who managed the horse loads, the porter loads, cooking, all those kinds of things. He did all that, and more. We couldn't have survived without him.

Then I thought the next thing to do was to make a map of the village. But the village was full of irregular, crisscrossing trails, going up and down and around and then turning back every which way. It was a rabbit warren. I could never get an accurate sense of where I was, because if I was in front of one house, I couldn't tell if that was the same house I had been in back of before, or an entirely different house. It was so complicated that I finally asked the *saciv* (secretary) of the Panchayat to walk around with me. As we passed by each house, he would tell me the name of the householder. So, I was able to make an extremely crude and distorted sketch of the village, not very accurate, but at least I had accounted for every house, each with a name attached to it. Later, with the support of local people we made a better map that showed how the trails actually spread within the village, but it was really hard work. It took me a month just to do what I thought would be a simple afternoon's task, but it wasn't simple at all.

The next step was to find who lived in each house—a census, showing ages, clan affiliation, where they were born, basic demographic information like that. At each house they always asked why I wanted to know whatever I was asking about. Then I would have to explain that I was a student in America, in the twenty-second grade, which they understood since a five-grade school had been started a year or two before, and they understood about grades. I explained that for me to graduate instead of fail, I had to write a book about their village. That struck them as very odd, because they didn't think there was anything at all interesting about their lives, which they perceived as mundane[47]. Anyway, after they had answered the question I had just asked, I might ask another question, and again they would say, "Why do you want to know that?" So it was pretty exasperating. No matter what I asked they didn't want to tell me anything. After some time then they began to be more trusting, and there was one guy who was kind of a political leader, and he decided that I was alright. So he spread the word in the village that, "It's ok, you can talk to him, just answer whatever he asks about and don't worry about him." After that they became more cooperative.

G: *How do you perceive your major research community, the Dolpalis, and where do you locate them in the larger cultural mosaic of Nepal?*

F: That's a complicated question which demands a complicated answer. The Tichurong Dolpalis are problematic to classify. They would be considered by mainstream Hindu Nepalis as Bhotias, but they specifically deny that and would say they are Taralis. But not that either, because if you ask, *"Tapaiko jat ke ho?"* they would say they are Magars. But not Magar like Hitchcock's Magars, and not Kham Magars either. They might say they are Kaike speaking, but even then Kaike is spoken in only three villages, out of the thirteen villages in the valley of Tichurong (nine are Tibetan-speaking and one is Nepali-speaking). They all claim to be Magars, but some spoke Kaike and some didn't, and they all spoke Nepali and Tibetan at least as second and third languages. To people who know about Nepal and don't know about Dolpa, I would say they are Magars, but if they really want to know, then I have to explain all these complications.

G: *And what about the place itself, the physical landscape?*

F: The landscape was very striking. Tichurong is a deep, steep valley cut by the Bheri River, flowing down from Upper Dolpa. Tarang was way up on the hillside of the left bank, probably a couple of thousand feet up from the river to the highest houses. The village was quite compact, but surrounded by fields in all directions. They had used rocks lying in the fields to build stone walls over the centuries. This is where they grew their *kodo* (millet) and *phapar* (buckwheat) and other crops, including *chinu chamal* (a kind of millet, but prepared like rice)

---

[47]   Their exact expression for this sentiment may be found in the Acknowledgments section at the beginning of this book.

and marijuana, which they use for seed oil but not for anything else (i.e., they do not use it to get high). The Himalayan peaks behind them and across the valley were covered with snow, more in winter than during the rest of the year. Their houses have flat roofs so if they have a lot of snow they have to climb up on the roofs with shovels and shovel off the roof. Otherwise snow will melt into their houses. It's high country and from my point of view it's strikingly beautiful, but from the point of view of the villagers, there was nothing special about it. It's just what they had seen all their lives. The Sherpas feel the same way about Mt. Everest.

G: *What was most striking about the Dolpalis? Is there anything that you found really amazing about their way of life?*

F: Yes, that was the main point of my study—that they were farmers, with a strong agricultural economy, all their crops and cattle, but at the same time they were also traders, and trade formed the second layer of their economy. Trading is what took them out of their valley into other parts of Nepal and, now, into the world. And that's what made them the intercultural brokers that they are. If they just stay there they wouldn't know anything else, but they also knew other languages and religions, and so on. That was the striking thing. In terms of daily life, when the women get on the rooftops and have shouting arguments with their characteristic gestures, they heap scorn on each other. That goes on every day. I don't know why their voices don't burn out because they just carry on at the top of their lungs. When I talk about it now, they laugh. They think it is so funny that I would remember that. Another thing that struck me is how hard the physical life was—plowing those fields (using only a single bullock behind the plow), carrying those loads of goods up from the Tarai—they carried them on their backs. It's a very hard life for the people there.

G: *In the field how did you maintain a regular diary or acquire any other particular records?*

F: I would scribble down notes during the day, but every night I would type them up on my little portable typewriter. Otherwise I would forget everything. For instance, while doing census work, I would type the names of the people and their ages, gender, place of birth, how many fields they have, how many animals, and information like that.

G: *What was the most difficult part of your fieldwork?*

F: Getting people to tell me things. They lacked cultural self-confidence because they knew that in some sense they were really Bhotias, but for some purposes they wanted to be considered really Nepalis. They tried to pretend they were both, and something more (Magars). Many of them used Nepali names to disguise their identities when they were in Nepali areas, and their own village names (Tibetan) when they were in the village or in Bhotia areas. They thought they were looked down upon as just rustic, uneducated, unsophisticated people by high-caste Nepali speakers. They were a little worried about that and didn't really want me to find out about all this, which meant they were always practicing 'impression management.' They wanted me to think what they hoped other people thought of them. They tried to do this through their "presentation of self in everyday life," as Goffman put it.

G: *Your wife also accompanied you till the end of your research?*

F: Yes, she was there the whole time, took notes sometimes on what she could learn about women. She sat with the women often and spent a lot of time with them, and helped one of them through a very difficult childbirth. It's hard to imagine any other American woman who could have done all that she did and survived. As I've said before, it was a hard life.

G: *Can you state how long your research lasted, when you submitted your dissertation, and how long it took to publish your book?*

F: First, I spent a month or two making preparations in Kathmandu, getting permits, equipment, etc., and then, after the two-week trek, reached the village on October 30, 1968. I stayed a full year there, thus fulfilling the anthropological preference for and tradition of doing fieldwork for at least a year, in order to see the seasonal agricultural activities, movement between animal pastures, and the annual ritual cycle. So we left also on October 30, 1969. By that time we had had enough. Except for a week's trek to Jumla, and Rara Lake, we had not left Tichurong the whole year. We returned to Kathmandu for five or six months, which were devoted to archival research (and the birth of my son in Shanta Bhawan Hospital). There were *lalmohar* documents to look at in Singha Durbar from the nineteenth century, such as those concerning the salt tax. The person who helped me do that archival research was Dor Bahadur Bista's middle son, Keshar Bahadur Bista, then a high school student, later a Minister. He was invaluable.

After all that, I spent a year (1970–71) writing up at Chicago. I was teaching part time (an interdisciplinary course called Introduction to Indian Civilization) and also writing the dissertation, but the truth is that I just kept postponing the writing. I should have been writing, but I kept thinking, "Oh, I heard somebody has an article somewhere; I should look at that article. I can't start writing until I read that article." Meanwhile, I had been offered a job at Carleton College that would begin the fall of 1971. The terms of the offer were that the salary would be eleven thousand dollars a year if I had finished the degree, but only nine thousand if I didn't. I thought, I can't possibly afford that two thousand dollar fine. I have to get it done.

So, I had to do something drastic. What I did was to change my work routine and to regard myself not as a budding scholar, but as a blue collar production line worker. I vowed that for five days a week I was going to produce five typewritten pages each day, which would add up to twenty-five pages a week. If I finished that quota by noon I could take the rest of the day off. If I didn't finish my quota by midnight, I had to stay up until I had done so. No excuses, no compromises. Saturday and Sunday I could take off, as weekend holidays. Now, if you do five pages a day, in one month you would have one hundred pages, and in two months you would have two hundred pages, and that was enough, so that is what I did. To keep me focused, I had a little sign over my desk which I recommend to people with writer's block. It says 'Don't get it right, get it written.' I wasn't satisfied with what I produced but I got the eleven thousand dollar salary even though I hadn't officially submitted it yet (my committee told Carleton that the dissertation was accepted).

After a year at Carleton I spent a summer in Mexico completely rewriting my dissertation. With the help of my typewriter (electric this time), I finally finished it and sent it off to Chicago. I still wasn't satisfied with it but my wife insisted I send it. Now, the university had a very, very strict policy about the formatting, font size, margins, and other editing and stylistic details for dissertations. In fact what they said was that you can type your own dissertation if you insist, but they strongly suggested using a typist from a list of typists who knew exactly what the university wanted. I accepted their suggestion, and I had to pay her for the job—I think it cost me $300. Then there is an administrative officer in the university whose job is to do nothing but look at dissertations, not to really read them, because he doesn't know anything about anthropology, or whatever the discipline might be. But my typist had done a good job and he approved my final copy (Fisher 1972).

Now, you have to not only write a dissertation, you also have to defend it orally in front of the department faculty. In December I went back to Chicago for the defense. I officially received my degree that fall, 1972, which happened to be ten years after my B.A. During those ten years I had received my B.A., served in the Peace Corps, worked with Sir Edmund Hillary, taught Nepali to new Peace Corps Volunteers, begun graduate study, conducted fieldwork, written my dissertation, and received my Ph.D. These were all things I wanted to do and enjoyed very much doing. I counted myself lucky, even blessed, to have accomplished them all.

I knew I would have to revise the dissertation for publication, so beginning in 1973 I worked on it, and kept working on it, until finally it came out in 1986, much revised, expanded, edited, and improved, but with the same title the original dissertation had: *Trans-Himalayan Traders, Economy, Society, and Culture in Northwest Nepal* (Fisher 1986b). The revisions took thirteen years, which is much too long. I should have done it quicker and not been so perfectionistic. I thought, "I want this to be very good," but even so I thought it could have been better. I usually feel that way about something I've written—disappointed. But then in this case, as in others, when I look at that book many years later, I think, gosh, that's pretty good after all. Did I really write that?

G: *Was your research supervisor familiar with the relevant literature on Nepal?*

F: You use that term, research supervisor, as if it were a common part of graduate education, but I never really had such an advisor, not even as a Ph.D. candidate. Before I went to Nepal and while I was here I had no supervisor. I had no advice, I had no support, I had nothing other than advice from friends like Dor Bahadur Bista and Harka Gurung. When I returned to the U.S. I reported to a committee for my dissertation but they knew nothing about Nepal, so I was my own boss.

G: *So then you can write anything regarding Nepal because nobody was there as a Nepal expert? No one could critique what you wrote about Nepal?*

F: They couldn't critique me about Nepal, but what they could do is to question, generally, if I say the Dolpalis do such and such, well, what is your evidence for this? Or they might say that another of my examples sounds similar to something in Mexico or Nigeria and they might say I should consider those examples comparatively. But the main advantage of the committee is not that they know the specific literature, but that they ask whether I make a coherent, convincing, theoretical argument as a whole in the dissertation, or whether my data support my theory. If I make points that are coherent and make sense, or if they are theoretically interesting, that's what they're looking for, and that's what I needed. But if they say something I've written is wildly off the map, then I'll say, well, Dolpa is just different, you are comparing apples and oranges, or something like that.

The invaluable critique I get on my work now comes mostly from the community of scholars interested in Nepal, especially Nepalis such as you, Chaitanya Mishra, Krishna Bhattachan, and other colleagues at Tribhuvan University, as well as those in America and from countries all over the world.

G: *What did you teach at Carleton, and at what level?*

F: Carleton is what we call a liberal arts college, a kind of institution unknown elsewhere in the world. Our goal is to produce well-rounded students, educated both broadly (in a variety of disciplines, such as sciences, arts, humanities) and deeply (majoring in one discipline, such as anthropology). Such colleges are almost always small compared to large universities; in the case of Carleton, about 1,800 students. We fortunately select our students from among the most highly qualified students in the country and around the world, including Nepal. We usually admit one or two Nepali students per year. It's a four-year college and the degree we offer is a B.A. I taught a variety of topics, including Introductory Anthropology, Anthropological Thought and Theory, Biography and Ethnography, Philosophy of Social Sciences, Growing Up Cross-Culturally, among others.

G: *You also taught courses like anthropology of humor and anthropology of dance. Can you briefly highlight what sort of courses these are?*

F: Well, I originated a course called anthropology of humor which considers humor and laughter as universals, found in all societies, but at the same time highly variable in interesting ways—just as with language. Everyone laughs, but not at the same things. The question is, therefore, what makes some things funny in one culture but not in another, or why something might be funny in one culture but insulting in another—like Sardarji jokes, or, in America, so-called Polack (even the name, Polack, is an offensive term for Polish) jokes. Questions like these are related to social structure. You don't want to be rude, but people may see humor that those inside the culture being made fun of don't think is funny. Humor can be a form of ethnic warfare. And there is always the question of crossing the line between something that might be funny but is not because it's just too grotesquely offensive, such as certain jokes (but not all) about Blacks or Jews or Punjabis. If you look cross-culturally, you find humor everywhere—Hispanic, Norwegian, Jewish, Japanese, Nepali, among many others. That's what the anthropology of humor is all about.

Dance is another typical anthropological approach to something that exists either universally, or almost universally. Why do some people dance in one way, why in couples, or in a dance line, or in ballet? What role does dance play in society? As with humor, there are many examples in the world to look at.

G: *Did you also teach Nepal-related courses?*

F: Yes, but not often courses exclusively about Nepal. In my courses I always used Nepal as an example of something or other. It could be linguistic, it could be family, it could be marriage, kinship, religion—anything. Since I know Nepal better than other places, I can give examples from there much better than I can from South America or Africa, which I've only read about. In that sense Nepal was important in all my courses. When Navin Rai came as a visiting Fulbright professor, he and I gave a seminar on Nepal, but generally courses were more widespread geographically or cross-culturally. Since anthropology is a worldwide science of humanity, they have to be.

G: *Don't you think it is necessary to incorporate Nepal directly in the syllabi?*
F: Certainly Nepal is included in the syllabi, but not necessarily to the exclusion of other places. It is actively taught and discussed, but that might be done more effectively in comparative courses, such as Himalayan Buddhism, which would be about Nepal and Tibet, or village Hinduism, about Nepal and India. Many of my students have graduated and then years later written to tell me all the examples about Nepal that I introduced and which they still remember.

G: *How would Nepal fit into a course like 'People and Cultures of South Asia'?*
F: The South Asia course considered M. N. Srinivas and Haimendorf's tribals, as well as many examples from Nepal. Himalayan Buddhism included examples of Sherpas, Dolpalis and also the Newars of Kathmandu and Patan. So Nepal was very well represented, but the course did not deal exclusively with Nepal. I generally like to examine Nepal in its wider cultural context with Tibet and India and not think of it as an isolated island unto itself. I think that's a danger Nepali anthropologists need to watch out for.

G: *How are the new anthropology/sociology graduates and postgraduates being produced in the U.S.? How are they being mentored in the field?*
F: First of all it helps if you go to a university that has a strong South Asian department or even, as at Cornell, various faculty interested specifically in Nepal. That's where you get mentoring as a graduate student, not just at the dissertation level, but also by taking courses or studying for exams. At a graduate university, the other graduate students at your level are all struggling with the same requirements. You are all trying to master the same material. You all get similar reading lists. You should all read certain classics of Nepali anthropology or South Asian anthropology or anthropological theory.

So, in a way, in the process of talking to each other and meeting each other, you mentor each other. I remember at Chicago we first-year students would meet every Saturday morning just to go over various readings for that week. Some of us understood some things better, others understood other things better, so collectively we all benefitted and learned more. As a Philosophy major, I had a lot of catching up to do, and this helped me more than anything. The chair

of the Anthropology Department even admitted that he expected us
to learn more from each other than from the faculty.

G: *You taught undergraduate students at Carleton; have you also supervised
any Masters or Ph.D. students researching on Nepal?*

F: Well, a couple of my undergraduate students came with me to
Nepal as research assistants. So that was a research experience for
them. Another example would be when other universities ask me
to sit on committees of their Ph.D. students. For example, there is
a Ph.D. student at the University of Wisconsin in Madison who is
doing fieldwork in Bhutan, studying professional arts like painting
and sculpture, and their relation to modernity. Madison didn't have
anyone in the South Asia area, so I'm helping them out with that, as
an external examiner.

G: *Apart from this did you supervise any graduate or postgraduate students
who did his/her research in Nepal?*

F: I'm often asked by graduate students from different universities, who
have similar interests and who have read some of my work, to discuss
their research plans. Sometimes I've been asked by universities in
places like Arunachal Pradesh or West Bengal to be a reader for
dissertations there, but they are not about Nepal specifically. In
such cases I don't know the particular student, but they send me the
dissertation, and I agreed to do that.

G: *Many people have interpreted your book* Trans Himalayan Traders *(THT)
[Fisher 1986b] in various ways. Can you briefly summarize it in your own
words?*

F: I would say a brief summation is that it is about a group of people in a
remote valley of northwest Nepal who are connected with the world
in fairly complicated and non-obvious ways. Relations with people
beyond their valley are mediated primarily through transactions
of one kind or another. They could be transactions of personality,
transactions of goods, like salt, or even of impressions—different
kinds of things. My problem was to analyze how those transactions
inform the culture and make the people there what they are. In a
significant way, if they didn't have the transactions, they wouldn't be
the same people.

G: *Instead of using the actual name (Sahar Tara) of your village, why did you choose to use a pseudonym for it? Also, how did you choose the word Tarangpur, because it sounds like a place in the Tarai.*

F: That's a good and relevant question. Every anthropologist has to consider the anthropological code of ethics, which is authorized by the American Anthropological Association. The code states that our primary obligation is to the people that we study, not to the funders, not to the universities, and not to the governments (including the Nepal government) or organizations which support our research. Our primary obligation is to the people we study. If there is a conflict between that and anything else, then the people always come first. That principle cannot be compromised.

Here's where the pseudonym comes in. If I say that the people in Sahar Tara poach *kastura* (musk deer), I can't ignore the fact that poaching is illegal. If I write about the poaching in my book and somebody in the government reads it, that might create a problem. They might go arrest the poachers. I feel it's my obligation to prevent that from happening, to protect the people I lived and worked with, and who trusted me. I want to tell the truth about the place, but I don't want to incriminate the people who live there. One way to avoid that is to make up different names, fictitious names, for particular people. But even that won't always work because people can be identified in other ways. Another is to hide the name of the location altogether, and that's basically what I did.

But, I have to admit in retrospect that anybody who wanted to find the village I call Tarangpur could easily do so. For one thing there's a map in the book that shows all the thirteen villages of the valley of Tichurong. All except Sahar Tara are listed with their real names. Now, if you are there and you see there are thirteen villages and only one doesn't seem to be represented on the map, which also shows the name of one village which no one recognizes, anybody can figure out they are the same place, especially since I've already told the reader that I have used a pseudonym for one of the villages. I didn't think all that through at the time, but I thought this will be my solution – certainly not an ideal solution, but at least it hides the identity to some extent and protects the people.

As far as the name Tarangpur is concerned, it's called Sahar Tara in Nepali—Sahar because it is a "city" in the context of Dolpa. Although it is a small village, it is the biggest village (roughly seventy-six houses) in the entire district of Dolpa, except for Dunai, the capital. Pur is a suffix meaning city (as in Gorakhpur, Singapore); Tarang is the Kaike word for Sahar Tara, hence the pseudonym Tarangpur. Now, nobody is going to know all that. It's mainly just a kind of cute etymology. But even so it omits the Tibetan term for Sahar Tara, which is Ba.

G: *Much anthropological work is less concerned with economic life, and more about ritual, culture, etc., but your book is about economic production and exchange in highland Dolpa. Why did you decide to make this the basis of your study? In Nepali society there are several specific trading communities such as Newar, Thakali, and Marwari, but your book seems to establish Magars as an equally successful trading community.*

F: Well, to get back to my actual fieldwork as an anthropologist, I wanted to understand as many different things as I could. So I have a lot of notes about ritual and politics and so on, which didn't end up in the book, but which I hope I'll be able to write about elsewhere. You ask why I decided to make economic life the focal point. The fact is I didn't decide it in advance: I had no preconceived notions about it. It's just that the longer I was there, the more I began to see this economic component as fundamental to understanding the rest of the culture, which was incomprehensible without it. In other words, the evidence dictated the analysis, rather than the other way around.

It's true that compared to the Thakalis and Newars, the Taralis are not as big or as successful. But the fact that they have been traders conditions them for new opportunities now, such as that given by *yarsagumba* [*Ophiocordyceps sinensis*], or Tibetan carpet manufacturing. They are somehow culturally ready for that. I think if they were just farmers they wouldn't have a clue about these things. Because of their transactional lives, they were culturally prepared for these other opportunities. Their experience in trading trains them somehow to recognize economic opportunities because when you are a trader you have to think, "Should I buy this? Should I sell that? And at what price? How can I maximize profits?" I think that way of thinking is helping them now. They may never be as big or as successful as Thakalis, but for becoming what they are in the process of becoming, I think trading is even more important now. In the context of the modern world, the importance of trading is even more important now than I thought it was forty-five years ago.

G: *You locate the Magars in their particular environmental setting, how they make their niche or choose their adaptive strategy. You could have grounded your study in the established theoretical approach of cultural ecology, but instead you chose Barth's transactional model. Can you explain why?*

F: Actually, I do think THT is relevant for cultural ecology. I have been considerably influenced by cultural ecology (and writers such as Roy Rappaport, Marshall Sahlins, and even Barth in some of his earlier work), and I probably should have acknowledged it more explicitly because it fits in well with the lines of my thinking. I suppose I didn't mention it much because cultural ecology was not much in vogue in Chicago—a good example of sociology of knowledge being dictated by institutional epistemologies.

G: *Ok then, is the engagement of these Magars explainable by 'economic necessity' or by 'ecological necessity' or something else?*

F: To say it is a necessity would vastly overstate the case. It's not a necessity; they could certainly live on their agricultural production and cattle and acquire salt through the old salt trade. But to maximize the situation they're in and acquire other kinds of goods not available locally—cotton cloth, tennis shoes, cigarettes, metal, sweets, shirts—they have to be prepared to give up something they produce, other than Phapar. They need to optimize their strategy to acquire them, involving not only cash, but also bartering. They were moved to do that as a way of getting things they need or want; according to local thought, needs and wants are the same thing. I would call it a 'strategy' for dealing with what they expect from life, nothing more than that.

G: *You are planning to publish a second edition of THT entitled* Trans-Himalayan Traders Transformed *by adding life history chapters of some of those Taralis. Some of it Hitchcock had sent to you. Can you mention what it is all about?*

F: Basically, I concluded that the modern turn for Taralis rests not on some broad, systemic cultural characteristics (such as transactions), but on idiosyncratic details of a few people who have converted local economic success into even more successful modern economic ventures. To show that's the case, I want to give a few examples of these particular Taralis. The most prominent one is Chandra Man Rokaya, whose life story, told in his own words, takes up more than half the book. Hitchcock had collected much of the material, then sent it to me many years ago, when he could no longer proceed with it. I brought it up to date with Chandra Man. It's ironic that in some ways he's been the most successful, and at the same time possessed none of the advantages of the others. That argues, counterintuitively, against my main point, but it also shows how difficult it is to generalize about situations like this.

G: *Those individuals represented in your life histories once engaged in trans-actional trade in Dolpa and are now established in business and politics in Kathmandu. How do you see the trajectory, shift and changes in their lives?*

F: It's a dramatic change for them. They have become educated, at least through SLC level, established businesses, mainly in the carpet manufacturing sector as well as in *yarsagumba*, live mainly in Kathmandu, and a few travel to countries in Europe, Singapore, Hong Kong and U.S. Even many of those still in the village are now literate, have cell phones, and fly back and forth to Kathmandu.

G: *Now I would like to ask about another book—*Living Martyrs: Individuals and Revolution in Nepal *(Fisher 1997). You somehow shifted from the usual anthropological tendency to continue ethnographic work in a different community, and instead all of a sudden you came out with a book focusing on the life history of Tanka Prasad Acharya and his wife Rewanta Kumari. Why did you move in this new direction?*

F: This was back in the mid and late eighties, before the *andolan* or anything like that came along. I remember thinking that here I was in the middle of a largely Hindu country, with a Hindu ruler and monarch. And it would be fair to say that the country was basically run by Bahuns and Chetris. They held the top positions, and the reins of power were pretty much in their hands. I realized I didn't really know much about that part of the country, at least not compared to the more Buddhist and Tibeto-Burman speaking groups along the northern border that I'd gotten to know. I thought I ought to learn more about Hindus, maybe by studying a village somewhere.

But I also knew that there are other ways of doing anthropological research, and the study of life histories is one of them. It's nothing new; it goes back as far as Boas and his students. Lots of people do them. I wondered how Bahuns, with their high caste and all that, might be changing in modern times, because I had lived with a Bahun family in Bijeswori in 1963. I thought of doing a life history with that traditional family, but I was more interested in a Bahun who was adapting to and becoming part of modern life, to see how that situation might look.

I don't remember the details, but while I was at TU, at one of the gatherings of Nepalis and Americans I ran into Meena Acharya, who had recently completed her Ph.D. at University of Wisconsin, and some of her brothers and sisters. They asked what I was doing, and I told them I wanted to do a study of Brahmanic culture, and Meena immediately responded, "Why don't you do my father?" I had never thought of that, but as I thought about it, it seemed both interesting and plausible, and Tanka Prasad and his wife were both keen to have me do it. That's how it got started. Of course they were both literate and could have written it themselves if they had wanted to. But they also knew very well that they would never do it; they just weren't organized and disciplined enough for a task like that. They were blessed with extraordinary qualities and talents, but writing a book was not one of them.

I was glad to have the help of the family because neither Tanka Prasad nor Rewanta Kumari were very good storytellers. I mean, they told good individual stories, but I was trying to construct more of a narrative. He would start one story, then switch to something else thirty years before, then another thing ten years later, etc. So I had to record all this and enter it on the computer, and then move all the text around so that it would tell a coherent story. I had to keep doing this, every time I talked to them. I also had to figure out what the chapters would be, because neither they nor anyone else lives their lives according to chapter headings. Tanka Prasad and Rewanta Kumari lived their lives one day at a time, as we all do.

Gradually, I realized I should have a chapter on childhood for each of them, so I gathered all the childhood fragments together, but even then you have to put them in the right order, showing how one thing leads to another. And then chapters on marriage, political activism, being in prison (for him), being out of prison (for her), being released from prison, becoming prime minister, being married to a prime minister—

assembling all these things was like putting together a giant jigsaw puzzle with thousands of pieces. I had to figure out which piece went where. You said the book appeared all of a sudden, but actually it took me more than ten years to finish it. It was a struggle.

I usually start writing a book because I think it's going to be easy. I do that with everything. In this case I thought just recording their lives as they passed through time would be easy, but it wasn't. Tanka Prasad was not only a Bahun, but he was also a political activist and a modernist. His life and persona contained everything I wanted to know, so I wanted to take his life, and hers, and make them the focus of the study rather than some community. It was a person-centered ethnography.

G: *Why Tanka Prasad when there were so many other possibilities?*

F: These things just sort of happen accidentally, not according to a finely worked out plan. You accidentally meet certain people and not others, then move in a certain direction rather than going somewhere else. It turned out to be a lucky series of accidents that I did this project in this way, since I was able to contribute something as an anthropologist, but also contribute to our understanding of the political history of Nepal. Tanka Prasad's full story had not been known before, at least not the way he saw it.

G: *Ok, can you now please briefly summarize the book?*

F: I would say this is the story of the relation of individual human beings and action to large, macro-scale movements like democracy in Nepal, government in Nepal, distribution of power in Nepal, the modernization of Nepal, the globalization of Nepal. So it's about that, and I think many things wouldn't have happened in Nepal had Tanka Prasad not taken the leadership role he did. He was President of Praja Parishad, the first democratic political party in Nepal. That's one point. The second point is to see that there's more to being a Brahman than automatically observing a hundred different dietary rules or worrying about pollution all the time.

The Brahmanical emphasis on the importance of education was fundamental, though, since Tanka Prasad read voraciously all his life. Without that intellectual curiosity he would not have become a political radical, determined to overthrow the autocratic and despotic

Ranas. He definitely wanted a modern, democratic political system from the time he was a child. So for him, part of the meaning of Brahmanism had to do with social justice, and being politically active and responsible for promoting it. He also wanted to show that there was no contradiction between being a Brahman and undertaking an active, modern political life and fighting for social justice. It was he, after all, who led untouchables into Pashupatinath.

In one sense he was very traditional in his life; he was not anti-Brahman by any means, but he did not hesitate to make changes to tradition too. In a way his wife was a better example because she was a very observant Bahun, much more so than he was, but even she made changes. Formerly, she would not eat tomatoes or onions, and other foods, but while he was in prison, she came into contact with other political wives who ate other things, so she thought, "Well, my husband is in prison and he's eating what's available, so sitting on the outside, I'm going to eat other things too," regardless of caste rules.

G: *What kind of comments and reactions did you receive on* Living Martyrs, *as compared to your first book?*

F: You probably know more about that than I do. On the back cover of the book there are a couple of quotes from Indian journals and newspapers, which were positive (they wouldn't put them on the book cover if they weren't positive!). There was also one which didn't quite make the book cover, by Pratyoush Onta, which dismissed my work as the product of "kuire ignorance," a racist slur which was unique in my experience. As far as I know, other reactions have been positive. The book has been out of print for ten years now, so lots of people don't even know about it. One development I am really proud of, though, is that the book was translated into Nepali, and published as *Jyuda Sahidharu* (Fisher 2000b). It was the first Western anthropology book translated, in its entirety, into Nepali. I was very gratified with this development since it meant that millions of Nepalis could now read the story of one of the heroes of the nation. Most Nepalis recognize his name, but know little else about him. Even one of Tanka Prasad's granddaughters said she picked up the book one evening and found it so fascinating she couldn't stop reading till she had finished it at dawn. While she was familiar with some of the material in scattered fashion, she said she had never known the whole story until it was assembled this way.

G: *Why do you think Onta's short* Kathmandu Post *op-ed commentary titled "Against Kuire Worship" (Onta 1997) is offensive or, in your terms, a "racist slur"? I read this piece and I also read the one in which you reacted to it some years later in the same newspaper (Fisher 2000a). Do you find the commentary itself problematic or are you just dissatisfied with the term he used,* kuire?

F: The commentary had little to say about the book and was mostly about the praise heaped upon it (and, by implication, on me, since I was the only *kuire* on the program) by the high officials assembled for the launch, including Prime Minister Sher Bahadur Deuba, who officially released it. Onta seemed offended at the attention paid to me (i.e., a *kuire*) as opposed to the neglect accorded Nepali scholars.

I take his point, although I don't see how I can be blamed for the reception I was given—did he expect me to denounce the Prime Minister on the spot? Moreover, he seemed to undercut his own point when he mentioned that the prestigious Madan Puraskar prize was awarded to a Nepali scholar Rajesh Gautam for his book on Tanka Prasad (Gautam 2046 v.s.)—not to me for my book! As far as the word *kuire* goes, my understanding is that it's a pejorative term used for light-skinned, blue-eyed people. Sure, it's used innocently by village urchins to refer to Western trekkers, but it doesn't seem to be the kind of terminology intended to promote mutual respect or scholarly discourse.

I admit to all sorts of ignorance, but *kuire*? Perhaps I'm spoiled, since in The Association for Nepal and Himalayan Studies (ANHS) we pride ourselves in our attempt to build a strong, supportive, diverse, international, active, and tolerant scholarly community (which includes many Nepalis), where we all learn from each other. Onta apparently prefers a different, more divisive and destructive form of association. Well, to each his own. In my experience, going back some fifty years, no one I've known, Nepali or *bideshi*, thinks of Himalayan scholars as divided into two groups (well…maybe Haimendorf did), as Onta seems to. Those of privileged high class, high-caste origin still wield great power. My job is to speak truth to power—his. If not me, who? If not now, when?

G: *In our daily usage we simply use* kuire *to refer to foreigners. As you know during the sixties, when bideshis flocked to Nepal, Nepali people perceived them differently in terms of culture and appearance. Many foreign anthropologists accept and call themselves bideshis or* kuires *in their texts. If so, how can this word, which is accepted by all, be considered a racist slur?*

F: *Bideshi* is a neutral term that can be used for any foreigner (including, for example, Indians), and those *bideshis* who are melanin challenged (not Indians) might use the term *kuire* humorously among themselves, the way African-Americans might use the term *nigger* among themselves, but no white person uses it publically to refer to a black person. *Kuire* is not used "simply" to refer to foreigners, which is why in your opening statement you referred to "foreign scholars" rather than "*kuire* scholars." *Kuire* is offensive because it's meant to sting—Onta's article was no joke. English has a rich vocabulary of insulting terms for 'others' (e.g., *wop* for Italians, *kike* for Jews), but none, surprisingly, that I can think of for Nepalis, so I'm unable to make the neat, parallel, mirror case. This is surely one of the very few instances where Nepalis are ahead of Americans in creating and using racist terminology. I'm sure Onta has something to teach us here.

G: *Have you gone through the popular book by historian Yogesh Raj* History as Mindscapes: A Memory of the Peasants' Movement of Nepal *(Raj 2010)?*

F: No, I know of Raj's high reputation as a scholar (as I know of Onta's), but I don't know this particular book.

G: *This book is about the life story of the peasant leader, Krishnabhakta Caguthi, locating him in time and in the role he played in the peasants' movement in Nepal. In the introductory section of this book Raj argues that*:

James Fisher's otherwise well-worked volume on life-story of the ex-premier Tanka Prasad Acarya provides scant information on the technique used in producing the text. From the scattered references to the method he followed, we know, for example, that the author firstly handed over a set of questions to the narrator before actual interviewing (Fisher 1997: 16) and that the interview was tape recorded. . . . When read with the examples given for narrator's autonomy in conversation,

Fisher 's assessment about his own role sounds modest. Unfortunately, he fails to discuss an outline of his technique, which could have helped others to establish their own methodologies in doing life-histories. (2010:14–15)

Do you agree or have anything to say about what he says?

F: I thank you for bringing this to my attention, and I think his critique has merit. My main defense would be that he too generously attributes scientific rigor to me when he says that I fail to discuss an outline of my "technique." Truth to tell, I never thought I had anything that I would dignify with the label "technique." I was far more pragmatic. My rule is: use anything that works. I shamelessly grabbed on to any seat-of-the-pants method available to get information, including sometimes asking family members to ask Tanka Prasad or Rewanta Kumari questions I did not seem to be able to successfully pose. I would defend that tactic to the extent that in the end it enhanced and clarified the narrative. Still, he's right that it would be useful to have well-described methodologies that others could use or modify. I just don't think that I'm qualified to supply them. Methodologically, I'm out of my league here.

G: *How do you evaluate Tanka Prasad compared to other political figures of Nepal?*

F: I would say two things. One is that politically he was never very successful in a populist sense. Yes, he was prime minister, and he accomplished much as prime minister and in his struggle against the Ranas. But he never won an election, not even in his own district. Now, BP Koirala won and Ganesh Man Singh won; compared with them, he was never successful in a populist sense. It is also true that he had a lot of political enemies, or at least opponents. What's interesting about this, though, and this is the second point, is that even his opponents all agreed that he was absolutely, uncompromisingly, incorruptibly honest. That can rarely be said of any politician, whether in Nepal or in any other country in the world. He deserves all credit for that.

One more point is that though he might not have been successful as a practicing politician, it was he who founded the first democratic political party in Nepal. They did not successfully overthrow the Ranas, but he scared them so much that they executed his friends (the Four Martyrs; the Ranas couldn't execute him because executing a Brahman would involve them in too much *pap*). He remained true to his principles. He refused to leave the jail when released, after ten years' imprisonment, unless his fellow political prisoners were also released.

He was very nationalistic. Other political leaders, like BP, Ganesh Man, and others, were products of India politically and educationally. Tanka Prasad always said he would never flee to India, even if it meant going to jail in Nepal. Again, he was not at all anti-Indian, he just wanted to be clear that he was firmly and irrevocably a Nepali, no matter what the consequences of that stance might mean for him. Other leaders respected him for that. Before BP went to New York for cancer treatment, he went to get *tika* from Rewanta Kumari. So BP respected Tanka Prasad as a father, or elder brother, to him and others (within the household, he was referred to by all, including me, as Bua). It was a matter of belonging to different generations, and BP acknowledged that.

G: *Well, this book was translated into Nepali also (Fisher 2000b). Was it well distributed and did it reach the wider Nepali masses? Do you know how many copies were sold?*

F: I honestly don't know about either the English or Nepali editions. His daughter, Meena Acharya, with Arvind Rimal as translator, organized the Nepali edition, but I didn't even know they had done that till she sent me a copy in the mail. I am told that the translation is extremely good. I told her to distribute copies to every member of the parliament, but I don't know if she was able to do that. I think translating it into Nepali was a very good idea because now most Nepalis can read it, although they would have to find a copy first.

G: *Your recent book,* At Home in The World *(Fisher 2013), is easily available now because of the Nepali publisher. Can you briefly say what this book is all about?*

F: The Peace Corps was perhaps President Kennedy's signature accomplishment. It was he who established it. He said America has to be part of the world, including what was then called the Third World, and that to understand it we have to go and live in it. We have to be a sympathetic audience for the rest of the world. Then, he said, when we Volunteers return to America, we need to help educate the rest of the country on what we've learned in these other countries. Among the 139 countries who have hosted the Peace Corps, Nepal was one of the first, and I happened to be in the first batch to come to Nepal. It was just a lucky accident of history for me—the right person in the right place at the right time. Furthermore, I call myself a packrat, which means if somebody hands me a note or article or document, I keep it. I store it away. I kept such things I got fifty years ago, and then found them in my files. I thought the founding of the Peace Corps in Nepal was an important event for both Nepal and the U.S., and as a member of the first group, with all sorts of documents (including my own extensive diary from those times) I was uniquely qualified to talk about all that. So I did.

Now, instead of focusing on the first group, I might have talked about the Ambassador or foreign policy or the Peace Corps bureaucracy or something else. But I thought it would be interesting to let other people—Nepalis and Americans—know what it was like to come here so long ago, when we were so naïve, not much educated about the country, and then show that it turned out to be a good idea. Lots of conservative people in America thought it was a terrible idea, but even they now agree that it worked out very well. No conservative politician has any objection to the Peace Corps now. Nepalis liked it. Americans liked it. Some countries, like India, later kicked the Peace Corps out because of some diplomatic disagreements, but nothing like that ever happened in Nepal. So if people want to know what America and Nepal were like in 1962, what Americans and Nepalis did, working together at the grassroots level, and what the Americans did in the following fifty years back in the U.S. when we were double agents (telling Americans about Nepal, after having told Nepalis about Americans), they can read about it. The two-way globalization process—that's basically what the book is about.

G: *All of your books were published outside Nepal, but this time your publisher was Himal Books from Nepal. Why did you decide to do that?*

F: Yes, my other books were published in the U.S. by University of California Press, and by Oxford University Press in Delhi. *At Home in the World* was first published by Orchid Press in Bangkok, as part of their Bibliotheca Himalayica series, and then reprinted by Himal Books.

G: *If it had already been published from Bangkok, why again from Nepal?*

F: I wanted Nepalis to be able to afford to buy the book. To give you a comparative example: in the U.S. the book costs twenty-five dollars in a book store, but in Nepal it's only six dollars (NRs. 590). There's a world of difference between six dollars and twenty-five dollars. This way Nepalis can read it. And the great thing about it for me is the quality of the Nepal edition. It's identical to the Bangkok edition in quality—of the print, the ink, the paper, photos and binding—everything. You have world class publishing here, which is something to be very proud of, especially when you compare it to how publishing was done here only a few decades ago. It was abysmal.

G: *Are globalization and Peace Corps separate entities? Don't you think the Peace Corps itself is a manifestation of globalization, since it belongs to America?*

F: Yes, the Peace Corps is certainly a part of this worldwide globalization, but it is a two-way process, because we were globalized by Nepalis. Then, having been globalized, we helped globalize the U.S., moving it away from its provincialism. There are thousands of examples of globalization going on, not only economically, but also culturally, socially, and even individually. I also said in the book that we as Peace Corps Volunteers were unaware of any of this. First of all, nobody talked about globalization; we didn't think about it and we didn't realize it was going on, or that we were part of it. Only now, looking back, can we see that that's what was happening. This process was starting and the Peace Corps was a good example of it.

G: *Was the recruitment of volunteers, including you, based on humanitarian or political grounds?*

F: Both. I would say that from the individual point of view it was very clear that some of us were motivated by adventure, others wanted to do good by answering "Kennedy's call," others wanted to see the world, some just wanted a job. From a political point of view (Kennedy's point of view), it was important in the sense that since ours is a very parochial country—for example, unlike Nepal, we are essentially a monolingual country—we needed to expand our political expertise. We live very far from any other country, other than Mexico, since Canada is almost the same, culturally, as the U.S. We are very far removed from Asian, African, and European countries. If we are going to exist in the world Americans have to learn about it, and what better way to do this than to send Peace Corps Volunteers, which cost practically nothing. So, send them out to the world, to countries like Nepal and India and even China, which has Peace Corps Volunteers now, whereas formerly we were bitter enemies. Politically it's good for Americans to be in these countries, and each country benefits. To get to know each other, learn each other's languages—only good can come from that. No one's motive was political in the modern sense of "political," involving parties; I would say motivation was political only in the special, globalization sense.

G: *Now let me ask about sociology/anthropology in Nepal. As you know the discipline was formally institutionalized in Tribhuvan University (TU) in 1981. You received a Fulbright 'Senior Lectureship' grant for two years (1984–1986) at TU. Did the university or any member of the Central Department of Sociology/Anthropology (CDSA) invite you, or did you apply for this grant personally?*

F: I had stayed in touch over the years with Nepali intellectuals and those interested in anthropology, and none more than Nepal's first anthropologist, Dor Bahadur Bista. I owe more to Dor Bahadur, both personally and professionally, than I can say. My life would not have been what it is without him. So when he was playing an instrumental role (along with Chaitanya Mishra) in the establishment of CDSA, we talked about the possibility of my coming to lend a hand to this new enterprise. I was wildly enthusiastic about doing so. The Fulbright Commission had a program to fill such needs. Dor Bahadur applied for the grant and, when he got it, asked me to take the job.

G: *How or in what way did you contribute to the recently opened department in TU? How did you see your role at CDSA then?*

F: To begin with, I was a regular lecturer teaching papers (what we call courses) there. But I was also part of discussions about the curriculum. These were not just technical questions about numbers of credits, but about what anthropology in Nepal should be. Dor

Bahadur felt strongly that anthropology in Nepal shouldn't just be a carbon copy of anthropology in the West; rather, it should be bent to the needs of Nepal. That meant that we should emphasize certain approaches, to development, for example, rather than, let's say, the cerebral, French rationalist approach of Claude Lévi- Strauss, which was all the rage then.

G: *Did you teach or develop any specific courses in the department? Who were your students? Were you happy with the way the department was functioning? Was there any kind of conflict among the faculty members? Among several, the one I have heard is that there were some members who advocated for separate departments of sociology and anthropology, whereas others were adamant that they should not be separated. Do you know about this or any other disputes?*

F: My recollection is that I taught anthropological theory and probably some sort of introductory course and also a course on Nepal. The students were just whoever had applied and been accepted. As with any student body, some were extremely interested in the material, others were quite indifferent to it and studying it only because they wanted an M.A. after their name. One problem is that for practical purposes there were no usable faculty offices, so no productive scholarship could be accomplished in Kirtipur. Instead, when we didn't have classes, we would sit outside and chat in the sun. (We called it *gham tapnu*, because the offices were so cold and miserable no one ever used them, and most of us didn't even have one.) That was fun but it didn't build a cohesive intellectual unit. Another problem, of course, is that often classes didn't meet at all, because of holidays or, more commonly, strikes. Since my own department at Carleton is a joint one, combining anthropology and sociology, it seemed natural to me to follow a similar intellectual organization at TU. I think the two disciplines are in many ways complementary. Anthropology tends to ask big questions not very rigorously, while Sociology pursues smaller issues with more methodological precision. I think dialogue between them can result in much enhanced and broader perspectives. As for arguments about this at the time, I don't have any solid memories about it. People may have had their own views on it, but everyone seemed content to let things slide along the way they were for a while. I think we regarded ourselves as lucky to have a department at all.

G: *In a book launch of your newly released book, the sociologist Chaitanya Mishra explicitly called you the father of the journal* Occasional Papers of Sociology and Anthropology, *published by the CDSA. What do you say about that? What and how did you contribute to the creation of that journal?*

F: Oh! First of all, it's very flattering to be described that way, but it's an exaggeration. The CDSA had just gotten started when I was here, under Chaitanya Mishra's leadership. I remember thinking that my colleagues at the university were a little intellectually isolated after leaving graduate school, and some had not yet pursued an advanced degree. They needed to be producing some research or engaged in scholarly activity, but there weren't many opportunities to do that in Nepal. I thought, well, here we have a new institution, a Central Department of Sociology and Anthropology, in a country for which that is a novel creation, and there are trained people there, so it just seemed sensible for the Department to have some support from the University for funding or for whatever it makes sense to have, such as a journal. I don't remember the exact chain of events but I guess I suggested that, and everybody thought it was a good idea. Then they asked me to edit the first volume, and I said, "Ok, if I can help in that way, no reason not to."

G: *Are you still affiliated with the CDSA in Kirtipur?*

F: When I left in 1986 there was an organization called SASON (Sociology and Anthropology Society of Nepal). I was elected to its board at the time. I wasn't going to be here physically, so it wasn't essential that I know day-to-day details about everything. I was just an interested and concerned external observer. Whenever I come to Nepal the Department asks me to provide a guest lecture, which I've felt honored to give. Some of the senior faculty now were graduate students in the eighties when I was here. It is gratifying to see the progress that they have made. So, affiliated? No. Informally engaged? Yes.

G: *What were the debates about the future of anthropology of Nepal at CDSA then?*

F: Pretty much what they still are: joint vs. separate departments, direction and content of the curriculum, how to recruit good students, how to produce more and better scholarship. The impressive thing is that, regardless of different opinions about issues growing out of different academic and personal backgrounds, everyone more or less got along and supported the departmental consensus, whatever that was.

G: *How do you see Nepali social science changing? Where do you think its heading?*

F: When we arrived here in 1962, I can't say there was any social science in the modern sense. There were traditional scholars, but no university. I've heard it said that Tribhuvan University was founded in 1959 but that doesn't mean that there was any physical presence in Kirtipur. There was certainly no sociology or anthropology. Gopal Singh Nepali got his Ph.D. from India and then taught in India the rest of his life, so he wasn't here either. Except for the occasional very odd example like that (since he was in absentia), there wasn't any academic social science, although there were brilliant private practitioners, like Dor Bahadur Bista and Harka Gurung.

There might have been economists. I wouldn't have known if there were or not. I can only really speak from my own experience as an anthropologist. Before 1984, several people in CDSA had been trained abroad, in India or elsewhere. Again, when I think back to 1984–86, no graduates had been produced but the department was starting, and it's been thirty years now. The CDSA is recognized as a growing concern. You have hundreds of students, the most popular department at TU, I'm told. You have turned out lots of M.A.'s, M.Phil.'s and even Ph.D.'s. The graduates are now teaching at different colleges all over the country. It has spread remarkably fast. Now, I can't tell exactly about the quality of the students or curriculum, but at least it's there, it's a presence. As for the future, if the department continues to be popular I guess it will just keep on growing, perhaps even splitting into two separate departments.

Then you have the problem of what those students will do for jobs. Already there are alternative jobs, not necessarily as sociologists or anthropologists. There are some jobs or positions with development organizations. They will pay hugely, probably, by comparison with other possibilities, so you have to be careful not to sell your soul to the development world, because they have their own agenda. Hard-core social science academicians are few in Nepal.

I think social science is going in the right direction in Nepal. Social scientists are contributing, critically, to development research within the country, both guiding it and executing it. There are many Nepali social scientists who have made their mark on the wider world of social science, and some have emigrated to foreign countries. They represent a loss to Nepal, but they are a force to contend with in many international conferences. They help keep Nepal on the intellectual map.

G: *What is your immediate research interest? What other thematic changes have occurred in your research in the meantime? How do you explain the changes that have occurred in your research focus?*

F: My research focus at the moment is to finish a book that deals with forty plus years of change in Dolpa. For that I will rely on what I wrote before, plus what I learned two years ago when I returned to Dolpa. I also want to do something similar with the Sherpa book. Those are immediate interests. Another derives from the fact that I grew up in a Southern, segregated American town where African-Americans were not even allowed to go to the movies. Our school system was not integrated until 1956, when I was a junior in high school, and the black students started coming to the white high school. By now it's been integrated for almost sixty years, but I was always fascinated to know how people adapted to that. At the time nobody objected, but I wanted to ask the people of my age if they had stories or memories from those years, or black people they knew or anything like that. I've interviewed several people with fascinating stories, and that's something I want to work on. I hope someone does something like that with Dalits in Nepal, since the situations are remarkably similar. Social science always needs to speak truth to power.

Theoretically, my Ph.D. was more concerned with the ideas of Fredrick Barth—not that I imitated him, but I was influenced by the way he thought about things. Nowadays I am more interested in Bourdieu, ideas about globalization, and I also continue to find interesting bits in Geertz and others. So I am always interested in following and participating in new developments in the theoretical world.

Some anthropological movements come like a tidal wave in the ocean and then just as quickly they're gone—like a tsunami. People get very excited about something, and then a few years later no one has heard of it. If I read somebody who puts things in a novel way, not quite thought of before, then I make a mental note and think whether I could use that in my own work. I took the example of globalization and applied it to the Peace Corps, which had not been systematically done before. The concept was not new, but the application was.

G: *Are you retired now?*

F: Yes, I retired from Carleton in 2009, when I was sixty-nine. Then I spent a year helping start a new college in Bhutan and retired from that when I was seventy. I don't want to pretend that Bhutan wasn't a job, since it was much harder than Carleton. For one thing I was teaching things I didn't know anything about, like demography, so I had to work very hard to master the material myself. They didn't pay me very much, but I wasn't there for the money; it was more in the spirit of the Peace Corps. (In fact, no one practices anthropology for the money; if money is your main goal, you go into business.) It was a wonderful year since I had been trying to get to Bhutan for forty-five years. I had always objected to the exorbitant prices they charged for their visas, so I took pleasure in the irony that in the end, rather than my paying anything at all, they bought my plane ticket and paid me to live there.

G: *Do you plan to do any more work related to Nepal?*

F: Yes. Now that I am retired from Carleton, I realize how demanding it was being there—intellectually stimulating, but also demanding, and now I am getting things done like *At Home in The World* and, before that, my Mahesh Chandra Regmi Lecture. I had been working on *At Home in the World* for a long time but I did it in little pieces which was frustrating because I wanted to get that monkey off my back. So, once I was through with Bhutan (where I edited a book on research by my students), I was able to finish *At Home in the World*. In a humbling and more than metaphorical sense, I had been working on that book for fifty years.

I'm also working on the Dolpa project. For more than forty years I wanted to go back to Dolpa, but I never did, not because I didn't want to, but because so many other interests and obligations kept cropping up—such as the Sherpas and Tanka Prasad and working at Tribhuvan

University. But now I am working on a 'Forty-Two Years Later' book, which should be out in the next year, and I want to follow that with a similar effort on the Sherpas book. My interest in these subjects has not decreased at all; in fact it has increased. I've also toyed with doing some work on Nepali humor and have collected some material (extremely funny!) on that, but I haven't done anything with it yet.

G: *I think we have to finish now; would you like to add anything more?*
F: I would just say that you have interrogated me so effectively that you have drawn out of me things I have forgotten for decades and had no memory of. But now, sitting here with you, I begin to think of things lost to memory, and I appreciate your probing and sensitive questions.

G: *Thank you, Professor. It's wonderful talking with you.*
F: It's been a real pleasure for me too.

Acknowledgement

I would like to thank Professor James F. Fisher for accepting my request for this interview and giving me his invaluable time during his short visit to Nepal. The interview text would not have come into fruition without his enduring engagement through email in the subsequent months. I am grateful to the two anonymous reviewers of this journal and to Pratyoush Onta for their comments on an earlier version, to Yogesh Raj for his editorial help in my introduction, and Kishor Pradhan of Martin Chautari for providing various technical assistance.

References

Fisher, James F. 1962. "An Anthropological Approach to Ethics." B.A. thesis, Princeton University.
Fisher, James F. 1967. "Schools for Sherpas." M.A. thesis, University of Chicago.

Fisher, James F. 1972. "Trans-Himalayan Traders: Economy, Society, and Culture in Northwest Nepal." Ph.D. dissertation, University of Chicago.

Fisher, James F. 1985. "The Historical Development of Himalayan Anthropology." *Mountain Research and Development* 5(1): 99–111.

Fisher, James F. 1986a. "Tourists and Sherpas." *Contributions to Nepalese Studies* 14(1): 37–61.

Fisher, James F. 1986b. *Trans-Himalayan Traders: Economy, Society, and Culture in Northwest Nepal*. Berkeley: University of California Press [reprinted Bangkok: Orchid Press, 2017].

Fisher, James F. 1990. *Sherpas: Reflections on Change in Himalayan Nepal*. Berkeley: University of California Press.

Fisher, James F. 1996. "An Interview with Dor Bahadur Bista." *Current Anthropology* 37(2): 349–356.

Fisher, James F. 1997. *Living Martyrs: Individuals and Revolution in Nepal*. New Delhi: Oxford University Press.

Fisher, James F. 2000a. "A Kuire's Query on Grovelling." *The Kathmandu Post*, 16 April, p. 4.

Fisher, James F. 2000b. *Jyuda Sahidaru: Nepalma Kranti Tatha Kyaktiharuko Bhumika*. Arvind Rimal, trans. Kathmandu: Tanka Prasad Acharya Smriti Pratisthan.

Fisher, James F. 2013. *At Home in the World: Globalization and the Peace Corps in Nepal*. Kathmandu: Himal Books.

Fürer-Haimendorf, Christoph von. 1964. *The Sherpas of Nepal: Buddhist Highlanders*. New Delhi: Oxford Book Co.

Gautam, Rajesh. 2046 v.s. Nepàlko Prajàtàntrik àndolanmà Nepàl Prajà-Pariùadko Bhåmikà. Kathmandu: Rajesh Gautam.

Onta, Pratyoush. 1997. "Against Kuire Worship." *The Kathmandu Post*, 12 June, p. 6.

Raj, Yogesh. 2010. *History as Mindscapes: A Memory of the Peasants' Movement of Nepal*. Kathmandu: Martin Chautari.

Turner, Ralph L. 1931. *A Comparative and Etymological Dictionary of the Nepali Language*. London: Routledge and Kegan Paul.

Biographical Note

Gaurab KC holds a master's degree in Anthropology from Tribhuvan University, Kirtipur. He has been affiliated with Martin Chautari, Kathmandu as a researcher. His research interests include migration, media, intellectual biography, disciplinary history, and the urban informal economy. His work on migration entitled *Maune: The Cultural and Economic Imaginaries of Migration* (2014) has been recently published from the Centre for the Study of Labour and Mobility (CESLAM). Email: <gauravdoti@gmail.com>

APPENDIX A

Kinship and Marriage Relations Among Entrepreneurial Taralis

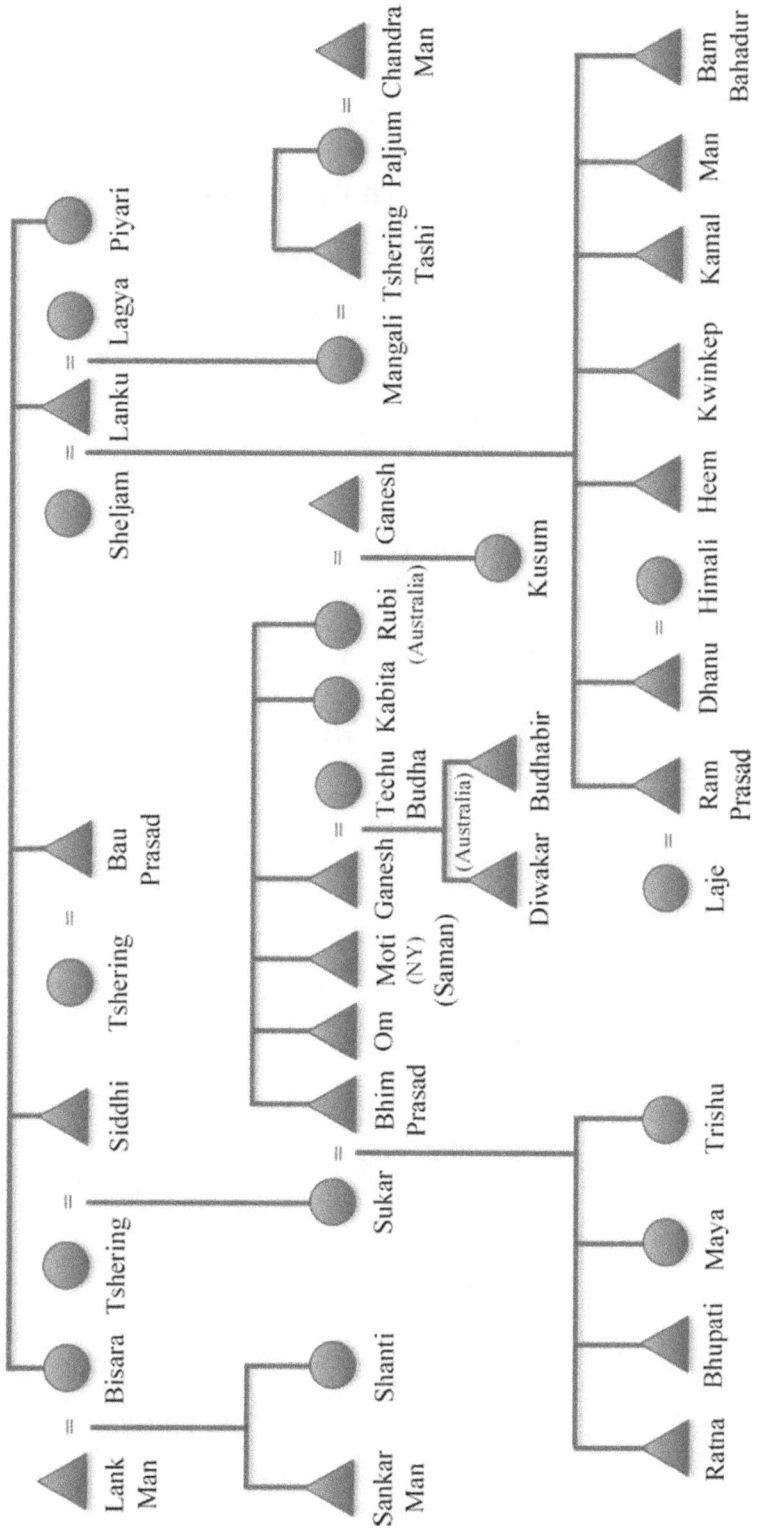

APPENDIX B

Chandra Man Rokaya's Genealogy

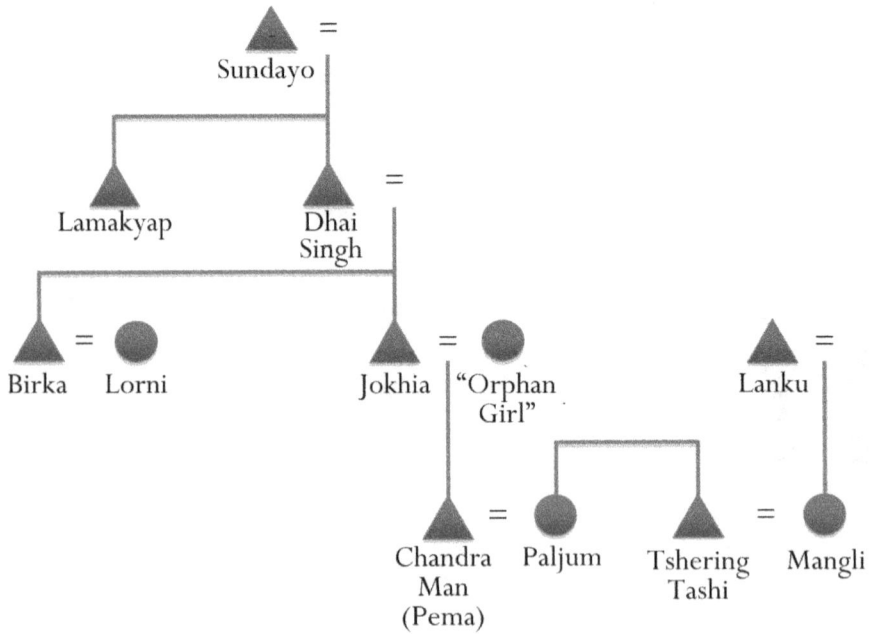

APPENDIX C

Advanced Education Pursued by Taralis during the Late 1960s and 1970s

	Location	Funding Source	Occupation
Bhim Bahadur	Baglung, Pokara	Government	Carpet Industry
Siddi Bahadur	Baglung, Pokara	Government	Shopkeeper
Lank Man	Balaju Boarding	Private	Carpet Industry
Kamal Bahadur	Tansen	Private	Carpet Industry
Bam Bahadur	Tansen	Private	
Shiva Nanda	Balaju Boarding	Private	Politics
Chandra Man	Pharping Boarding Nainital Univ., India	King Mahendra	Agriculture Development Bank

APPENDIX D

Months in Bikram Sambat, the Nepali Calendar*

Baisakh	mid-April to mid-May
Jeth	mid-May to mid-June
Asar	mid-June to mid-July
Saun	mid-July to mid-August
Bhadau	mid-August to mid-September
Asoj	mid-September to mid-October
Kartik	mid-October to mid-November
Mangsir	mid-November to mid-December
Pus	mid-December to mid-January
Magh	mid-January to mid-February
Falgun	mid-February to mid-March
Chait	mid-March to mid-April

* There is a fifty-seven-year difference (most of the time) between our commonly used Gregorian calendar and the Nepali calendar. Thus, our date of 2017 CE corresponds to 2074 BS in the Nepali calendar.

BIBLIOGRAPHY

Barnouw, Victor. *Culture and Personality*. Belmont, CA: Dorsey Press, 1963.

Bruner, Edward M. "The Opening Up of Anthropology." In *Text, Play, and Story: The Construction and Reconstruction of Self and Society*, edited by M. Bruner, 1–16. Washington, DC: The American Ethnological Society, 1984.

Budhamagar, Bhojbikra. *Magar Jaatiko Rajnitik Itihas* (Political History of Magar Caste). Magar Pragyik Samuha, Nepal: 2071 BS (2014 CE).

The Carpets from Nepal, 2009. A special issue for the New York International Gift Fair, 2009.

Daurio, Maya. "The Fairy Language: Language Maintenance and Social-Ecological Resilience Among the Tarali of Tichurong, Nepal." *Himalaya* 31 (2012):7–21.

de Sales, Anne. "The Kham Magar Country: Between Ethnic Claims and Maoism." In *Resistance and the State: Nepalese Experiences*, edited by David N. Gellner, 326–58. New York: Berghahn Books, 2007.

Fisher, James F. *Living Martyrs: Individuals and Revolution in Nepal*. Delhi: Oxford University Press, 1997.

——————. *Trans-Himalayan Traders: Economy, Society, and Culture in Northwest Nepal*. Berkeley: University of California Press, 1986; Bangkok, Orchid Press 2017.

Graner, Elvira. "Labor Markets and Migration in Nepal: The Case of Workers in Kathmandu Valley Carpet Manufactories." In *Mountain Research & Development* 25 (2001):253–59.

Hitchcock, John T. *The Magars of Banyan Hill*. New York: Holt, Rinehart and Winston, 1966.

Kautilya. *Arthashastra*. Bangalore: Government Press, 1915.

Oppitz, Michael. *Shamans of the Blind Country: A Picture Book from the Himalayas*. Frankfurt: Syndicate, 1981.

Regmi, Ambika. *A Grammar of Magar Kaike*. Munich: Lincom Europa, 2013.

_____. *Analyzed Texts in Magar Kaike*. Munich: Lincom Europa, 2014.

Ricoeur, Paul. "The Question of the Subject: The Challenge of Semiology," translated by Kathleen McLaughlin. In *The Conflict of Interpretations: Essays in Hermeneutics*, edited by Don Ihde, 236–66. Evanston, IL: Northwestern University Press, 1974.

Shah, R. K., "The Nepalese patuka in the prevention of back pain." *International Orthopaedics* 18 (1994):288–90.

Thakali, Santaram Hirachan. *Wigatako Dolpa* [Old Dolpa]. Kathmandu: Alka Printers and Publishers, 2064 BS (2007 CE).

Wallerstein, Immanuel. *World-Systems Analysis: An Introduction*. Durham, NC: Duke University Press, 2004.

INDEX